RANDALL HROZA

WORLDVIEWS IN COLLISION
THE REASONS FOR ONE MAN'S JOURNEY FROM SKEPTICISM TO CHRIST

RANDALL HROZIENCIK

WORLDVIEWS IN COLLISION
THE REASONS FOR ONE MAN'S JOURNEY FROM SKEPTICISM TO CHRIST

Paley, Whately Greenleaf Press

Worldviews in Collision:
The Reasons for One Man's Journey From Skepticism to Christ
by Randy Hroziencik

ISBN 978-1-947844-31-5

Copyright Randy Hroziencik, 2018. All Rights Reserved.

Published by *Paley, Whately, and Greenleaf Press*
an imprint of the Athanatos Publishing Group
www.athanatos.org

For more information about the author, including contact information, see page 245.

DEDICATION

Every author stands upon the shoulders of at least one person, and often several, who were extremely influential in his or her life. In that regard, I would like to dedicate this book to my three mentors in the faith.

When I first came to Bethel Baptist Church in Galesburg, Illinois, I had no idea that the two pastors on staff would become such powerful influences in my life. Even though I eventually completed seminary degrees in theology, Pastor Emeritus Lee Johnson was responsible for providing me with my theological education. By attending Pastor Lee's Bible study classes over the span of two decades, my faith benefitted beyond measure. Pastor Lee has been, and continues to be, a true servant of God, and is the single greatest Bible teacher I know.

The late Pastor Kirk Kendall taught me much about what it means to be a leader in the church, and I greatly miss his wisdom and guidance. One would have to search the world over to find a more Christ-like man – yet even then the search would be fruitless.

John Oakes served as my apologetics mentor. I became the first-ever graduate of the Certificate in Christian Apologetics program offered through the Apologetics Research Society, of which Dr. Oakes is the president. Although there are many great apologists working for the benefit of God's kingdom today, John is truly the best of the best.

ACKNOWLEDGEMENTS

The following people were kind enough to read through the first draft of this book, and then offer me the feedback that I needed to make this a more accurate, and more readable, resource for others. For that, I am truly grateful.

Roger Brown, Elder @ Bethel Baptist Church

Peter Fecht, Elder @ Bethel Baptist Church

Lee Johnson, Senior Pastor Emeritus @ Bethel Baptist Church

John Oakes, Ph.D., President of the Apologetics Research Society

Weston Oxley, Adult Ministries Pastor @ Bethel Baptist Church

Mark Templeton, Elder @ Bethel Baptist Church

I would also like to thank Anthony Horvath, Ph.D., the Executive Director of Athanatos Christian Ministries, for his willingness to publish this book. I have long admired this wonderful ministry, and am greatly impressed with Anthony's skill as an apologist. In the world of literary apologetics he is a giant.

Most of all, I would like to thank my wife, Deb, for always supporting my ministry. As a former nursing instructor with years of classroom teaching experience she has given me lots of tips on how best to reach an audience, plus she has always been willing to make sure that I have the time I need to work on ministry endeavors, be it teaching weekly in the classroom, presenting special lectures on apologetic topics, or writing this book. I cannot say thank you enough for your loving support.

This book examines the Christian worldview from science, logic, and history, demonstrating how the "Case for Christianity" not only makes sense of the world around us, but also refutes the other dominant worldviews today.

In his book *Worldviews in Collision*, Randy Hroziencik has put together a great addition to the genre of Christian Evidence. It is written at the senior high school or college level. There are a few things unique about this great book. First, Randy gives us an in-depth introduction to the variety of worldviews that pervade our world. He presents a fair and unbiased description of other worldviews such as pantheism, atheism, and dualism, rather than a polemical description which will turn off those who do not agree with us. He then gives us a clearly reasoned argument that the only picture which is rational and consistent with reality is the Christian worldview. In a post-Christian age, we need this kind of information. One of the great pluses of this book is that we are able to go through Randy's discovery with him, as he leads us through how he came to faith. The second part of the book is a classical presentation of the reasons for believing more specifically that the Bible is the Word of God and that Jesus is the Son of God. His is a Gospel-centered apologetic approach. This will be great material for anyone wanting to share their faith with non-believers. You may even want to loan your copy out, but be careful: You may not get it back.

John Oakes, Ph.D.
President of the Apologetics Research Society

TABLE OF CONTENTS

Introduction:	Is Apologetics Relevant Today?	1
Chapter 1:	The Four Main Worldviews	10
Chapter 2:	Science, Reason, & Revelation	48
Chapter 3:	"Eternity in their Hearts"	84
Chapter 4:	The Coming Messiah	101
Chapter 5:	The Jesus of History	121
Chapter 6:	The Christ of Faith	155
Chapter 7:	Faith & Reason	177
Chapter 8:	When Worldviews Collide: Paul in Athens	202
Chapter 9:	One Last Challenge to the Faith	225
	Bibliography	239
	About the Author	245

Introduction

IS APOLOGETICS RELEVANT TODAY?

For the Christian believer who desires to share his or her faith – which, by the way, should be everyone who professes Jesus Christ as Lord and Savior – the importance of building a case for the existence of God, the deity of Christ, and the divine authority of the Bible cannot be emphasized enough. We live in a culture of religious skepticism that constantly challenges those who live by faith, so if we are going to take the message of the Gospel to a lost world we need to "always be ready with an answer" (1 Peter 3:15) to the challenges posed by the unbelieving world. This is not a scriptural suggestion, but rather it is a command from God himself. It seems clear that God wants us, as Christian believers with a vitally important message to share, to be ready to engage in apologetics, which is the branch of Christian thought that is focused on evidences for the faith.

However, over the past few decades Christians have debated with each other regarding the usefulness of apologetics in our current culture. Skeptics of Christianity maintain that the Bible cannot be used in establishing the validity of the Christian worldview; the old "because the Bible says so" idea just doesn't work anymore. Since there are rock-solid evidences for the biblical worldview from science, logic, and history, Christians should be able to establish the truth claims of the Bible through an appeal to these areas of knowledge. But there's a problem with this: Our culture of religious relativism stresses the inadequacy of science, logic, and history to answer the big questions about God, Jesus, and the Bible. So, what are we to do?

We could attempt to show unbelievers the cohesiveness which exists between science, reason, and Scripture, but since non-Christians generally hold the Bible to be nothing more than outdated Hebrew mythology they typically reject this Christian claim. It's a vicious circle, really. We try to integrate science, logic, and Scripture into our apologetic methodology, only to find that unbelievers either view the Bible as an outdated myth, or they have no confidence in the ability to determine what is true. As a result of this unwillingness on the part of many unbelievers to examine the evidence for Christianity, the Christian believer may end up questioning the usefulness of apologetics. This is a common problem within Christianity today.

Yet despite these persistent claims that no one can really know anything for sure, or that Christianity is based upon nothing more than useless myths, I have personally experienced the power of apologetics in my life. Apologetics played a primary role in my coming to faith in Christ, and I've known many others in recent times who either converted to Christianity because of a thorough study of apologetics, or at the very least they had their already-existing faith strengthened tremendously because of the overwhelming evidence for God, Jesus, and the Bible. If apologetics can bring just one more unbeliever to faith in Christ, then it remains as useful as ever. Yes, as Christian believers we do need to be ever mindful of the fact that we live in a skeptical, relativistic culture marked by spiritual doubt, and we should learn to adapt our approach to engaging seekers and skeptics in light of this trend, but the various lines of evidence for the Christian worldview are still relevant today. In short, apologetics works. I've seen it impact numerous lives.

When sharing the faith it is sometimes necessary that Christian believers first establish the existence of God before they can effectively share the truth claims of Christianity in particular. There will be some unbelievers who are so hardened toward God and Christianity that, like the pharaoh of the Exodus, they seem to be totally closed off to the possibility of faith (Exodus 7:13, 14, 22; 8:15, 19, 32; 9:7, 34-35; 13:15). However, Christ himself called all believers to participate in the Great Commission (Matthew 28:16-20; Mark 16:15-18; Luke 24:46-47; Acts 1:8), which is the act of taking Jesus' message to the entire world. Sharing one's faith should not be directed just toward those who appear to be open to following Christ's teachings, but in fact should be aimed at everyone. Sometimes that means we will encounter religious skeptics who seem to be closed-minded toward Christian beliefs. I've experienced it more than a few times, but nonetheless the skeptic should be encouraged to go where the evidence leads in the search for truth. Ultimately, it is God who directs the unbeliever to faith (John 16:13), while the job of the Christian believer is to try to clear the roadblocks to faith that the skeptic may be experiencing (Colossians 4:5-6; 1 Peter 3:15).

This book is primarily focused on the relationship between faith and reason. We will begin by looking at the four major worldviews that exist in our culture today. This is crucial for the Christian believer, as it is very helpful to clearly understand what it is that non-Christians believe before we attempt to share our faith with them; a little knowledge can go a long way when sharing one's faith. The non-Christian worldviews of atheism, pantheism, and deism will be examined in the light of the evidence for God, Christ, and the authority of the Bible. We will then look at the major lines of evidence for God's existence, and then move on to the evidence for the identity of the Creator himself, who is both the Jesus of history and the Christ of faith. Establishing the existence of God prior to making the "Case for Christ" is oftentimes of paramount importance, as many skeptics outright reject a basic belief in God. Of course, sharing the evidence for God's existence is not enough. The Christian man or woman is only successful in sharing the faith when he or she proclaims Jesus Christ as Lord and Savior.

We will then examine the relationship between faith and reason. Sadly, it is often assumed by skeptics, seekers, and even some well-meaning Christians that we live either by faith or by reason, but never by both. I am confident that this notion will be put to rest in this book. As a practical application for the Christian believer who actively shares his or her faith with others, we will look at the example of the Apostle Paul speaking before the Athenian philosophers, as found in Acts 17:16-34. This account of one man's proclamation of the Christian faith to some very well-educated unbelievers is quite possibly the premier example of evangelism across worldviews. Finally, we will examine the Christian response to the problem of suffering, which is the most common objection to Christianity today.

Before going any further, however, it may benefit the reader to know a little bit about my spiritual background. The skeptic may find it interesting to know that I was once a member of their camp.

A SKEPTIC'S SEARCH FOR TRUTH

Several years ago in one of the adult education classes that I was attending in my home church, the teacher asked the class, "What song title best describes your spiritual journey to Christ?" I immediately knew that the answer for me was the Beatle's hit song *The Long and Winding Road*, because my spiritual journey from skepticism to Christ was a very long process, measured not in months but in years.

I grew up in Galesburg, Illinois, a small town nestled approximately half-way between Chicago and Saint Louis. I was raised in a good home in which moral values and respect for others were taught – not that I always put those values into practice. Despite being baptized as an infant, church was not a routine part of my early life. By the time I entered into junior high school I avoided church because I felt uncomfortable there, mostly due to my unfamiliarity with Christian terminology and practices. By high school I had adopted the full-blown skeptical position that organized religion was for weak people who needed someone to tell them what to think. I came to this conclusion after hearing the skeptical claims of some very influential acquaintances. I eventually labeled myself a freethinker, as many atheists do, but unlike atheists I always believed in God because I could not accept the idea that the universe could have begun merely by chance. I believed that molecules-to-man evolution was God's means of creating the diversity of life found on Earth, both living and in the fossil record, and I believed this to be an indisputable fact that is beyond question. I was sure that religious beliefs are of no importance to God, instead believing that God is only concerned with a person's moral values and treatment of others. I believed that Jesus was a great moral teacher, and I loved how Jesus stood up for the poor and the oppressed, but I did not believe that Jesus is God. I believed that the Bible is a holy book, but no more holy or truthful than the Qur'an, the Hindu and Buddhist writings, or the Book of Mormon. I believed that God would accept almost everyone into his presence upon death, with the possible exception of a few evil misfits like Adolph Hitler and Joseph Stalin. As you can see, a few of my beliefs were biblical, but most were not. I was theologically confused simply because I never took the time and made the effort to examine the evidence for the Christian worldview.

At twenty-three years of age I was accepted into a Radiation Therapy Technology residency program in Rockford, Illinois. The program lasted for one year, from September 1987 to September 1988, and it was the most intense year of my life. This was the year that began my spiritual journey from skepticism to Christ. Some interesting things happened that year. First of all, my biological sciences instructor turned out to be a devout Christian creationist. I admired her seemingly endless knowledge of anatomical science. She said more than a few times that the human body is way too complex to have evolved slowly in stages, and instead appeared to have been created instantaneously. As a result of my respect for her, I found myself questioning my evolutionary beliefs, and I began to think that if I could be wrong about origins, then maybe I've been wrong about some other faith-related issues as well.

I always knew that suffering existed in the world, and obviously I knew that people died, but during this year I was constantly confronted with the problem of suffering and death. I was warned that the program would be emotionally challenging, and it was. Although I hated to see anyone have to battle cancer, it was the children whom I treated that melted my heart – and caused me to have many intense conversations with God. During some of those conversations I was quite angry, to say the least. I could have gone the route of atheism, as many do because they cannot reconcile the problem of suffering and death with a loving God, but I always knew God existed because of the complexity of the universe and the existence of life; this was reinforced through my studies in the natural sciences during this time. I concluded that, regarding the problem of suffering and death, God knew something that I did not, which has to be the understatement of human history!

A strange thing happened near the end of that year. My fiancé Deb[1] and I went to a theater in downtown Rockford to see an up-and-coming comedian who was fast becoming all the rage in America. This comedian, who had been a Pentecostal preacher before he rejected his faith, went into a rant in which he repeatedly blasphemed Jesus and ridiculed the virgin birth. Deb, who had long been a Christian, was quite upset, but what was strange to me was that I also felt that he had crossed way over the line and was exceedingly inappropriate, and I felt this way apart from Deb's reaction. We abruptly left the performance. Now when I look back at that year I'm not surprised that I was also offended: God was at work in my life, although it would take some time before I would come to realize it.

Also near the end of that year Deb said to me, "You know, we're planning on getting married soon. It might be nice if you came to church with me and met the pastor and the congregation before the day of the wedding," and, of course, she was right. I was introduced to Pastor Don Reynolds, a true man of God who understands what it means to have a grace-based faith. Pastor Reynolds challenged me to examine the evidence for the Christian worldview, and I took him up on that challenge – much to my great benefit, of course. Also during those early days in the church I had the support of my wife and her mother, the late Marilyn Hodges,

---

[1] Deb and I were married after my graduation from Swedish-American Hospital's School of Radiation Therapy Technology. We have two grown children, Christopher and Heather. Christopher, who is married to Nicole, has given us two granddaughters, Alexa and Eleanor, while Heather, who is married to Anthony, has given us our third granddaughter, Jane.

who was the godliest woman I have ever known. They encouraged me as I explored what the Christian faith is all about.

Eventually my son Christopher and my daughter Heather were born, and anyone who has ever had a child or cared for a baby knows that it is impossible to look into the eyes of a newborn and not believe in the sovereignty of God. Also during this time, when I was still relatively new in my career as a radiation therapist, I began to notice that the patients I cared for who were the strongest emotionally and had the best attitude in their battle against cancer were those who freely confessed Christ as their Lord and Savior. I knew that this could not be a coincidence. I came to admire their faith, and I began to realize that their faith was not foolish, as I had once believed.

I came to a point where I knew that it would be a mistake to continue rejecting Christ and the truth claims of the Bible. The evidence for Christianity was just too overwhelming, and I had always said that in everything I examined I would try to put rational evidence before a personal agenda. Finally, when well into my twenties, I accepted Christ as my Lord and Savior. The song *The Long and Winding Road* contains the words, "The long and winding road that leads to your door." Interestingly, Jesus talks about a door in the final book of the Bible: "Here I am! I stand at the door and knock. If anyone hears my voice and opens the door, I will come in…" (Revelation 3:20).

Jesus was always knocking on the door to my soul, but it took me almost thirty years to open that door and invite him in. Since I have done that, I now know that Jesus truly is "the way and the truth and the life" (John 14:6). In the two decades since that time I have gone on to study under two of the best Bible and theology teachers ever to grace the church, Pastor Lee Johnson and the late Pastor Kirk Kendall, former pastors at Bethel Baptist Church in Galesburg, Illinois. I eventually completed a joint Master of Arts-Doctor of Philosophy in Theology through Trinity College of the Bible and Theological Seminary, an institution specializing in distance education. I was also the first person to complete the Certificate in Christian Apologetics program offered by the Apologetics Research Society, under the very capable mentorship of Dr. John Oakes, the most remarkable and gifted apologist I have ever known. Despite my thirst for learning about my faith, I am constantly amazed at how much more there is to learn, which is a truly humbling thought. Like Augustine many centuries before me, I have come to appreciate the approach of "faith seeking understanding." While this book will in no way address every question or concern offered by skeptics and Christian believers alike, I do pray that it will be of great benefit to those who use it.

MAKING THE CASE FOR CHRISTIANITY

Apologetics is the area of Christian thought that is concerned with making the case for the doctrines of the faith, whether it is the existence of God, the deity of Christ, the belief in the afterlife, and so on. Apologetics is derived from the Greek word *apologia*, which means "defense," or more literally "a speech for the defense." Not surprisingly, apologetics is often associated with a legal-type defense of the faith; it was a technical term in ancient Greek law that clearly had legal connotations.

Apologia is found seven times in the New Testament (Acts 22:1; 25:16; 1 Corinthians 9:3; Philippians 1:7, 16; 2 Timothy 4:16; 1 Peter 3:15), and when also considering the verb form *apologeomai* the term appears several more times in the New Testament. The Apostle Peter gives us the battle cry of apologetics: "But in your hearts revere Christ as Lord. Always be prepared to give an answer to everyone who asks you to give the reason for the hope that you have. But do this with gentleness and respect" (1 Peter 3:15). Ultimately, apologetics equips the Christian believer to share his or her faith more effectively with the unbelieving world. Apologetics, which has always been an important aspect of Christianity, has been a major part of my spiritual journey since my days as a seeker of truth.

APOLOGETICS: STILL RELEVANT TODAY

Make no mistake about it, apologetics is still relevant today. Although both skeptics and "faith only" Christians are adamant that apologetics has lost its relevancy, I trust that as you travel through the pages of this book you will see that this is definitely not the case. Beyond this chapter is a wealth of information which fleshes out the overall case for God and the Christian worldview. This book will likely find its greatest use as a tool for entering into dialogue with those who are either interested in, or even skeptical of, Christianity. Of course, it goes without saying that not everyone who reads this book will be impressed with the information that it contains. The Apostle Paul wrote, "The person without the Spirit does not accept the things that come from the Spirit of God but considers them foolishness, and cannot understand them because they are discerned only through the Spirit" (1 Corinthians 2:14). There is something amazing that happens in both the heart and the mind of one who comes to believe in the saving power of Jesus Christ: The intellect and the emotions are regenerated, and what was once unclear becomes clear. This is why the great theologian and apologist Augustine (AD 354-430) declared, "Believe, so that you may understand." That approach to faith may seem backward to most people today, as the unbelieving world maintains that if we are to believe in anything we must first understand why we should believe it. Yet what Augustine said dove-tails perfectly with what Paul wrote regarding the spiritual blindness of the unbelieving mind. For many unbelievers, the information contained within the pages of this book will have no effect whatsoever, until the grace of God combines with their willingness to entertain the truth claims of Christianity. Then, and only then, can the various lines of evidence for God's existence, the deity of Christ, and the truthfulness of the Bible come to clarity. It is my sincere desire that all those who read through this book will come to understand that Christianity is not a blind faith, but instead is a well-reasoned faith of great value, both temporally and eternally.

Chapter 1
THE FOUR MAIN WORLDVIEWS

Within Christian circles, and especially among those who enjoy studying the subject of apologetics, the term "worldview" gets thrown around a lot. But what exactly is a worldview? A worldview may be defined as the belief system that describes how people view the world around them, and their place in the world. Apologist James Sire further defines a worldview as being a set of presuppositions which we hold, regarding the basic makeup of our world.[2] Worldview provides the framework for tackling the big questions of life, such as the existence and nature of God, the problem of suffering, and what happens to us when we die. There are a number of different worldviews today, such as the biblical worldview, the naturalist worldview, the transcendentalist worldview, and so on, and oftentimes people use different terminology to describe the exact same set of worldview presuppositions – which can make it all very confusing, of course. Ultimately, however, the study of the different worldviews is crucial in understanding the beliefs of others, which allows the Christian believer to more effectively enter into dialogue with someone holding a different worldview.

Although scholars categorize worldviews differently, this book will focus on the four major worldviews in the West: Christian theism, atheism, pantheism, and deism. Each of these worldviews defines God differently. For the Christian, God is both one and personal. God not only has the attributes of personality – emotional and intellectual qualities such as love, compassion, the ability to exercise logic and reasoning, and so forth – but God also has the ability, and the willingness, to enter into a personal relationship with human beings. For the atheist, God is merely a figment of the imagination, created by human beings for the purpose of wish fulfillment.

---

[2] James Sire, *The Universe Next Door* (Downers Grove, IL: InterVarsity Press, 1997), 16.

In other words, God was created in the mind of man, rather than man being created in the image of God. For the pantheist, God (or, more accurately, god) is merely a force, perhaps best defined as spiritual awareness infused into nature itself. Pantheists would readily equate their god with the "Force" from the *Star Wars* saga. Finally, for the deist God is the Creator of the heavens and the earth, but God is "out there somewhere," aloof and not really interested in his creation or in the well-being of people. For deists, God is revealed in nature but not through any of the world's holy books, and especially not through Jesus Christ, as Christians claim God is most fully known. This is merely one quick peek at how the various worldviews differ.

CHRISTIAN THEISM

Christian theism is the belief in a personal God who is both active and interested in his creation, and is most fully revealed in the person of Jesus Christ, the second member of the Holy Trinity who is both Creator and Savior. Although Christian theism is only one of many versions of theism,[3] it is the form of theism that is most prevalent in the West today, and has been for the past two thousand years. At least half of the world believes in a sole Creator-God, as Christianity and Islam combined make up close to half of the world's population. Add to their numbers other religious followers who believe in one supreme God and it becomes apparent that a very significant percentage of the world holds to the belief in a sole Supreme Being who is actively involved in his creation. However, as mentioned this book will focus solely on Christian theism.

THE BELIEFS OF CHRISTIAN THEISM

As with every worldview or religion today, not every Christian believes the exact same things concerning their

---

[3] Theism is the belief in a personal God – that is, a God who has the attributes of personality. Besides Christians, other examples of theists include Jews, Muslims, Sikhs, Jehovah's Witnesses, and some within the Unitarian Universalist tradition.

faith. However, the following core beliefs form the basis for Christianity. Although there are numerous other beliefs within Christianity that could be covered, the following beliefs are sufficient to both explain what Christianity is about, as well as to differentiate this worldview from the other three described in this chapter.

The Nature of God

God is eternal: He had no beginning and he will have no end (Psalm 90:2; Revelation 1:8). God is immutable, or eternally the same (Malachi 3:6; James 1:17). God is Spirit (John 4:24), incorporeal and invisible (Exodus 33:20; John 1:18; Romans 1:20; Colossians 1:15). God is omnipotent, meaning he can do everything; there is nothing which God cannot do (Jeremiah 32:17). God is omniscient, or knows everything there is to know (Hebrews 4:13). This includes knowing not just the actions of every person who has ever lived, but even knowing every person's most intimate and guarded thoughts. God is omnipresent, or present everywhere at the same time (Jeremiah 23:23-24).

God is the Creator (Genesis 1:1), the source of all life (Psalm 36:9) who actively participates in his creation (Colossians 1:17; Hebrews 1:3). In fact, God's creation is one of his methods of self-revelation (Romans 1:20). God is self-existent, and does not depend upon anything outside of himself (Exodus 3:14). God is infinitely beyond us (Isaiah 55:8-9), yet amazingly he loves us deeply (John 3:16).

There is no other god besides God (Isaiah 44:6, 8); any other gods which are claimed to exist are merely false gods. Humanity has a sordid history concerning the acceptance of false gods. The belief in many gods, and similar false philosophies, has kept untold numbers of people in the dark concerning the knowledge of the one true God.

God is personal: He has the attributes of personality, and he is both able and willing to enter into a personal relationship with people, who are made in his image (Genesis 1:27). Among these attributes are knowledge (Isaiah 55:9) and emotions (Genesis 6:6). God is holy and just: Everything he does is morally perfect (Leviticus 11:44; Deuteronomy 32:4; Psalm 119:137). God is faithful (2 Thessalonians 3:3; 2 Timothy 2:13), true (John 14:6; 17:3), merciful (Ephesians 2:4; James 5:11), and sovereign over his creation (Proverbs 21:1). God is good (Mark 10:18).

The Trinity

One God is clearly revealed in Scripture (Isaiah 44:6; John 5:44; 17:3; Romans 3:29-30; 1 Corinthians 8:4; Ephesians 4:4-6; 1 Timothy 2:5; James 2:19), yet three separate persons are called God. This is the belief referred to as the Trinity, and it is a belief held only by Christians. Although the word Trinity is not found in Scripture, this teaching is clearly revealed through many verses such as 1 Peter 1:1-2 (God the Father), John 1:1-14 (God the Son), and Genesis 1:1-2 (God the Spirit). The Bible clearly teaches a three-in-oneness within the Godhead in other key places as well (Matthew 3:16-17; 28:19; 2 Corinthians 13:14).

God the Father is all the fullness of the Godhead invisible (John 1:18), God the Son is all the fullness of the Godhead manifested in bodily form (John 1:14; Colossians 2:9), and God the Spirit is all the fullness of the Godhead acting upon humanity (1 Corinthians 2:9-10). Isaiah 55:8-9 is especially relevant concerning the Trinity, for no matter how hard one tries to understand the three-in-oneness of God, this clear scriptural teaching is far beyond the ability of human beings to intellectually grasp.

Jesus Christ

Jesus Christ is God, the second member of the triune Godhead who lives in bodily form (John 1:1-14; Colossians 2:9-10). God is revealed directly to humanity through Christ (John 1:1-4), who alone is the author of salvation (John 14:6). Through Christ all things were created (John 1:3; Colossians 1:16). Christ has the authority to forgive sins (Mark 2:5; Luke 7:48), judge humanity (John 5:27), and defeat the evil deeds of Satan, the fallen angel who rebelled against God (1 John 3:8). Christ is the hope of all Christian believers, and he sustains everyone who calls him Savior (1 Corinthians 1:8).

At the incarnation, God entered the physical world as a man, exactly as foretold in Genesis 3:15, the first promise of the coming Redeemer. God became a man in the person of Jesus of Nazareth, yet he retained his divinity; Christ was, and is, fully God and fully human at the same time. This is referred to as the hypostatic union, the belief that the divine and human natures of Christ are neither mixed, alternated between, or combined into a new nature but rather exist in complete harmony with one another.

Christ was born of Mary, a virgin, through a supernatural conception (Luke 1:34-35). Despite his hypostatic union, Christ placed limitations upon his divine nature so as to fully experience his humanity (Philippians 2:5-11). Christ's birth was just like that of any other person's, and he grew to adulthood and experienced human life just as all people do (Luke 2:52). Jesus was subject to human limitations: He hungered (Matthew 4:2), he thirsted (John 4:7), he became tired (Matthew 8:24; John 4:6), he wept (John 11:35), he became angry (Mark 3:5), and he experienced temptation (Matthew 4:1) – although, unlike the rest of humanity, he did not sin (Hebrews 4:15).

God became man in Christ for many purposes: To reveal himself to humanity (John 1:18), to be a sacrificial atonement for the sins of the human race (Isaiah 53:6; Hebrews 2:14-18; 10:9-10), to destroy and deliver humanity from the works of Satan (Hebrews 2:14-15; 1 John 3:8), to present himself as a merciful and faithful High Priest (Hebrews 4:15-16; 5:1-2), and to present to all people the greatest spiritual and moral teachings ever known (Matthew 5-7). Of these purposes, Christ's death upon the cross as a sacrificial atonement for the sins of the entire human race – past, present, and future – was the ultimate reason why God became man. Christ's sacrificial death satisfied the divine penalty for sin and provided a ransom for fallen humanity. This was God's plan to redeem humanity from his divine wrath, which was instigated by a rebellious mankind (Matthew 20:28; 1 Timothy 2:6).

Christ was raised from the dead in a bodily resurrection (John 20:20; 1 Corinthians 15:20), and not just spiritually raised, as some have contended for the past two thousand years. Christ's resurrection confirms that Jesus was, and is, God. The resurrection of Christ is the linchpin of the Christian faith: Everything holds together because of the veracity of this doctrine (1 Corinthians 15:16-20). Christ's resurrection ensures the resurrection of all believers (1 Corinthians 15:20-22). Christians have a great hope that life does not end at the grave, because they have the assurance of Christ's resurrection. Christ's return will be the time when he gathers Christian believers to himself, so that they may reign with him forever in eternity (1 Thessalonians 4:16-17).

Christ now sits at the right hand of God the Father (Philippians 2:9-11; Hebrews 8:1-2). He prepares Heaven for those who believe in him (John 14:2-3).

The Holy Spirit

The Holy Spirit is the Great Comforter, the third member of the triune Godhead (Matthew 28:19; 1 Corinthians 6:11) who participated in creation (Genesis 1:2; Job 33:4) and testifies about Christ (John 15:26). The Holy Spirit is fully God, yet is distinct from both God the Father and God the Son. As God, the Holy Spirit possesses divine attributes: He is omnipotent (Romans 15:18-19), omniscient (1 Corinthians 2:10-11), and omnipresent (Psalm 139:7).

The Holy Spirit serves to connect people to God. He equips people for service (Judges 3:10; 14:6), he inspired the prophets (Numbers 11:29), and he guided the writers of Scripture (2 Peter 1:20-21). The Holy Spirit is active in producing the moral character of people; David serves as one such example (Psalm 51:11; 143:10).

The Holy Spirit brings Christian believers into intimate contact with God. Part of this involves the Holy Spirit's work of convicting individuals of their sins (John 16:7-8). The Holy Spirit is also the instrument of regeneration (John 3:5-6; Titus 3:4-6). When a person becomes a Christian believer for the first time, the Holy Spirit is given as a gift at the moment of conversion, sealing the person to Christ (Romans 5:5; Ephesians 1:13-14). Indwelling the Christian believer (1 Corinthians 6:19-20), the Holy Spirit illuminates Scripture (John 16:13), delivers people from the power of sin (Romans 8:1-2), and gifts each Christian with special abilities (Romans 12:5-6). These gifts are for the edification of both the individual believer and the body of Christ as a whole (1 Corinthians 12:7-11).

The common Christian expression "filled with the Holy Spirit," or simply "Spirit-filled," refers to the Holy Spirit being allowed to indwell, guide, and oversee the life of the Christian believer, influencing his or her thoughts and actions so that a more Christ-like character is developed (Galatians 5:22-23). Unfortunately, many Christians mistakenly believe that only Pentecostal and Charismatic Christians are to be concerned with becoming "Spirit-filled," but in reality all Christian believers should make the effort to live the Spirit-filled life.

Scripture teaches that Christ baptizes with the Holy Spirit (Matthew 3:11; Mark 1:8; Luke 3:16; John 1:33; Acts 1:5; 11:16). Once the Holy Spirit indwells the Christian believer, he will facilitate spiritual growth – that is, in conjunction with his or her willingness to receive such growth. The person who claims to have a secondary "blessing" or "baptism" of the Holy Spirit experiences a period characterized by a remarkable spiritual growth and enlightenment, which is ultimately attributable to the Holy Spirit who has always been present since the moment of salvation.

Divine Revelation

God has revealed himself to humanity throughout history, and he still does so today and will continue to do so for as long as people remain on Earth in their current state. God has provided humanity with the intellectual ability to recognize his existence and divine attributes through creation (Romans 1:20), the moral conscience (Romans 2:14-15), his sovereign rule over human history (Acts 17:26-27), and Scripture (Hebrews 1:1).

God's self-disclosure of himself through creation, the moral conscience, and human history are the three facets of general revelation. General revelation is distinct from special revelation, which is God's self-disclosure of himself through the written word, or Scripture. God's general revelation has been available to all people who have ever lived. For instance, all people have the ability to contemplate the magnificence of creation, and from that come to the conclusion that a powerful and awesome God exists. In short, an intelligent design, which is demonstrated throughout the entirety of the universe, requires an intelligent Designer. Creation is such a powerful witness to God's existence and power that no one can be excused for not making this obvious connection (Romans 1:20). The evidence for God's existence from creation will be covered in the next chapter.

God has also "hardwired" into every person a moral conscience, which bears witness to his existence and demands that all people are accountable to him (Romans 2:14-15). Although this inner knowledge of God is sufficient for all people to know of his existence, their disobedience to God establishes their guilt before him (Romans 1:32). This particular line of evidence for God's existence will be covered in the third chapter.

God has also revealed himself through his sovereign rule over human history (Psalm 105; Acts 17:24-28). God did this so that people would seek after him, and even find him (Acts 17:27). Every person who has ever lived was appointed by God to live his or her life at a specific time and place in history (Acts 17:26).

However, as useful as general revelation may be as an entry point in sharing the Christian faith with unbelievers, it is insufficient for salvation. People at some point need to know about Christ's sacrificial atonement for the sins of fallen humanity in order to obtain salvation for themselves (John 3:16; 14:6; 17:3; Acts 4:12; Romans 6:23).

For the Christian believer, the Bible is the inspired and inerrant Word of God. Scripture itself reinforces this teaching (2 Timothy 3:16-17; 2 Peter 1:20-21). Unlike many of the other religions of the world, the Christian claims that there is no further special revelation from God (Revelation 22:18).

The ultimate purpose of Scripture is to provide fallen humanity with the plan of salvation, which is found through the atoning work of Christ's crucifixion (John 20:31). This is certainly not the only purpose behind God's special revelation, but salvation is clearly the most important reason for God's Word.

Sin & Salvation

All people are born with a fallen nature, a residual condition resulting from the fall of mankind in the Garden of Eden (Genesis 3:1-24; Romans 8:20-22). The fallen nature of mankind is clearly revealed throughout Scripture, perhaps most forcefully in Paul's letter to the church in Rome (Romans 3:23; 5:12-19). The fall of humanity is a major belief within the Christian faith, as all other beliefs hinge upon it.

Salvation, which is God's rescue from the eternal death caused by the fall of mankind, is a free gift from God given to all those who trust in Christ and repent of their sins (Ephesians 2:8-9; 1 Timothy 2:5-6). Those who have accepted Christ will be with God forever after this earthly life has ended, and those who consciously reject Christ will be separated from him for eternity (Matthew 25:31-46; 1 Corinthians 15:50-54; Philippians 1:21).

The End of Days

The end of days was foretold by Jesus in Matthew 24, Mark 13, and Luke 21. Jesus said that many "birth pangs" will take place in the future. Many will claim to be the Messiah, and they will deceive many. Wars, famines, earthquakes, and pestilence will increase in frequency. Christian believers will suffer persecution, even to the point of death, but nonetheless will witness about Jesus to not only the masses, but even to "kings" or earthly leaders. However, many will turn away from the faith, and there will be betrayals by parents, brothers and sisters, and friends. There will be an increase in wickedness, and the heavens will display fearful events and signs. Many believe that these birth pangs are happening today.

Although this is not a comprehensive examination of Christian beliefs by any means, these basic doctrines of the faith are more than adequate to describe what it is that Christians believe, and what differentiates the Christian worldview from atheism, pantheism, and deism. In its shortest form, the Christian worldview is marked by the belief in a personal Creator-God who, despite being singular, is also triune in nature. This is not an illogical teaching, but rather is beyond logic itself – it escapes the full grasp of the human intellect (Isaiah 55:8-9). Mankind, although created in God's image, chose to rebel against their Creator, yet God in his immeasurable love and mercy enacted a rescue plan for rebellious, fallen humanity through the sacrificial atonement for sin by the second member of the Trinity, God the Son, who in his incarnation became Jesus of Nazareth. Each and every person who responds to God's free gift of salvation, which is the rescue from the deadly effects of the sin nature, will spend eternity with God when this life is over. Although there is much more to Christianity than just this very basic description, these are the main tenets of the Christian worldview.

THE ATTRACTION OF CHRISTIAN THEISM

What makes Christian theism so attractive to many people today? For starters, knowing that there is a benevolent Creator who cares deeply for each and every one of his creatures is a satisfying thought, especially when compared to the three other worldviews described in this chapter. In atheism there is no one to look out for us, and life ends at the grave. Pantheism is founded upon the intellectually and emotionally unsatisfying belief in an impersonal creative force. In deism the Creator suffers from a bad case of ADD and quickly abandons his creation after initiating the beginning of time, space, and matter-energy. Ultimately, however, I found that only Christian theism adequately answers the big questions of life. It is this pursuit of truth that challenged me to examine the evidence for God, Christ, and the Bible.

While still a seeker, I had a man say to me, "Randy, Christianity is such an emotional high that your life will never be the same again," and I had no doubt that what he was telling me was true. However, I wasn't interested in becoming a follower of Christ because I thought it would be emotionally uplifting, but rather I was intrigued by whether or not Christianity was true. Like Pontius Pilate standing before Christ, I was interested in knowing truth (John 18:38). I refused to send my emotions to a place where my intellect could not also go. If I were to become a Christian, I would first have to become convinced of the truthfulness of Christianity.

As will be demonstrated in the coming chapters, the evidence for Christianity is abundant. Although creation alone establishes the existence of God, creation by itself does not lead the unbeliever to the Christian faith. This is why the cumulative evidence for Christianity is so vitally important, as the evidence for God is powerful but ultimately meaningless without pointing one to Jesus Christ, who alone is the Author of Salvation (John 14:6). However, confirming the existence of the Creator is often a crucial step in leading a skeptic away from atheism and agnosticism[4] and preparing him or her to contemplate the overwhelming evidence for the Christian faith. This is why I have devoted chapters to both the evidence for God in general and Christianity in particular.

WHERE DOES CHRISTIAN THEISM FALTER?

In all fairness, however, I had to ask myself this question: If Christianity alone provides overwhelming explanatory power concerning the big questions of life, then why isn't everyone a Christian? Since I'm going to critique atheism, pantheism, and deism I need to be fair and address this ques-

---

[4] Agnosticism is the position in which one claims to be neutral regarding the existence of God. In other words, the agnostic is quick to say, "Maybe God exists, or maybe not – who can really know?" Agnosticism comes from two Greek words: *a*, meaning "no" or "without" and *gnosis*, meaning "knowledge." Therefore, the agnostic is "without knowledge" concerning the existence of God.

tion head-on.

I remember my days as a skeptic quite well. Admittedly, my memory isn't what it used to be, but it's not so bad that I can't remember back to my twenties. Even though I've been a Christian for over two decades now, that doesn't mean that I've buried the memories of skeptical days gone by. For me, Christianity was a very strange story back then. I viewed Christianity like this: An all-powerful, but invisible, Creator brought everything into existence in a short time frame, at some point in the distant past. (I never got into the age of the universe debate back then.) This Creator is a single being, yet somehow exists as three distinct persons. That one blew me away. Since mankind rebelled against the Creator – through nothing more than eating a stupid piece of fruit – God accepted the self-sacrifice of a man named Jesus, from Nazareth in Israel. In some way that was incomprehensible to me, Jesus' death made everything okay between God and people, but I just couldn't get my mind around God accepting a sacrificial death in order to make things okay again. Why did some poor man have to suffer on a cross for something that two other people did, especially when these two other people lived thousands of years earlier? (Plus, it was only a stupid piece of fruit!) In between the creation event and Jesus, there are all kinds of fascinating but strange stories such as an ark full of animals surviving a global flood and a young King David chopping off the head of a giant named Goliath. That was as far as I felt the need to go in my examination of Christianity, and that's not exactly going deep into the text. Yet that's as deep as many people are willing to go in their examination of the Christian worldview. Needless to say, that's not the fault of Christianity, but rather that's the attitude of people who don't want to give the biblical worldview a deeper look.

ATHEISM

The term atheism comes from two Greek words: *a*, the prefix which means "no" or "without," and *theos*, meaning "God." Therefore, atheism describes the position in which its adherents are "without God." The atheist is a person who does not believe in God, whether the God of the Bible or any other definition of a so-called "Higher Power." Likewise, the atheist denies the reality of anything supernatural, be it Heaven, Hell, angels, demons, or the existence of the immortal soul. Only nature, or matter, exists for the atheist, which is why atheism is often referred to as either naturalism or materialism. Although the term was once used in the Greco-Roman world in regard to Christians, who denied the existence of the pagan gods and goddesses, today the term typically involves the denial of a personal Creator-God, whether the God of the Bible or any version of a supernatural being in general.

Atheism, like the other worldviews, is based upon certain propositions.[5] First, matter exists eternally and is all there is; matter, not God, is "ultimate reality." Therefore, Carl Sagan's famous dictum, "The cosmos is all that is or ever was or ever will be," is held to be truth. Second, the universe exists as a uniform series of cause-and-effect relationships in a closed system. The universe began when time, space, and matter-energy exploded into existence for no apparent reason, and one thing caused another until here we are today, in a universe filled with cause-and-effect relationships with no over-arching purpose. Nothing outside of the universe, namely God, can be responsible for bringing this closed system of cause-and-effect events into existence. In short, the universe "just happened." Third, human beings are nothing more than complex machines, and human personality is merely an interrelation of chemical and physical properties that we do not yet fully understand. This means that our thoughts and emotions are nothing more than chemical reactions taking place within the brain. Fourth, life ends at the grave. Atheism does not offer the hope of eternal life that Christian theism does. Finally, ethical pronouncements are determined simply through our choosing. Mere mortals decide how they should behave, not God. Atheists do not base their ethics in what God would have us do, but rather upon

---

[5] James Sire, *The Universe Next Door* (Downers Grove, IL: InterVarsity Press, 1997), 54-64.

what we as human beings would like to see ourselves do. Atheism, no matter how it is lived out, holds to these five basic propositions.

ATHEISM THROUGH THE CENTURIES

Although polls continue to demonstrate that most Americans believe in a Higher Power of some sort, it is also noteworthy "that the fastest-growing segment of belief among the young is atheism, which has leapt in popularity in the new millennium."[6] Therefore, it is becoming increasingly necessary for Christian believers to "always be ready with an answer" (1 Peter 3:15) to the question, Does God exist?

There are several organizations which share the task of promoting atheism and skepticism toward religion, and they have more than sparked an interest in the atheistic worldview in today's society. American Atheists, Incorporated, the American Humanist Association, Atheist Alliance International, Atheists for Human Rights, the Council for Secular Humanism, Freedom from Religion, the Humanist Institute, the Secular Coalition for America, and the Skeptics Society are some of the more vocal groups promoting this worldview. Several state and campus societies, too numerous to mention, also exist for the purpose of spreading the atheist agenda, and internationally the list of societies is very long.

In order to better understand the atheist mindset, it is beneficial to have at least a basic knowledge of the history of belief versus unbelief in God. Going all the way back to ancient Greece, only a relative few philosophers held to naturalism, such as Thales, Anaximander, Heraclitus, Gorgias, Protagoras, and Pyrrho, but their influence was so powerful that it set a solid foundation for later skeptical thinking to build upon. However, the greatest Greek thinkers – Socrates, Plato, and Aristotle – were certainly not atheists, although they were not necessarily theists, either. Socrates (470-399 BC) left very little in the way of writing; we know about him primarily through Plato, his greatest student. It is believed by many scholars that he acknowledged the existence of God as

---

[6] Andrew Sullivan, "The Forgotten Jesus." Newsweek (April 9, 2012).

the Creator of everything. Plato (428-348 BC) has greatly influenced thinkers in every generation of history, and many Christians have acknowledged that his teachings align with the Bible more than any other ancient philosopher. Plato was the teacher of Aristotle (384-322 BC), who is not only considered to be one of the greatest philosophers of the ancient world but also one of its greatest scientists, especially in the discipline of biology.[7] Aristotle believed in the spontaneous generation of life from non-life and held to an evolutionary explanation for the diversity of living creatures, and like many of his fellow Grecians he held to a more pantheistic view of God. Much later in history, during the Renaissance (1400-1600), people renewed their interest in the writings and beliefs of the ancient Greek philosophers, in part giving birth to humanism in the West. Humanism, which was biblically-based in its beginning, merely states that humans are of great value, since we were created in God's image (Genesis 1:27). Eventually, however, some thinkers took humanism in a totally different direction, instead promoting the idea that evolution – not God – is what makes us special, as we are the one species who evolved in such a manner that we became gifted with great intellectual abilities. This led to the rise in skeptical thinking that is prevalent today.

During the Renaissance there was an increased accessibility and awareness of the great writings of the past due to both the Gutenberg movable-type printing press and a greatly increased literacy rate. This spawned an interest in acquiring knowledge, not just of biblical teaching – which in part led to the Reformation – but also of the Greco-Roman philosophers which, due to their emphasis on the supremacy of human reasoning, led to the continuing battle between God's revelation and man's speculation about reality. As a result of the controversy between the Roman Catholic Church and Galileo over whether it is Earth or the sun that is at the center

---

[7] This was during the time in history when science fell under the category of "natural philosophy," which is the investigation of the natural world through logic and reasoning. Empirical science, as we understand it today, did not develop until the time of the Enlightenment.

of the created universe, a rift began to develop between science and religion. The Bible does not say that Earth is positioned at the center of the universe, but some academic opponents of Galileo and the church leaders who were influenced by them read that belief into the Bible and used it as a weapon against him. This was the first of two major trials pitting science versus religion; the second trial, known as the Scopes Trial, would not happen until much later in history, in 1925. Around the time of Galileo there began a general trend of moving the source of truth away from the Bible and toward a dependence upon science, with the resulting claim of the supremacy of human reasoning over God's revelation.

During the Enlightenment (1600-1800) science was further elevated to the level of being the ultimate test for truth. Materialistic philosophers came to the forefront of academia, most notably the great skeptic David Hume. Hume presented arguments against miracles, and in general the materialist philosophers of the day encouraged people to assert themselves as freethinkers with no need of ecclesiastical authority or influence. Deism also became a very influential worldview throughout Western Europe and America during this time. Despite the advance of secular or non-religious thinking, most people still believed in a personal Creator because they could not conceive of a creation apart from a Creator. This would begin to change in the nineteenth century, however, with Charles Darwin's theory of evolution.

The 1859 publication of Darwin's *On the Origin of Species by Means of Natural Selection, or the Preservation of Favored Races in the Struggle for Life* divided science and religion far beyond what had previously been. Darwin's teachings became so popular that they were applied to every field of study, such as government (Karl Marx) and psychology (Sigmund Freud). Shortly after Darwin, the atheistic writings of German philosopher Friedrich Nietzsche became very popular throughout the West, influencing countless academics, lay readers, and, unfortunately, more than a few dictators in the early twentieth century (Lenin and Hitler). The move toward a liberal understanding of the Bible began in Germany in the nineteenth century, which was influenced in large part by Darwinism. This "Higher Biblical Criticism" of the more liberal German theologians was essentially Darwinism applied to Scripture, in the attempt to naturalize Christianity and rob it of its miraculous claims. Eastern religions such as Hinduism and Buddhism infiltrated the West in the nineteenth century as well. Some of these Eastern teachings were atheistic, while others were more pantheistic in nature, but either way they promoted a world devoid of the one true God. These Eastern ideas further challenged the clear teachings of the Bible in many ways; reincarnation is one such example.

During the twentieth century atrocities such as World Wars I and II and the Holocaust highlighted the problem of evil and suffering, causing many to question the goodness, and even the existence, of God. Combined with an explosion in human origins research from a strictly Darwinian viewpoint, and the ensuing Scopes Trial of 1925, many people were all too ready to give up on God. Many of the popular science and science fiction writers of the late nineteenth and twentieth centuries – men such as H.G. Wells, Isaac Asimov, Arthur C. Clarke, and Carl Sagan – were atheists or, at the very least, self-professed agnostics with a clearly atheistic agenda. They spread their philosophy through their writings, which the public could not seem to get enough of during this time. These men were also proponents of the extraterrestrial hypothesis, claiming that life had evolved not only here on Earth but throughout the universe as well. This idea teaches that human beings are really nothing special, just another evolutionary accident in the cosmos.

Today in the twenty-first century both religious pluralism and moral relativism have further eroded the acceptance of biblical teachings, continuing to weaken the belief in God and Christianity. Atheists continually state that religion is just a natural evolution of civilization. In other words, "God was made in the mind of man" rather than "man was made in the image of God." Atheists also state that one religion is just as good as another since they are all creations of the imagination anyway, and moral relativism is claimed to be proof that no moral Lawgiver really exists. The problem of evil and suffering continues to be an obstacle to belief in God for many. The tragedy of September 11, 2001 as well as multiple wars and natural disasters afflicting thousands worldwide continue to highlight the debate between belief and disbelief in a God who loves and cares for his creation. Darwinism has continued to erode the belief in a Creator among many, and is entrenched in academia. Few seem to question the theory, and even in the church it has been thoroughly assimilated by many professing Christian believers.

The current atheistic scene has been dominated by both American and British thinkers. At the top of the list of preeminent atheists is Richard Dawkins, a retired zoology professor from Oxford University who first gained notoriety with his book *The Blind Watchmaker*. Sam Harris is one of the leading atheists in America today. His book *The End of Faith* is a slam against all who believe in God, and especially those of the Christian and Islamic faiths. The American Daniel Dennett, author of *Breaking the Spell*, maintains that one of the great tragedies of our time is parents raising their children to believe in God. He states that this is a form of child abuse, and that it is a crime to teach the next generation to believe in God. The late Christopher Hitchens of England, the author of *God is Not Great*, has been a powerful atheistic influence worldwide. Never afraid to engage in dialogue with Christian believers, he was noted for his many formal debates with prominent apologists. The list of prominent atheists extends far beyond just these four men, of course, and almost every college or university in the world today can claim at least one professor who makes it his or her mission to spread the agenda of atheism. This is why the need for apologetics is so very necessary today.

THE ATTRACTION OF ATHEISM

What is it about atheism that can seem so attractive? After engaging in dialogue with more than a few atheists over the years, I've come to the conclusion that there are three primary reasons for people to adopt this position. First, there is the issue of accountability. As fallen creatures we naturally want to be the masters of our own universe. One who is sinful – which, by the way, is all of us by birth (Romans 3:23) – will never be interested in submitting to the authority of a Supreme Being unless one is first spiritually regenerated (1 Corinthians 2:6-16). Therefore, if a person decides that God does not exist, then he or she is accountable only to themselves. Denying God's existence is an easy way to avoid accountability to someone greater than one's self.

Second, the problem of suffering is a huge problem for atheists – and for all of us, of course. How can a good and loving God allow so much suffering in the world? I'll be honest and say that I sometimes struggle with this conundrum as well. The atheist is quick to say that if God wants to put an end to suffering but can't, then he's weak, and if God could put an end to suffering but won't, then he's malicious. Or, as a third option –and the only real option for the atheist– God simply doesn't exist, in which case no one can put an end to suffering. None of these scenarios is good, of course, but the atheist fails to realize that maybe there's more than just these three options. The Christian response to the problem of suffering is both philosophical and pragmatic, and it deserves the attention of everyone whether atheist, pantheist, deist, or otherwise. (See the final chapter for the Christian approach to the problem of suffering.)

Third, atheists have fallen for the erroneous idea that science has disproven the existence of God and the reliability of Scripture. However, nothing could be further from the truth: Science properly understood actually points us in the direction of the Creator. The following chapter will explore, and refute, this skeptical claim in significant depth.

WHERE DOES ATHEISM FALTER?

Of the various worldviews discussed in this chapter, atheism is the one worldview that is most directly refuted by the evidence for God and Christianity that is contained within the pages of this book. Whether from cause-and-effect, design, or any other line of evidence for God, the atheistic worldview is being seriously challenged today. The problem of suffering is perhaps the atheist's primary defense against a belief in God – at least the God of the Bible – and the belief that science eliminates the need for God may not be far behind, but ultimately I see atheism as being an accountability issue. Although the Christian worldview offers both intellectually sound and emotionally satisfying answers for the problem of suffering as well as the claim that science supposedly buries God, the only real way to effectively counter the problem of accountability is to combine a prayerful request for God's grace in the life of the atheist with solid answers to the big questions about God and faith.

PANTHEISM

Pantheism, which is derived from the Greek words *pan*, meaning "all" and *theos*, meaning "God" is the worldview which exclaims that "God is all," or, more accurately, "god is all." The pantheist holds that everything is god: The forests, the mountains, birds' in the sky and fish in the sea, human beings – everything is god. Unlike the God of Christian theism, the pantheistic god is impersonal, lacking the attributes of personality that the God of the Bible possesses. Pantheism is often combined with monism, the belief that everything is one and is directly connected to everything else. Therefore, the pantheistic monist claims that not only is everything god, but everything is one. Sounds a lot like the "Force" from *Star Wars*, doesn't it?

The World Pantheist Movement defines their worldview through nine statements of belief.[8] First, the universe is both revered and celebrated, as it is the totality of being in the past, in the present, and in the future. The universe is self-organizing, ever-evolving, and inexhaustibly diverse. The overwhelming power, beauty, and even mystery of the universe compel the deepest human reverence and wonder. Second, all matter, energy, and life are an interconnected unity of which human beings are an inseparable part. We rejoice in our existence and express this gratitude through intellectual

---

[8] Paul Harrison, "The WPM Statement of Principles."
https://www.pantheism.net/manifest.htm

study, celebration, meditation, empathy, love, ethical action, and the arts. Third, human beings are an integral part of Nature, which we should cherish, revere, and preserve in all of its magnificent beauty and diversity. We should strive to live in harmony with Nature. We acknowledge the inherent value of all life, human and non-human, and strive to treat all living beings with compassion and respect.

Fourth, all human beings deserve a life of equal dignity and mutual respect. To this end we support and work towards freedom, democracy, justice, and non-discrimination, and a world community based on peace, sustainable ways of life, human rights, and an end to poverty. Fifth, there is a single kind of substance (energy-matter), which is vibrant and infinitely creative in all its forms. The body and the mind are indivisibly united. Sixth, death is the return of our elements to nature, and the end of our existence as individual human beings. The forms of "afterlife" available to human beings are natural ones, such as our teachings living on through others and the continuation of our genome through our descendants. Our actions, our ideas, and the memories of us live on, according to what we do in our lives here on Earth. Our genetic traits live on in our families, and our elements are endlessly recycled in nature.

Seventh, we honor reality, and keep our minds open to the evidence of the senses and of the unending quest for deeper understanding that is attained through science. These are our best means of coming to know the Universe, and on them we base our aesthetic and religious feelings about reality. Eighth, every human being has direct access to Nature through perception, emotion, and meditation. There is no need for mediation by priests, gurus, or revealed scriptures (holy books). Lastly, we uphold the separation of religion and state, and the universal human right of freedom of religion. We recognize the freedom of all pantheists to express and celebrate their beliefs, as individuals or in groups, in any non-harmful ritual, symbol, or vocabulary that is meaningful to them.

From a Christian perspective, there is some that is good –

and some that is not so good – about these nine statements of belief. Regarding the first statement, although it is true that Christians are awed by the wonders of creation, we revere and worship only the Creator of nature, not nature itself. The Universe, which is often capitalized by pantheists so as to equate it with deity in some way, is considered to be the totality of being. However, nature is not all there is, a mistake that Carl Sagan made with his famous mantra, "The cosmos is all that is or ever was or ever will be." God, the Creator of everything, fashioned both the non-physical (supernatural) realm as well as the physical (natural) universe. Therefore, the universe is not everything that exists. Pantheists claim that the universe is self-organizing, but there is no self-organizing principle, law, or force that has been demonstrated by science. In fact, just the opposite is the case: The rule of entropy states that the universe is winding down rather than building up. Nature is moving from a state of order to a state of disorder, from more organizational complexity to less organizational complexity, and from more usable energy to less usable energy over time. In other words, the universe is winding down – it is devolving, not evolving. Although all people, regardless of their worldview, will generally agree that the grandeur of the universe encourages feelings of deep reverence and wonder, the Apostle Paul reminds us that we all should make the obvious connection between the Creator and the creation, and no one is without excuse for failing to do this (Romans 1:20). A few verses later Paul wrote that some people in his day were guilty of pantheistic worship, confusing the Creator with the creation (Romans 1:25), a charge that still stands today.

The next four statements contain elements of truth that many Christians would wholeheartedly agree with. However, in the sixth principle the pantheistic position on death is revealed, namely that death is the end of our existence as individuals. For the Christian death is only the end of the mortal, perishable bodies that we now possess (1 Corinthians 15:42-44), but death is certainly not the end of our existence. Scripture and the testimony of human history[9] constantly remind us that there is a non-physical component to our existence that survives death.

The seventh statement would lead us to believe that both our senses and the scientific method are the ultimate means of knowing about reality. As valuable as empirical knowledge and scientific verification are, without God's revelation in the written word there is little that we can know with certainty.

The eighth statement espouses a mystical approach to believing in all things spiritual. Although the mystical approach to faith holds some merit, the best means of establishing a worldview should involve rational evidences, at least to some degree. Christianity is a well-reasoned faith, not a blind faith that is accepted purely through mysticism apart from evidential support. Additionally, this particular statement of belief claims that there is no need for mediation by priests, gurus, or divinely-revealed scriptures. Although the assistance and teaching of trained clergy is often very helpful regarding spiritual matters, the guidance offered through biblical teaching is of paramount importance to the Christian. The Bible is the sole authority in spiritual matters for the follower of Christ.

As a Christian I am in full agreement with the final statement. Freedom of religion should be a right of every human being, and in that regard I agree that the Christian, the atheist, the pantheist, and the adherent of every other worldview or religion has both the God-given and the civil right to worship as he or she sees fit.

In summary, some of these statements are noble and

---

[9] The "testimony of human history" concerns the timeless belief that people possess a soul or soul-spirit that is immortal and lives on after death. This belief seems to transcend both time and culture, with people from throughout history, and in many diverse cultures, adhering to this belief. The thinking person should ask the question, "Where did this idea come from, and why does it persist?" Perhaps God has hard-wired this knowledge into each of us. Maybe that is what Solomon, in Ecclesiastes 3:11, is saying to us: "He [God] has also set eternity in the hearts of men…"

good. Others, however, miss the mark of truth, which is wholly found in the Christian worldview alone.

THE VARIETIES OF PANTHEISM

The World Pantheist Movement makes it very clear that pantheism is not based upon a monolithic creed,[10] which is not surprising as no worldview or religion ever is. There are three primary ways in which one may categorize pantheism, as based upon the relationship between the god-force and the universe as well as how the material world is viewed.

Pantheism versus Panentheism

This differentiation concerns how the god-force relates to the cosmos. Some pantheists believe that the god-force is identical with the universe. For these pantheists, the god-force and the universe are one and the same. These are the "pure" pantheists. They may differ among themselves as to whether the basic substance of the universe is material (scientific pantheism) or spiritual (religious pantheism), and also as to whether the totality of the universe possesses a consciousness that is greater than the sum of its parts. Many of the Eastern religions are based upon this version of pantheism.

On the other hand, those pantheists who believe that the god-force is present not only throughout the entire cosmos but also extends beyond the universe in ways beyond our understanding are termed panentheists. For the traditional pantheist, the god-force and the universe are identical, whereas for the panentheist the god-force somehow exceeds the totality of the universe. Stated differently, in panentheism the universe is the "body" of god, while the "mind" of god is the principle of logic and reasoning that is inherent in the cosmos. Most pantheists who come from a Christian or Islamic tradition are almost always panentheists, and many of the ancient Greek philosophers were panentheists as well.

---

[10] Paul Harrison, "Varieties of Pantheism."
https://www.pantheism.net/paul/variety1.htm

A Real Universe versus an Illusory Universe

Some pantheists accept that the material universe is real, while others believe it is an illusion. In general, scientific pantheists maintain that the universe is real, while religious pantheists hold to the belief in an illusory universe – only the god-force is real, while matter (atoms and molecules) are merely an illusion. Many within the illusory position are either Hindu's or followers of other Eastern religions. This does not necessarily mean, however, that those who hold to the illusory position neglect or despise nature. Many Chinese and Japanese Buddhists accept that nature has a kind of conditional reality that should be enjoyed in its transient (temporary) beauty.

Dualism versus Monism

Dualists believe that there are two types of substance in the universe. The first is matter, and the second may be described as mind, soul, or spirit. In other words, there exists both a material realm and a mental-spiritual realm. On the other hand, monists believe that only a single type of substance exists in the universe, which is described as matter-energy. Matter-energy is believed to be the only substance, since this is all that we can perceive through our senses. Therefore, dualists are religious pantheists while monists are scientific pantheists.

As can be seen from the above categories of pantheism, this worldview contains major differences among its adherents. Needless to say, this makes it very difficult to pin down the beliefs of pantheism precisely. Therefore, whenever I describe pantheism it must be kept in mind that there are significant variations that must be taken into account.

THE ATTRACTION OF PANTHEISM

What is it about pantheism that people find so attractive? Going back to the nine statements of pantheistic belief, it is really easy to see why many people in the world today find pantheism so appealing. It offers a mystical approach to understanding nature and the divine, without asking for any commitment or accountability to a specific set of beliefs or moral standards from God. Pantheism allows one to speculate about a higher power, the majesty of the universe, and our place in the cosmos without requiring reliance upon a holy book as an explanation for the way things are (or should be). In fact, the pantheist does not have to rely upon any one source of knowledge for providing answers to the big questions of life, and this eclectic approach to understanding our world is very attractive today.

Pantheism is a very noble worldview regarding ethics, environmentalism, and civic issues, and that should be positively acknowledged. I wish more people would think seriously about these things. I find pantheists to be wonderful people, and had God not intervened in my life I might very well be a pantheist today. However, as positive as pantheism may be in many ways, it does not satisfactorily answer the big questions of life like Christianity does. For me, my worldview choice is not based upon which one seems to be the most attractive, but rather it's about which one is demonstrably true.

WHERE DOES PANTHEISM FALTER?

As with the other non-Christian worldviews, the evidences for God and Christianity refute pantheism. Even apart from those evidences, however, there are three reasons why pantheism as a worldview fails the test of logic. First, why would an impersonal force be responsible for creating personal beings? Apart from the question of intelligent life on other planets, why would even one planet in this vast cosmos contain beings which are capable of thought, self-contemplation, and emotions when the supposed source of everything is impersonal? The evidence for God from design, which is made obvious from a thorough study of nature, points to a Designer who skillfully crafted the heavens and the earth with an eye for mind-boggling detail. Would an impersonal force be capable of designing a universe with that much pre-planning and attention to detail? The answer seems to clearly be no. Therefore, the complexity and interconnectedness of the creation itself refutes the pantheistic worldview.

Second, pantheism confuses the creation with the Creator, a mistake that the Apostle Paul discusses in his letter to the church in Rome (1:25). Since the god of pantheism is indistinguishable from the universe itself, there is no real difference between pantheism and atheism. The only difference between the two worldviews is that the pantheist assigns religious significance to nature while the atheist does not. The World Pantheist Movement defines scientific (natural) pantheism as "a form of pantheism that deeply reveres the universe and nature and joyfully accepts and embraces life, the body and earth, but does not believe in any supernatural deities, entities or powers."[11] This is, of course, nothing but atheism clothed in spiritual lingo. Scientific pantheism attempts to impose spirituality upon the atheistic worldview in the attempt to avoid the sheer hopelessness of atheism. Regardless of the term one chooses – religious humanism, religious naturalism, naturalistic spirituality, positive atheism, and so on – scientific pantheism is a cleverly-disguised way of holding a deep reverence in something that is believed to be greater than humanity, while at the same time denying the existence of the Creator. However, Scripture reveals that human beings were made in God's image (Genesis 1:27), and therefore we are of greater significance than even the entirety of the physical universe itself, which is composed of lifeless matter.

Third, as previously mentioned the pantheist claims that nature has a built-in self-ordering tendency or force that guides the evolution of the universe and life. However, the only tendency in nature which is observed is entropy, which is the scientific principle that describes the degradation of the universe. The cosmos always proceeds from a state of greater order to a state of lesser order, from a state of greater complexity to a state of lesser complexity, and from a state of more usable energy to a state of less usable energy, unless acted upon by an outside force. Entropy is a fact of science, as opposed to the assumed self-ordering principle of panthe-

---

[11] Paul Harrison, "Naturalistic (Scientific) Pantheism: Reverence of Nature and Cosmos." https://www.pantheism.net/paul/index.htm

ism which is based upon philosophical speculation. Pantheism, whether in its Eastern mystical or Western scientific versions, is an example of "science falsely so-called" (1 Timothy 6:20).

Ultimately, the same lines of evidence for Christian theism which so persuasively defeat atheism likewise dispel the notion of a pantheistic god-force which is supposedly responsible for organizing matter into complex functioning systems. Once again, the evidence for God and Christianity serves to refute this sometimes attractive, but nonetheless erroneous worldview.

DEISM

Deism has been referred to as "the isthmus between two great continents – theism and naturalism."[12] That is a very correct statement, as deism both proclaims the existence of a Creator-God while at the same time avoiding any accountability to him. In fact, this may be the great selling point of deism. Deists are intellectually honest enough to acknowledge that an intelligent design requires an intelligent Designer, but at the same time they are reluctant to admit that God is in control of his creation, especially regarding the affairs of humanity. It is, as the old saying goes, a case of having your cake and eating it, too.

Several Christian resources list theism, atheism, and pantheism as being the three most prominent worldviews, but it is clear that deism should be included as a fourth major worldview. Interestingly, many people who are deists by conviction may not even be familiar with this term. It has been demonstrated through various surveys that atheists are a relatively minor percentage of the American population; the vast majority of people in this country believe in God, or at least in a Supreme Being as variously defined. Yet so many people today are skeptical of the claim that the Bible, or any other holy book, is truly from God. Many of these skeptics

---

[12] James Sire, *The Universe Next Door* (Downers Grove, IL: InterVarsity Press, 1997), 53.

view all religious writings as being nothing more than the religious musings of primitive, ancient thinkers. The deist admits that the evidence for God's existence is all around us, yet at the same time denies that the Creator has revealed information about himself to us in the written word, using chosen people of the past as divinely inspired writers. Relatively recent articles on the rising prevalence of deism in America[13] and Great Britain[14] illustrate this point.

It is noteworthy, however, that some deists hold the Bible and other holy books in high esteem for the wisdom and moral teachings that are contained within their pages, while other deists have nothing positive to say about any holy book. Therefore, deists tend to be of two stripes. The first brand of deists are those who oppose the teachings of the so-called "revealed religions" – that is, those religions which claim that God has revealed himself, and his plan for humanity, within the pages of a special book or a collection of writings. These deists are intent on pointing out where they believe the revealed religions are in error. This is traditional deism. The second brand of deists are those who blend their deistic beliefs with Christian moral teachings. This is Christian deism. Traditional deism never gained a strong foothold in America, in large part due to the success of the first Great Awakening.[15] Worldview expert Glenn Sunshine is convinced that most deists in early America associated themselves with Christianity in some manner: "…deists typically saw themselves as Christians. They may have disagreed with the church, with the Bible – with any sense of organized religion, in fact – but they still kept many aspects of the Christian worldview in place…"[16]

Since our worldview determines what we think of as be-

---

[13] Steven Waldman, "Deism: It's Back!"
http://blogbeliefnet.com/stevenwaldman/2009/09/deism-its-back.html
[14] Sholto Byrnes, "Britain's Hidden Religion."
http://newstatesman.com/religion/2009/04/god-flew-deism-world-atheist
[15] John Eidsmoe, *Christianity and the Constitution: The Faith of Our Founding Fathers* (Grand Rapids, MI: Baker Academic, 1987), 41.
[16] Glenn S. Sunshine, *Why You Think the Way You Do* (Grand Rapids, MI: Zondervan, 2009), 139-140.

ing reasonable, deists coming out of a Christian tradition naturally brought much of the Christian worldview with them. Most deists in early America can be described as Christian deists simply because so much of their thinking was drawn from Christian sources.[17] Today, with most non-Christians holding a low regard for the Bible, the vast majority of deists fall into the traditional category.

DEISM THROUGH THE CENTURIES

Deism emerged from the political and scientific revolutions of seventeenth century Europe, and this philosophical movement was both an intellectual and emotional revolt against the supernatural worldview of the Medieval and early Renaissance eras, which were predominately Christian-based. There was a great desire among some of the intellectual and political leaders of this time to once and for all dispose of their reliance upon so-called "magic and mysticism," and to instead understand the world from a purely naturalistic-scientific perspective. During this time in European history several "enlightened" sources converged, brought on by both the scientific revolution and the rise of biblical criticism. Reason was in, and divine revelation was on the way out. In short, "Intellectual pursuit was the rage."[18]

Much of this desire to question biblical and church authority stemmed from the "Wars of Religion" which took place throughout Western Europe. The many battles between Roman Catholics and the newly established Protestant denominations caused much suffering and bloodshed, and as a result many Europeans became convinced that religious passions were a sure way to cause political and social upheaval. The societies of Western Europe, which extended to America, were ready for a worldview that emphasized rationality. Deism experienced a wide appeal throughout eighteenth century Europe and America, having great influence especially among the intellectual elite – those involved in political

---

[17] Ibid.
[18] Len Woods, *Handbook of World Religions* (Uhrichsville, OH: Barbour Publishing, 2008), 55.

leadership as well as the academics that strongly influenced them. This "Age of Reason" was largely facilitated by philosophers such as the Englishman Lord Herbert of Cherbury, the Frenchman Voltaire, and the German Immanuel Kant. Charles Darwin, who lived shortly after the end of the Enlightenment, is by several accounts believed to have held to deistic rather than atheistic teachings, keeping this worldview alive in England well into the nineteenth century.[19]

In America, almost all of the leading thinkers and statesmen were convinced of the existence of the Creator; there were scant few atheists in early America. As a result, deism became the philosophical challenge to Christianity early on in American history. Nonetheless, most Americans were traditional Christians during this time, with the average person not too terribly worried about the deistic tendencies of men like Franklin, Adams, and Jefferson.[20]

Deism is considered to have begun its decline in America around the beginning of the nineteenth century, despite the fact that many of the key leaders in American independence who adhered to deistic thinking were still in positions of power and influence during this time. Even well into the nineteenth century people such as Abraham Lincoln were influenced by deism. Lincoln's deistic influence came primarily through Thomas Paine's *The Age of Reason*. The most significant factor in the decline of deism in America was the deaths of Elihu Palmer (d. 1806) and Thomas Paine (d. 1809). These evangelists of deism were not replaced by anyone nearly as zealous as they had been.[21]

Another factor which contributed to the decline of deism, and the subsequent rise in atheism, was the 1859 publication of Darwin's *On the Origin of Species*, which in the minds of

---

[19] David Herbert, *Charles Darwin's Religious Views* (Guelph, Ontario, Canada: Joshua Press, 2009), 66, 95, 120-121, 155-156.
[20] Alf J. Mapp, Jr., *The Faiths of Our Founding Fathers* (New York, NY: Fall River Press, 2006), 153.
[21] John Lindell, "History of Christian Deism."
http://www.christiandeistfellowship.com/histdeism.htm

many seemed to provide the necessary proof that God was no longer necessary to account for the origin and diversity of life on Earth. Combined with the powerful influence of atheistic philosophers such as Friedrich Nietzsche and a trend toward religious skepticism in general, atheism took over as the dominant philosophy in intellectual and academic circles.

Another significant factor contributing to the decline of deism in early America is that this worldview did not organize into any significant groups, which almost certainly would have helped deism to continue flourishing.[22] On the other hand, once atheism began to take hold in America it formed into powerful groups such as the American Humanist Association. Finally, many theologians in the nineteenth century began equating deism with atheism, which not only discouraged deistic ideas within a still predominately Christian culture but also further encouraged atheism among the skeptically-inclined.

Deism never completely died out, however. The World Union of Deists has enjoyed much success at reviving this worldview. Additionally, several other deist groups have been formed in recent years, renewing interest in this once influential way of understanding reality.

THE ATTRACTION OF DEISM

What makes deism so attractive to many people? The ultimate strength of deism lies in the fact that deists are honest enough to admit that the evidence for God's existence is overwhelming, while at the same time sidestepping accountability to him. By denying the authority of holy writ – whether the Bible, the Quran, the Hindu or Buddhist writings, and so forth – deists decide for themselves how their lives will be lived, with no guidance from any form of religious scripture. This is a big attraction for many people.

Additionally, many deists struggle with the ideas of the Trinity and the dual nature of Christ, instead finding the belief in "one God in one person" to be much more logical. Since the Trinity and the dual nature of Christ are doctrines

---

[22] Ibid.

that surpass human reasoning, I get where deists are coming from on this. Nonetheless, from the time that I became a follower of Christ I have always felt that God exceeds human reasoning in many ways. God is an infinite Holy Being who is qualitatively different from us (Isaiah 55:8-9), yet at the same time incredibly similar to us (John 1:14; Colossians 2:9).

WHERE DOES DEISM FALTER?

Although deism may rightfully claim a place at the table of prominent worldviews, deism nevertheless suffers from two very serious faults. First, deists admit to the divine creation of the universe, but deny any other miraculous events from the hand of God. This seems to be a little too convenient. To maintain that God is responsible for the miraculous creation of the universe and everything in it, but then to deny that same God the ability to perform later miracles is not logical. This is clearly a case of assigning God the role of Creator, which the deist cannot deny, while simultaneously avoiding God's role as Judge, which the fallen and spiritually unregenerate person cannot accept. Although the deist should be credited with the willingness to admit that the universe was created by God, the refusal to admit that all is not well within the creation – that the world is in a fallen state and that the human condition is in need of redemption – is denied by the deist. To declare that God simply set the process of cosmic, chemical, and biological evolution in motion and then let the universe and life evolve into its present state seems far too convenient of a way to acknowledge the evidence for the Creator while at the same time denying the need for a Redeemer.

Second, deism is based upon the faulty notion that God should be capable of forming a universe which does not need his continual intervention. However, there is no reason to believe this idea because even the deist acknowledges that God is personal, and as a personal being God will likely choose to involve himself in the continual workings of his creation, just as parents are interested in involving themselves in the affairs and endeavors of their children. A personal God will undoubtedly choose to be personally active in his creation.

ANSWERING THE BIG QUESTIONS

How do the four major worldviews attempt to answer the big questions of life? Although we have already covered much of what the four major worldviews teach, it would be good at this point to further flesh out the beliefs of Christian theism, atheism, pantheism, and deism through an exploration of answers to the most important questions concerning God, man, and ultimate reality.

WHAT IS THE NATURE OF GOD?

Christian Theism: God is real, and is the Creator of the universe. God is personal, meaning that God not only has the attributes of personality such as intellectual and emotional capabilities, but also that God has the ability and the willingness to enter into a personal relationship with people, who are created in his image (Genesis 1:27).

Atheism: God does not exist, but rather God is a figment of the imagination of frightened people who need to believe in something greater than themselves. In other words, God is a crutch for weak-minded people. As some atheists say, "God was created in the mind of man," rather than God creating man in his image, as Christian theists believe.

Pantheism: God is an impersonal force that is essentially synonymous with the material universe. God, or more accurately god, is the accumulation of the physical forces of nature imbued with spiritual qualities, such as transcendent awe and wonder.

Deism: God is the Creator, but that is all. God reveals himself to people only through his creation, not through any holy book and certainly not through Jesus Christ, as Christians claim. God is aloof and "out there somewhere," not concerned with the state of his creation or the affairs of men.

HOW DID THE UNIVERSE ORIGINATE?

Christian Theism: God spoke the heavens and the earth into existence (Genesis 1:1; Psalm 33:9).

Atheism: The origin of the universe was a chance, random event, with no overarching purpose. The universe "just is," with no intelligence or planning behind it.

Pantheism: Everything emanates from the impersonal god-force of the universe. Therefore, everything is god, and for many pantheists everything is interconnected and one (pantheistic monism).

Deism: God brought the universe into existence, but at some point stepped back and allowed cosmic, chemical, and biological evolution to unfold, thereby creating all that we observe today. Regarding the origin and diversity of life, the majority of deists accept macroevolution, which is also known as large-scale or "molecules-to-man" evolution.

WHAT IS MAN?

Christian Theism: Man is the creative masterpiece of God, made in his image (Genesis 1:27). Man is designed for a personal relationship with God.

Atheism: Man is an evolutionary accident, evolved over countless eons of time. Man is merely another animal, no better and no worse than any other creature on the face of the earth.

Pantheism: Man evolved, but man ultimately shares with the god-force a spiritual oneness that the other creatures share in as well.

Deism: Man is the most complex, intelligent being of God's making. Deists maintain that man was created through the process of large scale, or molecules-to-man, evolution.

HOW CAN WE KNOW ANYTHING?

Christian Theism: Although God has created us with the ability to exercise logic and reasoning, which plays a key role in how we understand the world and our place in it, the ultimate source of knowledge is derived from God's revelation to us. God's revelation comes to us through creation, the moral conscience, and Scripture. As a result of God's revelation to us, we can have full assurance that what we know is, in fact, true.

Atheism: People can know things through the senses (empiricism) and through logical deduction (rationalism). Ultimately, however, our thoughts are nothing more than chemical reactions taking place in the brain, so our ability to know can never be fully trusted.

Pantheism: Only the recognition of the god-force, from which all things emanate, can be known with certainty. Many of the Eastern religions, which generally adhere to pantheistic monism, claim that everything other than the god-force is an illusion, and therefore cannot be known with certainty. Not all pantheists believe that the physical universe is illusory, however.

Deism: Essentially the same answer to this question as provided by the atheist worldview.

WHAT IS TRUTH?

Christian Theism: God is the basis for all truth, so whatever God reveals to us to be truth is, in fact, truth. God has revealed truth to us through the pages of the Bible.

Atheism: Truth is the best explanation for the way things are. Truth is founded upon sensory experience and logical deduction, and is therefore a human endeavor. When it comes to deciding what is true, there is no God involved.

Pantheism: From a practical standpoint, truth is determined exactly in the manner that atheists maintain it is. For some pantheists, truth is ultimately an illusory idea, as only the god-force from which everything emanates is real.

Deism: Again, from a practical standpoint truth is determined exactly in the manner that atheists maintain it is, but in this case truth may have a foundation in God. Many deists maintain that the Creator is responsible for giving us the ability to determine truth for ourselves.

HOW DO WE KNOW RIGHT FROM WRONG?

Christian Theism: God acts upon our inherent ability to know right from wrong (Romans 2:14-15), as well as providing us with the answer directly in writing, such as the Ten Commandments.

Atheism: Both experience and reason directs us in our ethical behavior. Morality and ethics are determined by man alone, as there is no God to rely upon in this matter.

Pantheism: From a practical standpoint, pantheists determine right from wrong exactly as atheists do. Apart from a personal God who reveals his moral intentions for humanity, right from wrong is always based in human reasoning.

Deism: Again, from a practical standpoint deists determine right from wrong exactly as atheists do. God may or may not play a role in morality and ethics.

ARE MIRACLES POSSIBLE?

Christian Theism: Absolutely. In fact, miracles are recorded for us throughout the pages of the Bible, from Genesis to Revelation.

Atheism: Miracles are not possible, as nothing can defy the physical laws of nature. If something appears miraculous, it is merely misunderstood as there is always a scientific explanation for every phenomenon.

Pantheism: Miracles may or may not be possible. For scientifically-minded pantheists, supposed miracles are nothing more than science misunderstood. For religiously-inclined pantheists, miracles are ultimately an illusory idea, as only the god-force is real.

Deism: Miracles are not possible, since like the atheist deists claim that nothing defies the physical laws of nature. After the initial act of creation, which was truly miraculous, no miracles have occurred.

WHAT HAPPENS WHEN WE DIE?

Christian Theism: Those who trusted in Christ as their Lord and Savior will enter into the presence of God when this life is over, and those who rebelled against the Creator will enter into an eternal separation from him.

Atheism: There is no afterlife, since life ends at the grave.

Pantheism: For some pantheists life ends at the grave, while for others the continuation of life occurs through the karma-reincarnation cycle, as taught in the Eastern religions. At the end of the karma-reincarnation cycle, the soul is absorbed into the god-force, at which point the soul becomes one with the god-force and the soul loses its individual identity. Since the soul loses its individual identity, this means that the end result is essentially the same as for those who claim life ends at the grave.

Deism: For some deists there is no afterlife, while for others there is some form of life after death, perhaps in a Heaven where everyone gains admittance (universal salvation).

WHAT I DISCOVERED

After examining the evidence for God, Christ, and the Bible, I came to the conclusion that Christianity is not an unreasonable faith, as I had once believed it to be, but rather just the opposite is the case: Christianity is a well-reasoned faith that is built on solid lines of evidence. Of course, if Christianity is shown to be true then atheism, pantheism, and deism are all false, regardless of how appealing they may be for many people.

This comparison of worldviews allows one the opportunity to examine the evidence for Christian theism. The Holy Spirit, however, must ultimately be behind any examination of the faith by a seeker or a skeptic. The work of the Christian believer is to attempt to respectfully persuade the unbeliever (1 Peter 3:15), thereby allowing the Holy Spirit to work fully in the hearts and minds of unbelievers. This is the job of the apologist.

Chapter 2

SCIENCE, REASON, & REVELATION

There are a number of evidences which point to the existence of a personal Creator-God, and this chapter addresses three of the most important of these: The evidence from cause-and-effect, the evidence from design, and the positive correlation between science and Scripture. As always, no one line of evidence is an island, entire of itself. All of these evidences combine into a comprehensive "Case for a Creator."

EVIDENCE FROM CAUSE-AND-EFFECT

The evidence from cause-and-effect, which is commonly known as the cosmological argument among philosophers and theologians,[23] declares that the universe (cosmos) must have had a cause, since nothing in the universe is self-caused. This includes the entirety of the universe itself. The principle of cause-and-effect states that everything which has a beginning must have a cause, and the cause always transcends the effect. Science clearly demonstrates that the universe had a beginning. Therefore, since the universe had a beginning it had a cause, and that cause transcends the universe itself. We must ask ourselves what could possibly transcend the universe. Many are inclined to agree with the late R.C. Sproul: "The world that we perceive with our senses must therefore have a necessary first cause, otherwise known as the Creator God."[24]

---

[23] The term "cosmological argument" is the more scholarly term for the evidence from cause-and-effect. The word "cosmological" is derived from two Greek words: *cosmos*, meaning "world" or by extension "universe," and *logos*, meaning "reason" or "rational account." The cosmological argument therefore attempts to provide a rational account for the universe. This particular line of evidence for God's existence may be especially interesting to the unbeliever who enjoys scientific reasoning.

[24] R.C. Sproul, *Defending Your Faith* (Wheaton, IL: Crossway Books, 2003), 88.

The evidence for God from cause-and-effect has a long history. Aristotle was the first thinker of merit to utilize this line of reasoning for God's existence, some three and a half centuries prior to the time of Christ. Much later, the medieval theologian Thomas Aquinas utilized the evidence for God from cause-and-effect in the West while Arabian philosophers did the same in the East. Still later, during the Enlightenment or "Age of Reason," philosopher Gottfried Wilhelm Leibniz relied heavily on this line of reasoning, and jumping far ahead to the present day the preeminent Christian philosopher William Lane Craig is widely known for his use of cause-and-effect as a major line of evidence for God's existence. In short, this has always been a well-utilized line of reasoning for God.

In its most basic form, the evidence from cause-and-effect is summarized in three statements: (1) Whatever begins to exist must have a cause; (2) the universe began to exist; (3) therefore, the universe must have a cause. That's pretty basic, so let's explore this particular evidence for God's existence in more detail.

How do we know that the universe had a beginning? As it turns out, this has been an area of debate for quite a long time. Throughout much of history, the belief in an eternal universe – that is, a universe without a beginning – was very common. If the universe had no beginning, then this particular line of evidence for God is "dead in the water," as they say. Although we will explore both the science and the Scripture behind the beginning of the universe shortly, for now we can say with great confidence that the universe did, in fact, have a beginning.

Was the beginning of the universe caused or uncaused? Once again, according to the principle of cause-and-effect everything which has a beginning has a cause. Since the universe had a beginning, it must have had a cause. The claim that the beginning of the universe was uncaused would entail that the universe sprang into existence out of nothing, and for no reason, but it would be absurd to think that this happened since a basic rule of logic is that nothing never produces something.

Did the cause of the universe come from within the universe itself, or from outside of the universe? The cause of the beginning of the universe cannot lie within the universe itself, for in cause-and-effect relationships the cause always transcends the effect, as previously noted. Therefore, the cause of the universe had to come from outside of the universe. This means that the cause of the universe is supernatural, which literally means "beyond nature" or beyond time, space, and matter-energy. If the cause of the universe originated from within the universe, and the universe had a beginning, this would mean that the cause of the universe sprang into existence at the same time that the universe did. Of course, this is nonsensical, as causes always precede their effects.

Does this cause from outside of the universe need a cause itself, or could it be independent of the cause-and-effect relationship? Stated differently, either this cause from outside of the universe was caused to exist by something else, or this cause does not depend upon anything else for its existence. Although the principle of cause-and-effect states that everything that has a beginning has a cause, what if the first cause of the universe was itself eternal, or without a beginning? The universe had a cause, because it had a beginning, but that does not mean that the cause of the universe had to have a beginning. If it is not caused – in other words, it is eternal as it lies outside of time – then there are very serious theological implications involved. The Bible describes the one true God who brought the universe into existence as being eternal, or beyond time itself:

> *Lord, you have been our dwelling place throughout all generations. Before the mountains were born or you brought forth the whole world, from everlasting to everlasting you are God (Psalm 90:1-2).*
>
> *"I am the Alpha and the Omega," says the Lord God, "who is, and who was, and who is to come, the Almighty" (Revelation 1:8).*

Since the universe had a beginning it had a cause, and by extension everything within the universe had a cause as well. But the cause of the universe is itself uncaused. Countless people throughout history have recognized the identity of this first cause as being the God who reveals himself in Scripture.

SCIENCE AND THE BEGINNING

The strength of the evidence from cause-and-effect lies in both its logic and its appeal to science. The reasoning behind this line of evidence is very straightforward and convincing. At this point, an examination of four of the most important scientific pointers to the beginning of the universe is in order.

The First Law of Thermodynamics

Also referred to as the law of the conservation of mass and energy, this law states that both matter and energy can be neither created or destroyed naturally, although one may be converted into the other as demonstrated by Einstein's Theory of Special Relativity, the famous $e = mc^2$ equation. Isaac Asimov declared that the First Law of Thermodynamics "is considered the most powerful and most fundamental generalization about the universe that scientists have ever been able to make."[25] Since matter-energy may not be created naturally, yet it is clear that matter-energy exists, it therefore had to originate somehow. It is logical to maintain, therefore, that matter-energy was created supernaturally, "in the beginning" (Genesis 1:1a) before this law was put into place. No new matter-energy is being created, which agrees with the words of Scripture: "Thus the heavens and the earth were completed in all their vast array. By the seventh day God had finished the work he had been doing; so on the seventh day he rested from all his work" (Genesis 2:1-2). This is a very illuminating correlation between science and Scripture.

---

[25] Fred Heeren, *Show Me God: What the Message from Space is Telling Us about God* (Wheeling, IL: Day Star Publications, 2000), 128-129.

The Second Law of Thermodynamics

The Second Law of Thermodynamics tells us that the contents of the universe are becoming less ordered over time, and the amount of usable energy in the universe is also decreasing over time. Although the first law tells us that matter-energy cannot be created naturally, the second law tells us that matter-energy is degrading over time. In short, the universe is wearing down, a phenomenon known as entropy. Therefore, it is impossible for the universe to be eternal, as it could not have been dissipating or winding down forever. The Second Law of Thermodynamics is accurately described in Scripture (Psalm 102:25-26; Isaiah 34:4; 51:6), once again confirming the positive relationship between science and the Bible.

The Expansion of the Universe

The expansion of the universe, as poetically described in Scripture (Psalm 104:2; Job 9:8; Isaiah 40:22; 42:5; 44:24; 45:12; 48:13; 51:13; Jeremiah 10:12; 51:15; Zechariah 12:1), has been scientifically confirmed through the phenomenon of red shift. Red shift is attributed in large part to the work of Edwin Hubble in the early part of the twentieth century, and merely confirmed what the biblical writers already knew millennia earlier.[26] Using the most powerful telescope in the world, Hubble observed that the universe is continuously expanding. He discovered that a galaxy's velocity is proportional to its distance: Galaxies that are twice as far from Earth are moving away twice as fast. Additionally, the universe is expanding in every observable direction, which indicates that the universe is expanding from a common starting point. If the expanding universe could be put into reverse and shrunk back down, it should come to a near-infinite point, referred to by cosmologists and astrophysicists as the "event horizon," or the starting point of the universe. This is, of course, powerful proof of a beginning point to time, space,

---

[26] Ralph Muncaster, *Examine the Evidence* (Eugene, OR: Harvest House Publishers, 2004), 163-164.

and matter-energy.

Cosmic Background Radiation

In 1965, two scientists from Bell Labs, Arno Penzias and Robert Wilson, attempted to detect microwaves from outer space, and inadvertently discovered an electronically-detected "noise" of extraterrestrial origin. This was five years after SETI – the Search for Extraterrestrial Intelligence– began under the initial name Project OZMA, so as would be expected there was much excitement generated at first. However, the noise did not seem to emanate from one location in the universe, but rather came from all directions simultaneously. Therefore, the noise that they heard was of a natural origin, as opposed to being attributed to advanced, thinking beings from elsewhere in the universe. Penzias and Wilson went on to discover that this detectable noise was radiation which had been left over from the creation event itself – sort of a "fossil remnant" of the initial beginning of time, space, and matter-energy. This discovery of cosmic background radiation lent very strong support to the beginning of the universe. More recently, NASA's COBE satellite was able to detect cosmic microwaves emanating from the furthest reaches of the known universe. The uniformity of these microwaves demonstrated the homogeneity of the early universe, shortly after the initial moment of creation. As the universe cooled, yet maintained its expansion, small fluctuations began to form as a result of temperature differences. These temperature differences verified calculations that had been performed in the attempt to demonstrate the hypothesized cooling and development of the universe just fractions of a second after its creation. These temperature fluctuations in the universe provide not only a more detailed description of the first moments after the initiation of the creation event, but more importantly provide a powerful line of evidence for the creation event in general – and, by extension, evidence for the Creator.

SKEPTICISM & CAUSE-AND-EFFECT

Due to the formidableness of the evidence from cause-and-effect, skeptics are often quick to attack this particular line of reasoning for God's existence. Nonetheless, these skeptical attacks may be effectively countered.

An Oscillating Universe

An argument against the beginning of the universe is found in the oscillating universe theory. This theory was devised as a way around the problem of a universe with a beginning, which clearly contains theological implications – namely, God's existence. British physicist John Gribbin is refreshingly honest about this: "The biggest problem with the Big Bang theory of the origin of the Universe [in other words, that the universe had a beginning] is philosophical – perhaps even theological – what was there before the bang? This problem alone was sufficient to give a great initial impetus to the Steady State theory [which is the theory that the universe is eternal]."[27]

Gribbin confirms that the theological implications of a beginning of the universe are problematic, as the evidence from cause-and-effect is only difficult to embrace if one holds to naturalism. Gribbin continues: "…but with that [Steady State, or eternal universe] theory now sadly in conflict with the observations, the best way round this initial difficulty is provided by a model in which the universe expands from a singularity, collapses back again, and repeats the cycle indefinitely."[28] This idea is nothing new, which should not be surprising as few things ever are (Ecclesiastes 1:9). Astrophysicist and old earth creationist Hugh Ross relates that both Hindu philosophers and Roman naturalists in the ancient world devised the idea long before the so-called "Age of Science."[29]

---

[27] Hugh Ross, *The Fingerprint of God* (New Kensington, PA: Whitaker House, 1989), 97.
[28] Ibid.
[29] Ibid.

Proponents of the oscillating universe theory claim that the universe is eternal, but only *appears* to have had a beginning because the universe is undergoing an eternal or neverending series of expansions and contractions. According to these theorists, at a certain point the universe can no longer expand, at which time it begins to contract back to a near-infinitesimal point, only to begin the expansion phase all over again. From our perspective as observers of the universe, utilizing the best scientific tools at our disposal, the universe appears to be expanding for the first and only time. However, proponents of this theory say that in reality the universe is only expanding during our particular "bounce," as each cycle of the expansion-contraction theory is known. Perhaps in previous bounces (universes) there were different life forms unlike anything we know of today, and maybe in future bounces there will be new forms of life that are unimaginable to us, each following a unique evolutionary pathway. According to oscillating universe theorists, this current bounce is marked by our existence, but even then many people hold to the idea that human beings are only one of countless life forms throughout the universe.

However, the oscillating universe theory is based upon pure speculation. It is a convenient way to avoid the problem of positing a Beginner of the universe. Furthermore, it is besieged by a host of scientific problems, most notably the Second Law of Thermodynamics and the absence of any known mechanism or force which could aid in the bounce. Despite these scientific obstacles, the ideological motivation to avoid a beginning to the universe – and hence the necessity of a Beginner – is incredibly powerful. Surprisingly, in 1973 two Soviet scientists, Igor Novikov and Yakob Zel'dovich, provided scientific evidence against the possibility of oscillation. They pointed out that a uniform isotropic compression, which has been hypothesized as the means of contracting the universe from the point of maximum expansion, "becomes violently unstable near the end of the collapse phase, and the collapsing medium breaks up into fragments."[30] They went on to state that "oscillation provides no escape from an ultimate beginning in the finite past."[31] As Soviet scientists who were supposed to be devoted to the propagation of Marxist ideology, which is inherently atheistic, it was refreshingly honest of these two men to admit the faulty scientific reasoning behind this theory.

The evidence against the oscillating universe theory is devastating. The following five points offer a sound refutation of this idea.[32] First, a cyclical expansion and contraction of the universe would result in an ever-increasing radius, which would be traceable backward to a first cycle, and hence an ultimate beginning of the universe in the first place. Second, the observed density of the universe appears to be only half of what would be necessary to force a collapse of the expansion-contraction cycle. Third, there is no mechanism or force known that could trigger a cosmic contraction. Fourth, isotropic compression becomes violently unstable near the end of the collapse phase, and is ruled out as a possible explanation for the bounce back. Finally, the observable entropy in the universe is such that a bounce becomes impossible after a certain number of bounces, ruling out an infinite number of expansion-contraction cycles. Despite this particular attempt to refute a beginning of the universe, and hence a Beginner, the oscillating universe theory falls flat in light of its scientific errors.

Misunderstanding Cause-and-Effect

It is common for skeptics to ask the question, "If God made the universe, then who or what made God?" Their line of reasoning is that if everything requires a cause, then something or someone must be responsible for God's existence. However, the principle of cause-and-effect does not state that everything has a cause, but rather everything which begins to exist has a cause. If God did not begin to exist, but rather is

---

[30] Ibid.
[31] Ibid.
[32] Ibid.

eternal – a point which is both declared throughout the Bible (Psalm 90:1-2; 1 Timothy 1:17; Hebrews 13:8) and is reasonably ascertained through examining the evidence from cause-and-effect – then God himself does not need a cause. In fact, God alone is eternal, and is the only uncreated or uncaused entity. The entirety of the universe is finite and therefore caused, but God does not fit into that classification. God is eternal, infinite, immaterial, and immutable. God is uncaused, a philosophical concept which is impossible to adequately wrap our minds around. God, through the words of the prophet Isaiah, declares his infinite character:

> *"For my thoughts are not your thoughts, neither are your ways my ways," declares the LORD. "As the heavens are higher than the earth, so are my ways higher than your ways and my thoughts than your thoughts" (Isaiah 55:8-9).*

The erroneous belief that God himself had to have a cause is based upon a faulty understanding of both the principle of cause-and-effect as well as the nature of God. It is a common misunderstanding that should no longer be appealed to by skeptics.

Quantum Physics

Some skeptics have claimed that nothing can actually produce something, and they appeal to quantum physics as the "hero" which makes that possible:

> *According to contemporary quantum physics, virtual particles can pop into existence in what is called the "quantum vacuum." They are called "virtual particles" because they cannot be observed directly, although their indirect effects can be measured. Because the quantum vacuum doesn't appear to be an object – according to our ordinary notion of object – it is sometimes said that virtual particles literally come into being out of nothing.*[33]

However, we must ask the question, "Where did this

---

[33] James R. Beebe, "The Kalam Cosmological Argument for the Existence of God." http://www.apollos.squarespace.com/cosmological-argument/

quantum vacuum come from?" No matter how we may think of this quantum vacuum, it is most definitely *something*, even if non-physical (immaterial) in nature. However, even proponents of the quantum vacuum say that it gives every indication of being a physical object with a complicated structure, and the term "structure" itself further implies that it is physical in nature. "[The quantum vacuum] is simply the lowest energy state of the quantum field, and the quantum field is a physical object with a very complicated structure, a structure that is specified by a set of equations that contain a variety of apparently arbitrary numbers."[34]

When the quantum vacuum is no longer in its lowest energy state, particles do appear to pop into existence, but in actuality there are physical events taking place which merely give the appearance of the creation of these particles from out of nothing. True "nothingness" has no physical or non-physical properties. "Nothingness" cannot be studied by science, because there is absolutely nothing to study! Quantum physics, although fascinating, is an area of physical science that still leaves many questions unanswered, and due to its almost supernatural nature many open-minded physicists are quick to say that this branch of science will likely point us in the direction of the divine.

SCRIPTURE AND THE BEGINNING

The Bible opens up with the words, "In the beginning God created the heavens and the earth" (Genesis 1:1). Therefore, right at the very beginning of Scripture is the proclamation that God created everything. The entirety of the universe was actually brought into existence at a definite point in the very distant past, however long ago that was.[35] As opposed to many ancient thinkers who believed that the gods formed the world out of eternally pre-existing matter, this proclama-

---

[34] Ibid.

[35] I personally utilize resources from both young earth and old earth creationist ministries, and rather than focusing on the age of the earth I instead emphasize the evidence for a beginning of the universe, the incredible design in nature, and the fact that life comes only from life.

tion by Moses was radical in its day – and is, in the minds of many, clear evidence that God is behind the words of Scripture. In fact, it would be a long time before the human race as a whole would begin to see that Genesis opens up right where it should: "In the beginning…"

The Israeli scientist Gerald Schroeder, known worldwide for his expertise on the relationship between science and the Hebrew scriptures, relates how difficult it was for modern scientists to finally accept a beginning point for the universe:

> In 1959, a survey was taken of leading American scientists. Among the many questions asked was, "What is your estimate of the age of the universe?" Now, in 1959, astronomy was popular, but cosmology – the deep physics of understanding the universe – was just developing. The response to that survey was recently republished in Scientific American – the most widely read science journal in the world. Two-thirds of the scientists gave the same answer. The answer that two-thirds – an overwhelming majority – of the scientists gave was, "Beginning? There was no beginning. Aristotle and Plato taught us 2400 years ago that the universe is eternal. Oh, we know the Bible says, "In the beginning." That's a nice story; it helps kids go to bed at night. But we sophisticates know better. There was no beginning."[36]

The evidence for a beginning of the universe was already well-established by 1959, but it would be another six years before Penzias and Wilson would discover cosmic background radiation –the "fossil remnant" of the creation event– which seemed to solidify the case for a beginning point to time, space, and matter-energy. By this time in history it seems that more than one-third of the respondents should have been adequately versed in at least the scientific basics of a universe with a beginning. Of course, this demonstrates that sometimes it takes a long time for paradigm-changing information to take hold.

---

[36] Gerald Schroeder, "The Age of the Universe."
http://www.geraldschroeder.com?AgeUniverse.aspx

As it turns out, the Bible had it right all along: There was a beginning to the universe. Genesis 1:1 is not the only verse which speaks of this beginning, for the Holy Spirit inspired many different biblical authors to write of the creation event, from both the Old and the New Testaments (Nehemiah 9:6; Psalm 89:11; 115:15; 124:8; Isaiah 40:21; 42:5; 45:18; Jeremiah 10:12; 51:15; John 1:1-2; Acts 17:24; Colossians 1:16-17; Hebrews 1:10; Revelation 4:11). It is thrilling, to say the least, to find this positive correlation between science, reason, and faith.

WORLDVIEWS IN THE LIGHT OF CAUSE-AND-EFFECT

What does this line of evidence for God's existence mean in light of the four major worldviews that we explored in the first chapter? While the evidence from cause-and-effect on its own does not necessarily sound the death knell for either atheism or pantheism, neither of these worldviews look especially healthy after considering the theological implications of cause-and-effect. Since the atheistic worldview claims that there is no God or gods that transcend nature, those who claim atheism for their worldview must somehow explain away the implications of an uncaused cause of the universe, one which originates from beyond time, space, and matter-energy. Pantheism does not fare any better in the light of this evidence, since the cause of the universe had to originate from outside of the universe itself. Pantheism maintains that the universe and the god-force are one. In order for the god-force to be able to create the universe it would also have to create itself at the same time – which is a nonsensical idea since "from out of nothing comes nothing" and truly nothing existed before the initial moment of creation.

However, it must be noted that the evidence from cause-and-effect also lends support to the belief in the so-called "god of the philosophers," which is the god of deism. Cause-and-effect demonstrates the existence of the uncaused, timeless, independent First Cause of the universe. It is up to the other evidences for God to further flesh out the identity of this First Cause. However, the evidence from cause-and-effect has hit both atheism and pantheism hard, and now only deism remains somewhat intact. Deism will eventually be severely challenged through the remaining lines of evidence for God, however.

As a young man in my late twenties I became solidly convinced that the existence of the Creator is beyond doubt, based in large part upon the science and logic of the evidence from cause-and-effect. Later on, when the correlation between science and Scripture became evident to me, I began to gravitate more and more toward the truth claims of the Bible, and then it was only a matter of time before I bowed my knees before the King of the Universe himself, Jesus Christ. If this particular path of coming to Christ happened to me, in which the evidence from cause-and-effect played a significant role, then I suspect that it has happened to others as well. This is why evidences for God can be such a powerful means of sharing the message of Christ. Just like I was in my mid-twenties, many people are not ready to hear about Christ's sacrificial atonement for the sins of humanity until they are first convinced of the reality of the Creator. Only then do some people move beyond a general belief in God and become ready to thoughtfully consider the truth claims of Christianity.

EVIDENCE FROM DESIGN

Design is a powerful line of evidence for God's existence which links nature with common sense. The evidence from design looks at both physical science, such as the intricate system of planets within the Milky Way galaxy, as well as biological science, such as the high level of complexity within the DNA molecule, and asserts that an intelligent design requires an intelligent Designer. Whether appealing to examples from astrophysics, microbiology, or everything in between, the universe displays intelligent design at every turn. It is no wonder that the Apostle Paul does not excuse the atheist for denying the obvious evidence for a Designer (Romans 1:20).

The evidence from design has a long history. A few decades before the birth of Christ, the Roman orator and statesman Cicero utilized design to challenge the naturalistic ideas that were being proposed even in his day. In his book *On the Nature of the Gods* Cicero claimed that the intricate design that is displayed throughout nature pointed to a Designer. Although several different schools of philosophical thought existed in Cicero's time, the two most dominant were Epicureanism and Stoicism. Interestingly, a century later the Apostle Paul confronted both Epicurean and Stoic philosophers in Athens, and Paul began his presentation of the Gospel message to them by sharing the evidence for creation. Although Epicurus, the founder of Epicureanism, proposed an elaborate system of naturalistic evolution, Cicero argued against that notion by reasoning that the beauty and purpose of nature was so majestic that it could only have arisen through a conscious intelligence of inconceivable power. Like Paul after him, Cicero needed only the God-given gift of logic and reasoning to come to this conclusion, not a microscope and a telescope. Today, however, in addition to the gifts of logic and reasoning a complex system of scientific investigation exists which further solidifies the "Case for a Designer." Cicero, so far as we know, did not have the technology to peer into the heavens or marvel at the inner workings of the cell, but nonetheless his ability to reason was more than adequate for him to formulate his concept of intelligent design.

Skipping far ahead to the eighteenth century, William Paley penned his masterpiece *Natural Theology*, in which he put forward his famous "watchmaker argument." Writing thirty years after the skeptical philosopher David Hume, who is known to history as the man who challenged the evidence from design in modern times, Paley maintained that if a person were to come across a watch lying on the ground, he or she would have to logically conclude that it had been intentionally designed by someone. The reason for this is that the watch is just too intricate; its parts exhibit an interconnected cohesiveness and design that cannot be explained as the result of metals in the ground forming together by sheer chance. To think that possible would be sheer lunacy. As intricate and interconnected as the parts of the watch are, consider how much more complex is nature as a whole. The cell has proven to be an exquisitely designed system, far exceeding the complexity that it was thought to possess in Paley's day. Yet naturalistic evolutionists have somehow been able to convince a large segment of the general population – as well as themselves – that all systems found in nature are ultimately attributable to chance, random processes, despite these systems exhibiting a complexity that far exceeds anything that can be humanly designed. This successful plot by naturalists to promote their view of origins has been simultaneously disheartening and baffling.

The next major figure to radically impact the origins debate was Charles Darwin. Darwin was required to read Paley's *Natural Theology* during his theological studies at Cambridge. Although an admirer of Paley, Darwin nonetheless spent the remainder of his life attempting to demonstrate how the appearance of design in nature could be explained apart from the creativity of God. Darwin's appeal to natural selection, which is the ability of living organisms to pass on favorable traits to their offspring, became the primary tool of his theory of origins. As it turns out, although natural selection is an actual process in biology, in reality it only serves to maintain an already existing creature's current state, rather than building a living creature from the ground up. Stated differently, natural selection promotes the maintenance of already existing creatures, not large-scale evolutionary changes that bring a creature into existence in the first place.

In the past few decades, the modern intelligent design movement became established through the publication of key works, notably Michael Denton's *Evolution: A Theory in Crisis* and Phillip Johnson's *Darwin on Trial*. Additional resources, far too numerous to mention, have also contributed to the rising interest in the Darwinism versus Intelligent Design debate.

The list of naturalistic evolutionists today is long, but perhaps the name that is often thought of as being at the top of that list is Richard Dawkins, the retired Oxford zoologist who is considered by most to be the preeminent evangelist of atheism in the world today. Dawkins is riding the wave of Darwinism that was begun over a century and a half ago. In fact, one can say that his atheistic worldview is founded upon the conviction that Darwin proved naturalistic evolution to be true. Despite the advances of modern science, many of which cannot be logically interpreted without appealing to an intelligent Designer, Dawkins and those like him are stuck with the very refutable arguments of atheism.

REASON & DESIGN

The more complex an event or structure is, the less likely that it just happened by chance. For example, the presidential faces on Mount Rushmore are too complex to be the result of wind and water erosion. Anyone who is told that random processes in nature could form the artistic design seen on Mount Rushmore would have their intellect insulted. If the faces on Mount Rushmore show signs of having been designed on purpose, then how much more incredible is it to believe that the DNA code, which is unbelievably complex and information-rich, happened merely by chance, without the input of an intelligent Designer? Amazingly, the academic and skeptical communities – which overlap far too often – propose that the structures of nature evolved into their current states of complexity apart from any form of creative design.

Complexity and design in nature is really a very simple matter: One does not have to be a scientist by training to readily see that the structures of nature, whether seen through the telescope, the microscope, or with the naked eye, are too complex to be the result of chance, random processes in nature. The Apostle Paul made this point very clear in his letter to the church in Rome (Romans 1:20). Following Paul's lead in a time closer to our own, the subtitle of William Paley's *Natural Theology* reveals the purpose of intelligent design: *Evidences of the Existence and Attributes of the Deity, Collected from the Appearances of Nature.* Well ahead of the Darwinism versus Intelligent Design controversy, Paley provided the impetus for scientists, theologians, and scholars from all disciplines to thoughtfully consider the evidence of design in the world. Nature, according to both Paley and Paul, appears designed for a reason: It is.

Design appeals to our innate sense of truth. Some may try to deny design, as atheists do, or attribute it to alien creators, as ancient astronaut theorists do, or even soften it by saying that nature itself has a built-in self-ordering mechanism, as many pantheists do. Nonetheless, the reason for intelligent design is clear: The designs of nature are attributed to an intelligent Designer. For those who uphold intelligent design, the fact that it is a common sense approach to origins holds much merit.

SKEPTICISM & DESIGN

The lack of precise methods for distinguishing true design in nature has, in large part, kept intelligent design out of mainstream science. Being able to absolutely confirm intelligent design in nature through either mathematical or empirical means – as opposed to identifying structures which appear to be designed but are, in fact, attributed to chance, random processes – is the main point of contention between design theorists and naturalistic evolutionists. Along this line, intelligent design author William Dembski notes the error of the Enlightenment astronomer Johannes Kepler. Kepler was convinced that the craters on the moon were intelligently designed by "moon dwellers."[37] However, we now know that they were formed through chance, random processes in nature (namely, meteor impacts). Therefore, it is important for design theorists to make certain that a precise methodology exits which can confirm design, and proponents of intelligent design are quick to acknowledge this. There is no disputing this very valid point. Fortunately, intelligent design theorists have made considerable advances recently in developing ac-

---

[37] William A. Dembski, "Intelligent Design." http://www.designinference.com/documents/2003.08.Encyc_of_Relig.htm

curate methodologies for scientifically testing the presence of intentional design. In fact, some of the so-called "special sciences," such as forensic science, cryptography, archaeology, and the search for extraterrestrial intelligence (SETI), already utilize some of these methodologies.[38]

Opponents of intelligent design point out that it is possible that a creation event occurred without intelligent design following that event, and likewise it is possible that intelligent design occurred, or even continues to occur, without a point of creation for the universe. In the former scenario, God initiates the creation of time, space, and matter-energy but then backs away and allows the laws of nature to guide the universe into its present condition through the process of cosmic, chemical, and biological evolution. This is the deistic position on origins. In the latter scenario, the universe is eternal, and a self-ordering evolutionary force proceeds to form out of eternally pre-existing matter the structures of the universe as we know them today. This is the pantheistic position on origins. In Western civilization the pantheistic view goes back at least to the time of the Stoics, who believed that "the world is full of signs of intelligence but was not created,"[39] while the deistic view goes back to roughly the time of the Reformation, some five hundred years ago. These opponents of intelligent design are saying that an initial creation event does not demand design, and design does not demand an initial creation event, and they want everyone to know this – and this is a point which cannot be dismissed. However, this is not really a weakness of the evidence from design so much as it is a philosophical point to be noted. Intelligent design theorists do admit that it is logically possible that God could have created a world with no signs of intelligence in it, and it is likewise logically possible that the world is eternal and uncreated yet shows signs of having been designed. The point that intelligent design theorists want to proclaim is this: Philosophical and scientific evidences clearly demonstrate

---

[38] Ibid.
[39] Ibid.

that the universe was both created *and* designed. The evidence from cause-and-effect combined with the evidence from design forms a one-two punch that sends both atheism and pantheism reeling backward into the proverbial ropes. Deism does not fare so well from this combination punch, either.

One very important point needs to be brought up when considering the evidence from design. The Enlightenment philosopher Immanuel Kant, despite never rejecting design in nature, did object to overextending its use, to make it more than it should be. He was adamant that design in nature only establishes an "architect" who fashions out of pre-existing matter the structures of nature. For Kant, the argument from design does not establish the existence of a Creator who brought everything into existence from out of nothing.[40] Once again, however, this is no problem for the Christian theist, as the evidence from cause-and-effect readily refutes the idea that the universe is eternal. This is why the combination of cause-and-effect and design can be so persuasive. Cause-and-effect demonstrates that the universe was created from nothing, while design establishes that the Creator is intimately involved in the creation. This combination of evidences oppose the deistic concept of an aloof, uninterested Creator who merely allows the established laws of nature to take over after the initial moment of creation. Atheism and its essentially synonymous counterpart pantheism are effectively refuted through cause-and-effect, while deism is refuted primarily through the evidence from detailed design. All other lines of evidence for the existence of God further solidify the "Case for the Creator."

The great skeptic David Hume was known to say that many structures in nature only appear to be designed, but in fact are not. This line of thinking has persisted to this day.

---

[40] It must be noted that Immanuel Kant lived well before the modern scientific confirmation of the beginning of time, space, and matter-energy. In his day it was common for many philosophers to argue for a universe that was eternal, or without beginning.

However, one has to simply study biology, chemistry, and the physical sciences to see that there really is design in nature. For example, the DNA chain is an incredibly complex system of coded information, and could not reasonably have arisen through chance, random processes in nature. In fact, useful information only comes from one source: Intelligence.

Unintelligent natural causes, which are the only type of causes that exist in the eyes of naturalistic evolutionists, are merely the interactions of the properties of matter-energy with the laws of nature. These interactions are governed by the laws of physical chemistry and do not have the ability to look ahead and guide evolution in a desirable path. However, a guided, desirable path is exactly what seems to have taken place as countless systems in nature exhibit an interconnected, symbiotic relationship that seems to defy the odds of happening through sheer chance alone. It is true that unintelligent natural causes produce patterns which are both random and regular, and it is also true that purely material causes can move matter in a uniform pattern and start and stop the movement suddenly. However, when not acted upon by an outside force, physical systems will move from a state of order to a state of disorder, per the rule of entropy or universal decay. Naturalistic evolution, however, generally holds that nature self-orders itself by means of an as-yet-unknown force or principle, or simply through chance, random processes in nature. Despite this confidence by many naturalistic evolutionists in either chance or the unknown, all that has ever been observed in nature is entropy. This self-ordering theory is simply not supported by the observable evidence, and chance, random processes fare no better, either. Structures that contain vast amounts of ordered information, such as DNA, had to arise through intelligent planning.

DNA: IRREFUTABLE EVIDENCE FOR DESIGN

The existence of precise information encoded in the deoxyribonucleic acid (DNA) molecule is clear evidence of intentional design in nature. To believe that the DNA molecule simply evolved by chance is to accept an impossibility that no rational person, if he or she took the time to thoughtfully consider the matter, would embrace. "The amount of information that could be stored in a pinhead's volume of DNA is equivalent to a pile of paperback books 500 times as tall as the distance from Earth to the moon, each with a different, yet specific content."[41] The preeminent atheist Richard Dawkins admits that DNA has "enough information capacity in a single human cell to store the *Encyclopedia Britannica*, all 30 volumes of it, three or four times over,"[42] and, for the computer geek, a pinhead of DNA can hold 100 million times more information than a 40 gigabyte hard drive.[43] Yet naturalistic evolutionists are adamant that this molecule simply evolved over eons of time through chance, random processes in nature.

In intelligent design theory, the term "irreducible complexity" gets thrown around a lot, and for good reason. Irreducible complexity, which became a commonplace term as a result of Michael Behe's wildly popular treatise on the subject of design, *Darwin's Black Box*, demonstrates that it is impossible for biological systems to be built from the ground up by natural selection working through small changes. Instead, biological systems demonstrate over and over again that all of their many complex parts were functioning from the beginning of their existence to the present time. The evidence for this is based upon the irreducible interconnectedness of the individual parts. In order for a biological system to function, all of the parts had to be in place from the beginning, or the system could not work. Regarding DNA, there is an unmistakably high degree of irreducible complexity in its ability to accurately reproduce itself.

When a DNA molecule undergoes reproduction, the encoded information is precisely copied into a new strand. This

---

[41] Russell Grigg, "A Brief History of Design." https://www.creation.com/a-brief-history-of-design
[42] Jonathan Sarfati, "DNA: Marvellous Messages or Mostly Mess?" https://www.creation.com/dna-marvellous-messages-or-mostly-mess
[43] Ibid.

copying is far more precise than pure chemistry can account for, however: Only about one mistake occurs out of ten billion copies. This is due to an editing "machine" that is part of the DNA molecule. This machine proofreads the code, and corrects for errors that might have arisen had there been no error-checking system in place.[44] This proof-reading machine had to be in place from the beginning, otherwise DNA would not have continued on to the present time, and certainly not in its remarkably consistent form.

Regarding the origin of the DNA molecule, the noted philosopher of science Sir Karl Popper admitted that the DNA code cannot be translated without relying upon certain products of its translation. "This constitutes a baffling circle; a really vicious circle, it seems, for any attempt to form a model or theory of the genesis of the genetic code."[45] It is incredibly baffling, but only if one is locked into accepting purely naturalistic explanations for the origin of DNA. Only when the possibility of a supernatural origin for the DNA code is considered can we put an end to this mystery.

Needless to say, the reluctance to consider a supernatural explanation for the origin of DNA can lead to some improbable and unnecessary hypotheses. Sir Francis Crick, one of the co-discoverers of the DNA molecule, was devoted to atheism long before his landmark discovery. Crick was the Richard Dawkins of his generation. In 1961, the year before he and fellow researcher James Watson discovered the DNA molecule, "Crick resigned as a fellow of Churchill College, Cambridge, when it [the college's administration] proposed to build a chapel."[46] Interestingly, Crick's distaste for religion was one of the reasons that led to his discovery of the molecule: He believed that DNA would provide the evidence that life simply evolved by chance, random processes. How-

---

[44] Ibid.
[45] Ibid.
[46] Gary Bates, "Designed by Aliens? Discoverers of DNA's Structure Attack Christianity." https://www.creation.com/designed-by-aliens-crick-watson-atheism-panspermia

ever, the staggering amount of precisely encoded information is anything but proof for naturalism, and I cannot help but wonder if Crick secretly came to the realization that God was directly responsible for this incredibly information-rich code.

Enter directed panspermia. Panspermia is derived from two Greek words: *pan*, meaning "all" and *sperma*, meaning "seed." Therefore, panspermia is the idea that the seeds of all life are to be found throughout the universe. At the initial moment of creation or shortly thereafter, life in the form of cells and molecules developed and were spread throughout the universe, as it expanded. Crick actually preferred the idea of directed panspermia, which maintains that the "seeds" constituting all of the life forms here on Earth were directed to this planet by intelligence from beyond our sphere – intelligence which does not include God, of course. Crick, in his book *Life Itself*, proposed that primordial life was shipped to Earth billions of years ago by an advanced race of extraterrestrial beings,[47] who, in Crick's view, had either evolved naturally or had originated through directed panspermia via an even earlier intergalactic civilization. One can see how that could quickly turn into an almost infinite regress of alien creators. Crick acknowledged the futility of his view on origins when he wrote, "Every time I write a paper on the origins of life, I swear I will never write another one, because there is too much speculation running after too few facts…"[48] Had Crick honestly and openly considered the evidence from cause-and-effect and design, he might never have had the problems that he wrestled with concerning the origin of life.

SCRIPTURE & DESIGN

The following verses are only a select few of many that address the reality of intelligent design. Job is not only one of the oldest books in Scripture but is also one of the most

---

[47] Ibid.
[48] Ibid.

fascinating from a scientific perspective; nature is described in great detail in some of the later chapters. Near the end of the book, God quizzes Job over some of the more interesting facets of nature, and then reminds Job of his finite limitations when he poses the question, "Where were you when I laid the earth's foundation? Tell me, if you understand" (Job 38:4). As intelligent as Job surely was, he was no match for the wisdom of the infinite and all-powerful Designer.

King David penned the following verse long before astronomy became a formalized science: "The heavens declare the glory of God; the skies proclaim the work of his hands" (Psalm 19:1). When contemplating the wonders of intelligent design, sometimes we can view creation through the microscope or, as the psalmist would have greatly appreciated in his time, the telescope. Either way, the magnificence of creation is startling.

The Apostle Paul is adamant that no one can be excused for failing to see the evidence for intelligent design: "For since the creation of the world God's invisible qualities – his eternal power and divine nature – have been clearly seen, being understood from what has been made, so that people are without excuse" (Romans 1:20). Christian theists from Paul's day to the present are convinced that atheism is a worldview developed in large part as a way to avoid accountability to the Creator.

On that note, deism has been a convenient way for some people to affirm the existence of a Creator while at the same time avoiding accountability to him. Paul declares Christ as the Creator, "For in him all things were created; things in heaven and on earth, visible and invisible, whether thrones or powers or rulers or authorities; all things have been created through him and for him" (Colossians 1:16) before revealing Christ's personal concern for his creation: "He is before all things, and in him all things hold together" (Colossians 1:17). The false god of deism is not interested in his creation– he is not interested in sustaining the universe, but rather observes it from afar, if at all – yet it is clear from Scripture that Christ oversees creation, and is concerned with the details of human affairs. John 3:16 is the verse which perhaps best exemplifies Christ's loving concern for humanity: "For God so loved the world that he gave his one and only Son, that whoever believes in him shall not perish but have eternal life." Clearly, the God of John 3:16 is not the false god of deism.

In the final book of Scripture, the Apostle John praises God for his creation: "You are worthy, our Lord and God, to receive glory and honor and power, for you created all things, and by your will they were created and have their being" (Revelation 4:11). The fact of intelligent design should be obvious (Romans 1:20), but we must strive to go beyond mere knowledge of the Creator's existence and offer him the praise that only he deserves.

As mentioned, these are only a relative few of the many verses which touch upon intelligent design. These verses may not impact a skeptic, or even a seeker, until after he or she has first thoughtfully considered the scientific reasoning from both cause-and-effect and design. Sometimes we need logical evidences pointing us to the Creator in order to prepare us for the path to Christ the Savior.

WORLDVIEWS IN THE LIGHT OF DESIGN

Design, like cause-and-effect, is a very formidable line of evidence for the existence of God. The evidence from design points us in the direction of a personal God, not merely a god-force as pantheism proclaims or a distant, unconcerned god as deism maintains. The incredible level of complexity and detail found in nature, not to mention the symbiotic relationships that exist between many living creatures, points to a God who (1) clearly exists; (2) is a God of inconceivable intelligence who engages in planning, unlike impersonal forces which do not engage in detailed forethought; (3) is a God who is concerned with the details of his creation, rather than being an aloof deity who is uninterested in this world. Therefore, like the evidence from cause-and-effect, intelligent design has much to say about atheism, pantheism, and deism – and it's not good for any of them.

While still an unbeliever, prior to my investigation of the Christian faith I could see the evidence for design in nature, especially design in the human body. Although I studied a wide variety of topics during my time in radiation therapy training, human anatomy was always the branch of science that I was the most passionate about. I loved anatomical studies, and had I been able to continue on as a full-time student after graduating from my program I would have enrolled in an anatomical science degree program. My yearlong internship in radiation therapy is when I transitioned from being an evolutionist to a creationist, although it would be some time longer before I would become a Christian. The evidence for God's design is written all over the human body, and fortunately I had a biology instructor who wasn't afraid to point that out.

SCIENCE & SCRIPTURE

Rather than being opposed to each other, as is often claimed by skeptics, both science and Scripture actually support one another. The following scientific facts have a high level of scriptural support, demonstrating that both science and Scripture have the same author.[49] Although many skeptics claim that the Bible is pre-scientific, if not downright unscientific, whenever the Bible addresses scientific matters it is accurate, despite its great antiquity. The following examples illustrate this scientific accuracy not just centuries but millennia prior to modern scientific confirmation.

A BEGINNING OF THE UNIVERSE

"In the beginning God created the heavens and the earth" (Genesis 1:1). All ancient Near Eastern cultures – with the exception of the Hebrews, that is – believed the universe did not have a beginning. Only in the first half of the twentieth century did scientists finally begin to recognize that time, space, and matter-energy came into existence at a particular

---

[49] Ralph Muncaster, *Examine the Evidence* (Eugene, OR: Harvest House Publishers, 2004), 159-167.

point in time. Even Albert Einstein found the concept of a beginning difficult to accept when first presented with the evidence, as he originally held to an atheistic worldview. When confronted by the overwhelming evidence for a beginning of time, space, and matter-energy, he eventually accepted the fact that the universe is not eternal, a concept that his ancient Hebrew ancestors understood fully well.

The Hebrew word for "created" is bara, which means "creation from nothing." Bara signifies that something has been brought into existence when their formerly was nothing at all. "Starting from nothing" is a very good description of what modern cosmologists have termed a "singularity," which is the starting point of the universe. This concept is discussed once again by the writer of Hebrews: "By faith we understand that the universe was formed at God's command, so that what is seen was not made out of what was visible" (Hebrews 11:3). The original starting point for the universe was invisible, as it simply did not exist, and from that point God brought everything into existence – just as the Bible teaches, and no other ancient Near Eastern writing does.

THE EXPANSION OF THE UNIVERSE

"He stretches out the heavens like a tent" (Psalm 104:2). The universe is expanding, as demonstrated by cosmologists and astrophysicists in the early twentieth century and into today. Ancient cultures, with the exception of the Hebrews, did not consider the concept of an expanding universe. Why would an eternal universe expand, anyway? Other verses discuss the expanding universe:

> *He sits enthroned above the circle of the earth, and its people are like grasshoppers. He stretches out the heavens like a canopy, and spreads them out like a tent to live in (Isaiah 40:22).*
>
> *This is what God the LORD says – the Creator of the heavens, who stretches them out, who spreads out the earth with all that springs from it, who gives breath to its people, and life to those who walk on it (Isaiah 42:5).*

> *This is what the LORD says – your Redeemer, who formed you in the womb: I am the LORD, the Maker of all things, who stretches out the heavens, who spreads out the earth by myself (Isaiah 44:24).*
>
> *It is I who made the earth and created mankind on it. My own hands stretched out the heavens; I marshaled their starry hosts (Isaiah 45:12).*
>
> *But God made the earth by his power; he founded the world by his wisdom and stretched out the heavens by his understanding (Jeremiah 10:12).*
>
> *He made the earth by his power; he founded the world by his wisdom and stretched out the heavens by his understanding (Jeremiah 51:15).*
>
> *He alone stretches out the heavens and treads on the waves of the sea (Job 9:8).*
>
> *The Lord, who stretches out the heavens, who lays the foundation of the earth, and who forms the human spirit within a person (Zechariah 12:1b).*

It is amazing to see how the biblical writers, under the inspiration of God's Spirit, could note such amazing facts of cosmology in their own time, millennia before modern science confirmed these points. Yet so many today believe that the universe is nothing more than an accident, a "quantum fluctuation" of sorts.

A SPHERICAL EARTH

"He sits enthroned above the circle of the earth" (Isaiah 40:22). Earth was believed to be flat in many cultures of the ancient world, and was a belief that continued for quite some time in history, yet the Bible has always described a spherical Earth. Modern science did not catch up to this fact until the time of Copernicus, in the early sixteenth century.

GRAVITATIONAL SUSPENSION OF EARTH IN SPACE

"He suspends the earth over nothing" (Job 26:7). Earth is suspended by gravity in space, a fact not accurately described by science until relatively modern times. Some of the ancient cosmologies had Atlas holding the world on his shoulders (Greece), or Earth resting on the backs of giant elephants, themselves standing on the back of a giant turtle (India). The law of gravity exerting itself between solar bodies is revealed in Scripture, although not in modern scientific terminology. Once again, science finally caught up to this fact at the time of Copernicus.

THERMODYNAMICS

The science of thermodynamics focuses on the power and nature of heat energy, and as it turns out the first two laws of thermodynamics have much to say from a biblical perspective. Both the conservation of matter-energy, as described by the first law, and the rule of entropy (universal decay), as described by the second law, provide food for thought regarding origins. Once again, both of these points have been discussed previously in the section on cause-and-effect, but are worth examining again.

The law of conservation of energy indicates that matter and energy can be neither created nor destroyed naturally, just converted from one to another. However, it is obvious that matter and energy exist, so how did matter and energy get here in the first place? If matter and energy did not come into existence naturally, then it had to be created supernaturally – that is, from beyond the laws of physics. The law of conservation of energy speaks clearly to God's completed creation:

> *By the seventh day God had finished the work he had been doing; so on the seventh day he rested from all his work. Then God blessed the seventh day and made it holy, because on it he rested from all the work of creating that he had done (Genesis 2:2-3).*

> *Now we who have believed enter that rest, just as God has said, "So I declared on oath in my anger, 'They shall never enter my rest.'" And yet his works have been finished since the creation of the world. For somewhere he has spoken about the seventh day in these words: "On the seventh day God rested from all his works" (Hebrews 4:3-4).*

It seems clear to me that matter and energy, along with time and space, were brought into existence before the current laws of physics that govern the universe were put into place. Yet many naturalists insist that time, space, and matter-energy could only come into existence through the current laws of physics, not before they were enacted. Yet scientists cannot peer far enough back into the past to see the beginning point of the universe, so we cannot rule out the divine origin of time, space, and matter-energy; in fact, that's where the evidence clearly points us.

The rule of entropy demonstrates that everything in nature progresses from a state of order to a state of less order, from a state of usable energy to a state of less usable energy, or from a state of greater complexity to a state of lesser complexity over time, within a closed system – and naturalists believe that the universe is a closed system since there is no God outside of time, space, and matter-energy who can adjust the physical constants of the universe at will. So, if the universe is supposedly eternal, as many throughout history have believed, then why does the universe remain today when it is clearly decaying over time? Examples of entropy include stars burning out, heat dissipating, and bodies decaying after death. There are many references to the rule of entropy in the Bible, such as the following:

> *In the beginning you laid the foundations of the earth, and the heavens are the work of your hands. They will perish, but you remain; they will all wear out like a garment. Like clothing you will change them and they will be discarded (Psalm 102:25-26).*
>
> *Lift up your eyes to the heavens, look at the earth beneath; the heavens will vanish like smoke, the earth will wear out like a garment and its inhabitants die like flies. But my salvation will last forever, my righteous-ness will never fail (Isaiah 51:6).*
>
> *For the creation was subjected to frustration, not by its own choice, but by the will of the one who subjected it, in hope that the creation itself will be liberated from its bond-*

age to decay and brought into the freedom and glory of the children of God (Romans 8:20-21).

It is amazing to see this positive correlation between Scripture and the facts of science, as the two are so often believed to be diametrically opposed to one another. So many skeptics today maintain that the universe has been upwardly evolving since its beginning billions of years ago, yet both science and the Bible accurately describe a universe which is winding down, not building up.

THE HYDROLOGICAL CYCLE

Although the hydrological cycle was not fully explained until the eighteenth century, Scripture gives an accurate description of how water cycles through its various stages, albeit in common (non-scientific) terms:

He draws up the drops of water, which distill as rain to the streams; the clouds pour down their moisture and abundant showers fall on mankind (Job 36:27-28).

All streams flow into the sea, yet the sea is never full. To the place the streams come from, there they return again (Ecclesiastes 1:7).

Although many ancient cultures viewed rain differently, often as a blessing or even as a curse from the gods, it is satisfying to know that Scripture renders an accurate account of the hydrological cycle, millennia before modern scientific understanding of this process. Another satisfying correlation between science and Scripture.

THE STARS ARE UNCOUNTABLE

Ancient people believed that the stars were countable, mostly because they had a very limited view of the heavens and could only see a very, very small fraction of the number of stars just in our galaxy alone. Shortly after the time that the Apostle John wrote the final book of the Bible, Ptolemy was busy cataloguing the stars, which he had numbered to 1,100 in his time. In the early twentieth century scientists, with the help of extremely high-powered telescopes, realized that the number of stars was in the billions. A few decades later scientists came to the realization that there are about a billion galaxies in the known universe, each containing a billion stars. Today we know that if we were to count the stars at the rate of ten per second, it would take 100 trillion years to count them all – clearly an impossibility. However, Jeremiah wrote six centuries before Christ that the stars are uncountable: "I will make the descendants of David my servant and the Levites who minister before me as countless as the stars in the sky and as measureless as the sand on the seashore" (Jeremiah 33:22). If Ptolemy could catalogue a little over a thousand stars in his day, it would not have been any different for Jeremiah in his time. Yet Jeremiah nonetheless wrote that the stars are uncountable.

CURRENTS IN THE OCEAN

Matthew Fontaine Maury, the father of oceanography, read the following verse that describes "pathways in the sea" or what we now call ocean currents: "This is what the LORD says – he who made a way through the sea, a path through the mighty waters" (Isaiah 43:16). Taking that verse literally, Maury searched the oceans and discovered – and then mapped – major currents that have been used as routes for sea travel ever since.

GLOBAL WIND PATTERNS

Utilizing satellite technology, we now recognize the existence of global wind patterns, yet the Bible discussed the existence of these patterns nearly three millennia before our time: "The wind blows to the south and turns to the north; round and round it goes, ever returning on its course" (Ecclesiastes 1:6). Why would Solomon believe that the winds would return to their course? Why should there even be a course for the winds? That's a level of knowledge that, despite his great intellect and eye for observation (1 Kings 4:29-34), it seems that no one could really know without the aid of special (revealed) knowledge.

LAND LYING FALLOW

Today, agriculturalists recognize the importance of allowing land to "rest" every seven or so years, in order to allow nutrients to replenish the soil. The ancient Hebrew's clearly knew the value of this practice long before our time, however: "But in the seventh year the land is to have a year of Sabbath rest, a Sabbath to the LORD. Do not sow your fields or prune your vineyards. Do not reap what grows of itself or harvest the grapes of your untended vines. The land is to have a year of rest" (Leviticus 25:4-5). This practice mirrors the seven-day creation week, in which God worked for six days and then rested on the seventh day.

ENGINEERING NOAH'S ARK

The dimensions of Noah's ark turn out to be the optimum construction for a barge-type vessel that is required to float through rough seas: "This is how you are to build it: The ark is to be three hundred cubits long, fifty cubits wide and thirty cubits high" (Genesis 6:15). In fact, modern shipbuilders use these same dimensions when constructing barges that will likely sail through rough waters.

CIRCUMCISION ON THE EIGHTH DAY

Although it is unclear why God chose circumcision as the sign of his covenant with Abraham (Genesis 17:11), it is of interest that circumcision has definite medical value. Also of interest is the fact that the best time to circumcise a newborn is on the eighth day after birth, when the levels of vitamin K and prothrombin – both of which are key factors in blood-clotting – are at the ideal level. Certainly it was no accident that God, the Creator of all biological systems, chose this day: "For the generations to come every male among you who is eight days old must be circumcised, including those born in your household or bought with money from a foreigner – those who are not your offspring" (Genesis 17:12).

QUARANTINE, STERILIZATION, & CLEANLINESS

When the Black Plague was killing much of Europe in the

Middle Ages, nations turned to the church for an answer, and fortunately the church turned to the pages of Leviticus 13, which describe the procedure for dealing with infectious disease. As a result of adhering to God's commands, the Black Plague was brought under control in areas that put these biblical guidelines into practice.

Although germ theory and sterilization were not well-understood until the time of Joseph Lister, near the end of the Civil War, the Bible had already prescribed the correct procedures for dealing with childbirth (Leviticus 12), infectious diseases (Leviticus 13), bodily discharges (Leviticus 15), and the handling of the dead (Numbers 19). As a result, those individuals and institutions who kept the health commands found in the Mosaic writings did tremendously better than those who failed to abide by the wisdom of Scripture.

WHAT I DISCOVERED

Once I began to really dig into apologetics, it became exceedingly clear to me that the evidence for God's existence was overwhelming. Although I had never held to the atheist position, it was encouraging to know that the foundation of the Christian faith is truly rock solid: God does exist. I knew for sure that atheism was out of the picture, and both pantheism and deism looked to be on really shaky ground. Although it would still take some time for me to progress to the next level – that of accepting Christ as Savior – I was off to a good start, and I always enjoyed the investigation.

Overall, the evidences examined in this chapter collectively establish the case for God's existence. The evidence from cause-and-effect by itself is enough for many people to proclaim with great confidence that God exists, and the evidence from design demonstrates that this God is the God of Christian theism, and not merely the impersonal god of pantheism or the false god of deism. The correlation between science and Scripture builds upon the firm foundation of the previous two lines of evidence, pointing us soundly in the direction of the God of the Bible. Therefore, the order of the evidences for God's existence addressed in this chapter constitutes a logical progression which firmly establishes the reality of a personal Creator-God.

It must be stressed that the evidences outlined in this chapter, as well as those discussed in the chapters to follow, are meant to be combined into a comprehensive case for the God of Christian theism, with no single line of evidence forming a water-tight "Case for Christianity" all by itself. As with anything, the greater the number of convincing evidences there are, the stronger the case that is being established.

Chapter 3

"ETERNITY IN THEIR HEARTS"

In this chapter we will look at evidences for the God of Christian theism which are much more personal in nature, since they are directly concerned with what it means to be a human being created in God's image. We will explore the evidence from morality, the dual nature of human beings, aesthetics, human thought, meaning and purpose in life, the enduring belief in the afterlife, and religious experience.

EVIDENCE FROM MORALITY

The so-called "moral argument" for God's existence is founded upon the belief that all people, throughout all time and place, inherently know the difference between right and wrong. In other words, all people who have ever lived exhibit a basic universal standard of moral behavior. The basic codes of moral conduct, which includes prohibitions against murder, rape, incest, torture, and so on, seem to be generally the same for all humanity, regardless of one's culture or period in history. Christian believers are adamant that the only reasonable explanation for this phenomenon is that the moral law, which is inherent in all of us, demands a moral Lawgiver.

Christian believers point out that morality apart from God lacks the solid foundation that is able to withstand trials and temptations. Of course, the secular claim is that morality works just fine without God. To be sure, there are many atheists who live their lives in an ethically upstanding manner, but the question is not really, "Is it possible to lead a moral life apart from God?" so much as the question is, "What is the foundation for true morality?" This is the crux of the issue.

It is not necessary to read the Bible in order to understand right and wrong, as morality is an inherent part of our being.

Romans 2:14-15 reveals that God has instilled a moral code into each and every one of us, which is why the Apostle Paul could state with confidence that Gentiles – who do not have the civil laws of Judaism – are still able to conduct themselves in an ethical manner because they possess an even greater law, which is the moral law that is part of the fabric of all human beings: "Indeed, when Gentiles, who do not have the [civil] law, do by nature things required by the [civil] law, they are a [moral] law for themselves, even though they do not have the [civil] law. They show that the requirements of the [moral] law are written on their hearts, their consciences also bearing witness, and their thoughts sometimes accusing them and at other times even defending them" (Romans 2:14-15). Therefore, people from all worldviews (including atheism) will have the same basic moral instincts. Of course, we need to be cognizant of the fact that some people suffer from pathological conditions that may render the normal, healthy moral instinct impaired, while others seem to be exceedingly evil, but in general this is not the normal state of the human moral character.

General moral intuitions should be treated as reliable and trustworthy. Most people consider their five senses, along with their ability to reason, as being reliable, and we should do the same regarding our moral intuitions as well. We have basic moral instincts that almost always guide us ethically in the right direction, or at least make us very uncomfortable when we go against them. That is to say, we have an inherent moral compass that guides our behavior, and this should be every bit as obvious as the evidence from design in the universe.

If we were to suggest to someone that their moral conduct is in error, the ethically normal person may very well not even attempt to refute that suggestion, if in fact he or she knowingly is at fault. Instead of denying the moral principle in question, most people will argue that what they did does not violate the moral principle in question. This phenomenon is best explained in the context of objective moral values, and objective moral values are best explained through an appeal to an innate moral law. An innate moral law, in turn, is best accounted for by the existence of a moral Lawgiver.

Every normally-functioning human being can grasp the basics of morality. Even in ancient cultures, theft and murder were condemned while adherence to marriage vows and honoring one's parents were encouraged. Ancient people, just like us today, knew that maintaining certain inherent standards allowed for a healthier society. These standards are "hard-wired" into each of us, as Paul states in Romans 2:14-15. There have always been cultural differences regarding morality, of course, but the basic core issues seem to have always been the same. Just as God equipped us with the inborn ability to know that there is a realm beyond nature (Ecclesiastes 3:11), perhaps we can also state with certainty that God has inherently equipped us with the ability to understand right and wrong – and use that ability to be our "brother's keeper" (Genesis 4:9).

SKEPTICISM & MORALITY

It has often been said that people can be good apart from God, and I have no dispute with that claim. Personally, I have known more than a few atheists or skeptics who live their lives with impeccable moral standards. Outwardly they are truly upstanding citizens who would not hesitate for a moment to help someone in need or to do the morally right thing. In fact, some of these folks make me, an evangelical Christian, look bad in more than a few ways. But that's not the point of the evidence from morality. This line of evidence merely states that the foundation of morality only makes sense in the light of God, who created human beings "in his image" (Genesis 1:27) and therefore hard-wired into each of us the knowledge of right and wrong. Christian believers are adamant that naturalistic evolution is not capable of accomplishing that grand feat. Instead, naturalistic evolution leads to concepts such as "survival of the fittest" and "might makes right." Altruism, which is the selfless concern for the well-being of others, is at odds with these evolutionary concepts and instead gives every indication of being part of what it means to be created in God's image.

Right or wrong, I tend to not utilize the evidence from morality when talking to a seeker or a skeptic, and for me the reason is simple: Regardless of how clearly I try to make the point that this line of evidence is not a personal slam against an unbeliever's morality, it is often misunderstood in that way. My best friend was a skeptic, and he was one of the best people I've ever known.[50] The one time that I tried to appeal to the evidence from morality he felt like I was insinuating that he was immoral in one or more ways, which was definitely not the case. Yet the potential for this misunderstanding is always there when utilizing this line of evidence–so tread carefully when working morality into your apologetic discourse.

DUAL NATURE OF HUMAN BEINGS

How do we account for the simultaneous beauty and horror that is found within the human condition? For every Mother Teresa that exists in the world today, why is there an Adolf Hitler lurking just around the corner? Why do some people give their lives for the safety and well-being of others, when seemingly just as many people are more than happy to throw a fellow human being under the proverbial bus? Why are people both saints and sinners? It seems that the amusing image of the person with a godly angel on one shoulder and the Devil on the other is, in fact, closer to the truth than we would care to admit.

How do the various worldviews and religions account for this phenomenon? Atheism, which relies upon the foundation of naturalistic evolution, is quick to explain why bad things happen in the world: Human beings are evolved from primitive, savage creatures and have not yet overcome the effects of their evolutionary history. Nature is "red in tooth

---

[50] I use the word "was" because he has since passed on. He was a good man who did what was right more often than most of us, and yet he was a skeptic. Never let it be said that skeptics are always self-centered and immoral people.

and claw," and that is why the lion is more than happy to take down the antelope. But when it comes to beauty and altruism, atheism struggles for an explanation. Beauty and altruism fly in the face of naturalistic evolution, for the two concepts are at odds with each other. Since both pantheism and deism also rely upon the principle of cosmological, chemical, and biological evolution, neither of these worldviews fare any better than atheism in explaining the dual nature of human beings. Christian theism, however, offers an extremely satisfying explanation for this phenomenon.

The book of Genesis opens up with the account of how everything came into existence, including mankind who was the pinnacle of creation. In fact, the Bible says that God created mankind "in his image" (Genesis 1:27), setting human beings apart from all other creatures. What it means to be created in God's image is a point of debate among theologians, but we can say with a very high level of confidence that being created in God's image is a positive thing – it is an honor that sets us apart from every other creature. Yet, despite this wonderful attribute something is clearly wrong: We do not always act godly, and in fact we oftentimes struggle just to act decently. Once again, we must ask ourselves why we are both saint and sinner. The book of Genesis gives us the answer.

Moses, writing under the inspiration of God's Spirit, revealed in this incredible book that all people suffer from a fallen nature, which is a residual condition resulting from Adam and Eve's rebellion against God (Genesis 3:1-24). Although we may not understand exactly how the fallen nature is passed from generation to generation since the time of Adam, it is clear that the mode of transmission is not nearly as important as is its pervasive reality. The doctrine of the fallen nature of mankind is clearly revealed throughout Scripture, perhaps most forcefully in Paul's letter to the church in Rome (Romans 3:23; 5:12-19). Therefore, human beings are simultaneously saints created in God's image, and sinners by birth. The Bible describes why people have a dual nature, and no other worldview or religion makes as much sense regarding this phenomenon.

The dual nature of human beings is something that caught my attention early on in my investigation of the Christian worldview. After thinking about this issue for some time, it eventually came down to one of two scenarios for me: Either human beings are evolved creatures, or we were created but then something went wrong. Can naturalistic evolution explain why we are a combination of Mother Teresa and Adolph Hitler? Not really. As previously noted, evolution thrives on concepts such as "survival of the fittest" and "might makes right," but it doesn't explain altruism and self-sacrifice. Additionally, the evidence for naturalistic evolution is sorely lacking, so I wasn't buying into this explanation for the dual nature of people. However, creation in God's image followed by a rebellion – and consequent fallen nature – does explain this dual nature. You can imagine how intrigued I was when I read for the first time the account of the fall of mankind in the Garden of Eden (Genesis 3). Talk about an "aha" moment!

EVIDENCE FROM AESTHETICS

In addition to the previous evidences for the existence of God, some apologists also include aesthetics, which is the evidence from beauty. It has been noted that, "Philosophers rarely advocate arguments from beauty for the existence of God, and those who do advocate them rarely spend more than a few paragraphs in their cause."[51] I definitely agree with this observation. Having read many of the popular-level books on Christian evidences for many years, it is true that the evidence from aesthetics is rarely appealed to – make that *very* rarely appealed to. Apologists should be using this line of evidence on a regular basis, as it compliments' the more traditional evidences for God's existence very well.

Naturalism lacks explanatory power when it comes to the

---

[51] Peter Williams, "Aesthetic Arguments for the Existence of God." http://www.quodlibet.net/articles/williams-aesthetic.shtml

beauty that is found in nature. Instead, as previously mentioned naturalism is only concerned with concepts such as "survival of the fittest" and the continuation of the species. Naturalism does not offer any real explanation for the beauty that is found in nature, perhaps because beauty often serves no real purpose other than to make us pause long enough to consider the thing of beauty itself. Beautiful things in nature may be living or non-living. An example of living beauty would be the peacock's feathers, while an example of non-living beauty would be the Horsehead nebula (an interstellar dust cloud) in the far reaches of space. Regarding beauty among living things, we must ask ourselves how naturalistic evolution could generate such beauty. Some naturalists will counter with the argument that beauty in living things serves an evolutionary purpose. For instance, peacocks in ages past who possessed the most beautiful feathers were able to attract a mate more easily, and therefore reproduction for them was much more successful compared to those peacocks that lacked beauty and thus found it more difficult to contribute to the continuation of the species. However, beauty "cannot be accounted for in terms of survival value, natural selection, and the like."[52]

In the minds of countless people, the explanation for beauty only makes sense when viewed in a Christian theistic framework. Naturalistic explanations of the world, which rely upon chance, random processes, give no reason to expect beauty to arise in either living or non-living things. Christian theism, which invokes intentional design to explain beauty, offers a truly reasonable explanation for this phenomenon.

Aesthetics is one of those rarely thought about, and definitely under-utilized, evidences for the existence of God, but it really caught my attention the first time I encountered it. It just plain makes sense. Although it isn't the first line of evidence for God's existence that I would appeal to in an evangelistic encounter with a seeker or a skeptic, it does make for

---

[52] Ibid.

a refreshing supplement to an already well-established case for God's existence.

EVIDENCE FROM HUMAN THOUGHT

Human thought or cognition may be defined as that group of mental processes which are concerned with attention, memory, problem-solving, decision-making, and the ability to produce and understand language. Those who appeal to human thought as an evidence for God's existence do so based upon three premises: (1) Human thought can only be reliable if designed, rather than being attributable to chance, random processes in nature; (2) human thought is reliable; (3) therefore, it is reasonable to conclude that human thought is designed.

The first premise above is true, because if human thought were to be merely the result of random biochemical reactions, then we would have no reason to believe that our mental faculties are reliable; we would not be able to trust our own thinking abilities. No one could really trust their thoughts if they are merely attributable to chance, random processes of biochemistry.

How can we verify the reliability of our thought faculties? It turns out that there is no way to objectively cross-check our ability to think: We must assume that out thinking faculties are reliable. If we did not, then we would be engaged in a sort of self-aware madness that would give us no reasonable foundation with which to properly conduct our thought life. When we begin with the premise that our thinking faculties were designed, we then have a reasonable basis to accept their reliability. Is it possible that naturalistic evolution could in any way account for human thought? Chance, random processes of nature cannot realistically produce such intricately complex phenomena as human thinking abilities. Human thought seems to be clearly attributable to intelligent design.

The second premise above is necessary if there is to be any kind of reasonable discussion on the topic. If our thinking faculties are not reliable, then there is no reason to truly accept anything at all. Therefore, as based upon the first two premises, we can logically conclude that human thought is designed rather than evolved, and this argument serves as one more line of evidence for God's existence.

Either we were created by God, or we evolved by chance. If we evolved by chance, then we can forget about having this whole God and Christianity conversation – it's meaningless if we can't trust our own thoughts. But if we're created by God, then everything changes: We can be confident that the Creator endowed us with the ability to know things with great certainty, and that includes the existence of the Creator himself. I like this line of evidence. It's a little on the heady side, but it makes great sense.

EVIDENCE FROM MEANING & PURPOSE

It has been pointed out over the centuries by numerous philosophers, theologians, and thinkers of all stripes that God has designed us for a relationship with himself. We were meant to be close to God. Therefore, we should expect God to have "hard-wired" into each one of us the longing for that relationship, and this does, in fact, seem to be the case. The psalmist wrote, "As the deer pants for streams of water, so my soul pants for you, my God" (Psalm 42:1). Saint Augustine once wrote, "You made us for yourself, O Lord, and our hearts are restless till they rest in you," and closer to our time Blaise Pascal acknowledged the universal need for God as well: "There is a god-shaped vacuum in the heart of every man, and only God can fill it." Even the preeminent atheist of the mid-twentieth century, Bertrand Russell, knew in his heart that he also had that divine need. He was not afraid to admit that he always seemed to be searching for something beyond what the world contains. The longing for God seems to be present for everyone, regardless of their worldview choice.

This "restless desire" that can only be satisfied through a personal relationship with God is reasonably explained by creation, for God created mankind in his image (Genesis 1:27). Atheists may insinuate that this phenomenon is adequately explained by biochemistry and psychology – perhaps an emotional or biochemical imbalance of some sort – but those who find rest in God are adamant that nothing else fills this longing. Not drugs or alcohol, not sensual desires, and not even healthy, loving human relationships can adequately fulfill this need. Only a personal relationship with God can do that. Pascal noted that humankind has tried unsuccessfully to fill this void with everything around them, but apart from God nothing works. C.S. Lewis also noted this phenomenon: "Creatures are not born with desires unless satisfaction for those desires exists. A baby feels hunger: well, there is such a thing as food...If I find in myself a desire which no experience in this world can satisfy, the most probable explanation is that I was made for another world."[53] Not only does Lewis offer evidence for God from meaning and purpose in life, but he also argues for the existence of Heaven. With the existence of Heaven, we not only have confidence in the reality of God, but also confidence in the continuation of ourselves beyond this life. Although some may argue that the existence of God proves the existence of Heaven, technically one does not necessitate the other. For example, the Sadducees of ancient Judaism believed in God but not in the afterlife, while Buddhists – who are oftentimes atheistic – maintain a belief in the afterlife. Lewis, however, notes that our longing for God is inextricably tied to Heaven, and that is a very comforting thought indeed.

I enjoy thinking about the evidence for God from meaning and purpose in life, because it goes beyond the usual intellectual evidences for God such as cause-and-effect and the cohesiveness of science and Scripture. If God not only exists but created us in his image, then it makes total sense that he would hard-wire us to know him, and to give us the ability to experience him directly – and not just know about him through logic and reasoning. *Knowing about God* is com-

---
[53] Ibid.

mendable, but simply *knowing God* is infinitely better.

ENDURING BELIEF IN THE AFTERLIFE

According to atheists, when a person dies, that is it: The body begins its descent into decay, and the mind immediately ceases to exist. Game over. Life ends at the grave. Sayonara. There are probably many more clichés that could be used, but the point is this: Atheism insists that there is no afterlife. Human beings, and in fact all living creatures, are merely biological machines with no immortal or spiritual component that survives death. Since atheism denies the existence of God and anything spiritual, there can be no immortal soul which continues on after this life.

The late Grant Jeffrey, a prolific author who specialized in apologetics and end-time issues, discusses one of the best, and most-enduring, evidences for the existence of the immortal soul:

> *Perhaps the strongest evidence supporting the truth of immortality is that virtually every tribe, nation, and culture throughout history has expressed a strong faith in the reality of a life after death. In addition to the almost universal belief in God, the conviction that we will live again after our earthly bodies return to dust is the strongest and most commonly held belief of humanity. For thousands of years the vast majority of people have approached their personal valley of death with the firm expectation that they will ultimately rise from death and live forever in a better world. The longing for eternal life is the strongest instinct found in the heart of every human.*[54]

Jeffrey was absolutely correct in stating that the longing for eternal life is found within every human heart, for he is simply restating what Solomon wrote approximately three thousand years earlier: "He has also set eternity in the human heart…" (Ecclesiastes 3:11). God has hard-wired us to know that we will live on after this life is over.

---

[54] Grant R. Jeffrey, *Journey into Eternity* (Toronto, Ontario, Canada: Frontier Research Publications, Inc., 1999), 21-22.

R.C. Sproul supported Jeffrey's assertion that the strongest support for the truth of immortality is to be found in human history. He pointed out that the greatest thinkers throughout time have struggled over the question of life after death: "From ancient times the keenest minds of mankind have sought intellectual evidence for the survival of the soul or spirit beyond the grave...Scholars have given the question serious attention because it is the most serious of all questions."[55]

This universally inherent knowledge of eternity is one more line of evidence for God, for if Heaven exists then there is both a natural and a supernatural realm of existence. Although one may argue (unsuccessfully) that the natural realm could be the result of chance, random processes in nature, the existence of a supernatural realm only makes sense in the light of God's existence.

This particular line of evidence is definitely anthropological in nature – it's inherently built into mankind. I'm convinced that the atheist has to actively suppress this evidence for God and the spiritual realm; the continuation of life after death seems to be a part of who we are. Have you ever been to a funeral? Most of us, unfortunately, will answer yes. Rarely do you hear someone proclaim that the deceased is now "dead as a doornail" – that would be extremely poor etiquette, of course – but rather most people seem to be fairly convinced that life in some way, shape, or form will continue on after death. It's a natural part of who we are as human beings.

RELIGIOUS EXPERIENCE

A question that has often been asked by both Christian believers and unbelievers alike is whether or not religious experience is a valid line of evidence for establishing the existence of God. Many, especially within the skeptical crowd, are convinced that religious experience is not a valid means

---

[55] R.C. Sproul, *Reason to Believe* (Grand Rapids, MI: Zondervan, 1978), 146.

of knowing about anything spiritual with any degree of certainty. Some skeptics may acknowledge that the classical arguments for God, such as the evidence from cause-and-effect and the evidence from design, hold some weight in the debate over God's existence, but most are reluctant to acknowledge any such legitimacy for religious experience.

THE BATTLE OVER RELIGIOUS EXPERIENCE

Most people tend to think of our sensory perceptions as being valid, whereas religious experience is usually viewed as being very subjective. "The same experience can be received very differently by different people. In fact, what one person interprets as a religious experience may be completely explained by science for another person."[56] This is, of course, the basis for much of the debate between skeptics and those of faith. What some people claim as being a religious experience is, for many skeptics, nothing more than psychological factors at play. This is the major argument against religious experience as a valid means for knowing that God exists.

As a rebuttal to the skeptical claim that religious experiences are subjective in comparison to sensory perceptions, it has been rightly noted that "our sense perception requires subjective interpretation."[57] Sensory perceptions are simply the data that must be correctly interpreted by the mind – otherwise they are essentially useless without that interpretation. Therefore, by nature religious experience must be subjective.

If we are open to the possibility of religious experience, then it may become a valid means of not only *knowing about God*, but simply *knowing God*. "God does not limit accessibility to him. However, we may limit our own accessibility to God if we fail to be open to the experience."[58] As beings created in the image of God, we should expect to have the "seed of faith" that opens us up to knowing God. It would be

---

[56] Jeffrey S. Tunnicliff, "Can We Trust Religious Experience to Help Us Know God?" http://www.renewaloffaith.org/basics/talking/relexp.pdf
[57] Ibid.
[58] Ibid.

ludicrous to believe that God would create us in his image (Genesis 1:27), desiring a personal relationship with us (John 3:16), and also instilling "eternity in our hearts" (Ecclesiastes 3:11), and then not expect God to somehow provide us with the ability to experience him in a personal way.

RELIGIOUS EXPERIENCE & RATIONALITY

As I believe most of us already know, the evidences outlined in this chapter are not guaranteed to lead one from skepticism to Christ. It simply does not work that way, however well-intentioned apologists may be. It is not unusual for people to believe what they want to believe on a matter, with or without evidence for their view. People may wish to remain in their current state of unbelief, even in the face of overwhelming evidence for Christianity, simply for emotional reasons.

However, sometimes this type of apologetic information works very well. More than a few former atheists and skeptics of the Christian faith have come to know Jesus Christ as their Lord and Savior, and many of these new Christian believers eventually went on to make a very profound impact for God's kingdom. The following list of Christian authors who were once an atheist or an agnostic demonstrates that people still require this type of information in order to accept the Christian worldview.

C.S. Lewis: Lewis was raised in the church, but fell away from the faith in his early teens, when he began to view the faith as being nothing more than a chore and a duty. It was also around this time that he began to study occult topics, although he never actually became a devoted occultist. He did, however, label himself an atheist. Later in adulthood, Lewis slowly re-embraced Christianity largely because of the rational arguments offered by his friend J.R.R. Tolkien, and through the influence of G.K. Chesterton's classic work *The Everlasting Man*.

Josh McDowell: McDowell's early life was marked by abuse and the resultant low self-esteem common to those living in a very difficult environment. As the child of an alcoholic father, he abandoned any thought of having a personal relationship with God the Father. In college he researched the historical evidence for Christianity in order to prepare a paper against the faith, but he found – much to his great surprise – that the evidence actually supported Christianity, and as a result he abandoned his harsh agnosticism to accept Christ as his Lord and Savior.

Hugh Ross: Ross, a physicist and astronomer by training, is the founder of Reasons to Believe, an old earth creationist ministry that delves into a variety of scientific and general apologetics. At a young age, Ross studied the religions of the world in an attempt to determine which one, if any, offered the best explanatory power concerning the big questions of life. Ross found that only Christianity makes sense of the facts of both science and history.

Lee Strobel: Strobel was a hard-core atheist who began studying the evidences for and against the Christian faith when his wife converted to Christianity. He was originally convinced that Christianity would fail miserably when scrutinized through the lens of science and logic, but instead he discovered that only the Christian worldview makes sense of the facts of both science and history.

Holly Ordway: The author of *Not God's Type*, which chronicles her conversion from atheism to Christianity, Ordway began her trek to faith at the age of thirty one, when through a series of events she came face-to-face with the evidences for the Christian worldview. Prior to her conversion to faith in Christ she was convinced that the Christian worldview offered no real explanations for the important issues of life, but later admitted that her naturalism was, in fact, the worldview which offered nothing of importance.

Many other examples of well-known Christians who were once atheists or skeptics could be included in this list, but the point should be clear: The need for scientific, logical, and historical evidences for the Christian faith will never go out of style, despite living in a skeptical, relativistic world. Although the prevalence of relativist thinking – the idea that truth is what each person decides it should be, as summed up in the motto, "true for you, but not for me" – people still live with the either-or logic that is based in absolute truth, and as a result these types of evidences will always have a place in determining one's worldview.

The evidence for God from religious experience goes hand-in-hand with the evidence from meaning and purpose in life, in that since God created us in his image it makes total sense that he would hard-wire us to know and experience him directly, rather than just knowing about him through logical deduction. After all, if God has the attributes of personality he should desire a personal relationship with the crown of his creation.

WHAT I DISCOVERED

Over the years I have found that regardless of how much I enjoy the reason-heavy evidences for God's existence, especially cause-and-effect, it's these more personal lines of evidence in this chapter that oftentimes seem to be the most encouraging to me in my faith journey. Maybe it's because these particular lines of evidence are where faith and reason collide in the most obvious way. Although I would never consider discarding the reason-heavy evidences from the previous chapter in my personal approach to apologetics, I have found that the human heart is oftentimes more open to the evidences in this chapter than those found in the previous one. Although it can be said that we should never allow our emotions to go to a place where our intellect cannot also go, conversely it can be said that we should never allow our intellect to go to a place where our emotions cannot also go as well. Christianity needs to be both intellectually stimulating and emotionally satisfying. One without the other simply will not work, and that is why we need this mix of reason-heavy and more personal lines of evidence for God.

We have now made our way from a general belief in the First Cause of the universe, as found in the previous chapter, to the Creator who fashioned human beings "in his image" in this chapter. We are slowly progressing from the general belief in God to the God of the Bible, and now we will begin to look at the identity of the Creator himself. As we do this, both atheism and pantheism will be even further refuted, and deism – which remained somewhat intact, although very badly bruised, after chapter two – will now be thoroughly refuted as well.

Chapter 4

THE COMING MESSIAH

When it comes to building the case for Christian theism, some lines of evidence seem to fit more of a supporting role, such as archaeology, whereas other lines of evidence may be classified as "major weapons" of evangelism. Fulfilled messianic prophecy is one of those major weapons, and may be what most convinces an open-minded seeker that Scripture originates from the mind of God. The Old Testament is filled with prophecies about the coming Redeemer, who was initially foretold at the time of the fall of mankind in the Garden of Eden (Genesis 3:15). These Old Testament messianic prophecies include many details about the life and death of the coming Messiah, and they were completely fulfilled in the person of Jesus Christ. For many people this has been the tipping point in their examination of the evidence for Christianity.

FULFILLED MESSIANIC PROPHECY

Fulfilled messianic prophecy is often thought of as being a form of "hard evidence" since it is concerned with probable statistical events. Generally speaking, the hard evidences are those that come from the realm of mathematics and the physical sciences. "Prophecy can provide hard evidence of God, Jesus, and the Bible because it can be evaluated using "absurdly conservative" assumptions and still prove (statistically) the supernatural inspiration of the Bible."[59]

Prophecy as a line of evidence for Christian theism lies in its value to perform two functions.[60] First, fulfilled prophecy may assess the probability of random occurrence as the explanation for a specific event prophesied in Scripture. This is known as the "specificity" of prophecy, and for some apolo-

---

[59] Ralph Muncaster,, *Examine the Evidence* (Eugene, OR: Harvest House Publishers, 2004), 296.
[60] Ibid.

gists this is where mathematical probability and statistics really come into play. Second, fulfilled prophecy may assess the number of consecutive correct prophecies made without error. Once again, for some apologists mathematical probability and statistics provides the final decision for the probability of the number of examined prophecies as a whole.

There are three basic criteria for statistically evaluating prophecy.[61] First, the prophecy under question must be of sufficient specificity, and unlikely that a person of reasonable intellect would conclude that the fulfillment of the prophecy would yield a probability of at least one in ten. This criterion eliminates the vagueness offered by popular psychics. Second, the prophecy must be from one source and confirmed by a separate source that would receive no benefit from the prophecy being fulfilled. This criterion eliminates deceitful ulterior motives that could be used to benefit the party claiming a fulfilled prophecy. Third, the prophecy must be based upon a reliable source, which includes both the source of the prophecy and the source confirming the prophecy. Since the Bible itself is both the source (Old Testament) and the confirmation of the source (New Testament), it must be demonstrated that the Bible is a reliable source of information, which we will look at shortly.

NUMBER CRUNCHING: THE GOOD AND THE BAD

Although the certainty of statistical proof may be debated, "scientists generally accept a standard that anything with a probability of less than one chance in 10^{50} is regarded as impossible."[62] Therefore, if the probability of Jesus having fulfilled numerous Old Testament prophecies approaches a number similar to this figure, then we can exclaim with confidence that Christ really is "God made flesh" (John 1:14). That is the useful aspect of assigning numbers to prophecies. Although some people may not be easily convinced by number crunching, others seem to be hard-wired to more readily respond to the evidences from the hard sciences (mathemat-

---

[61] Ibid.
[62] Ibid.

ics, physics, engineering, cryptology, etc.) and may find the so-called "number game" to be quite convincing.

However, on the flip side we should ask ourselves just how accurate is the number which was assigned to the probability of the individual prophecy. I personally find "number crunching" to be a bit unsettling. It seems to me that the probability of a New Testament situation or event happening that was foretold in the Old Testament is something that should just be obvious, just as the "Case for an Intelligent Designer" is something which we inherently understand, whether we acknowledge it or not (Romans 1:20). But, in the spirit of fairness, I also have to point out that those who assign numbers for prophetic probability most likely have done their homework and utilized a significant degree of research to back up the numbers. So, in the end there will be some who are bowled over by the numbers game while others are just plain skeptical of it.

PROPHECY AND THE CASE FOR CHRIST

The messianic prophecies examined in this chapter[63] must fulfill the first two criteria above, in that they need to be specific, statistically improbable by purely natural means, and historically confirmed, and they can only come out of documents which are solidly dated, so that no one can reasonably claim that these prophecies have been rigged after the fact. As will be demonstrated in this chapter, the Bible has a remarkable track record when it comes to fulfilled messianic prophecy.

THE ANCESTRAL LINE OF CHRIST

According to the Old Testament, Messiah would be descended from the lines of Shem (Genesis 9-10), Abraham (Genesis 22:17-18), Isaac (Genesis 26:4-5), Jacob (Genesis 28:14), Judah (Genesis 49:10), Jesse (Isaiah 11:1-5), and David (2 Samuel 7:8-16). The fulfillment of this prophecy is

---

[63] The messianic prophecies examined in this chapter are adequate to demonstrate the significance of this line of evidence for Christian theism, but is not an exhaustive study on this topic.

seen in Luke 3:23-38 (Mary's genealogy) and Matthew 1:1-17 (Joseph's genealogy).

First we will explore the genealogy of Jesus through Luke's Gospel, which details the family line of Mary, the mother of Christ:

> *Now Jesus himself was about thirty years old when he began his ministry. He was the son, so it was thought, of Joseph, the son of Heli, the son of Matthat, the son of Levi, the son of Melki, the son of Jannai, the son of Joseph, the son of Mattathias, the son of Amos, the son of Nahum, the son of Esli, the son of Naggai, the son of Maath, the son of Mattathias, the son of Semein, the son of Josek, the son of Joda, the son of Joanan, the son of Rhesa, the son of Zerubbabel, the son of Shealtiel, the son of Neri, the son of Melki, the son of Addi, the son of Cosam, the son of Elmadam, the son of Er, the son of Joshua, the son of Eliezer, the son of Jorim, the son of Matthat, the son of Levi, the son of Simeon, the son of Judah, the son of Joseph, the son of Jonam, the son of Eliakim, the son of Melea, the son of Menna, the son of Mattatha, the son of Nathan, the son of David, the son of Jesse, the son of Obed, the son of Boaz, the son of Salmon, the son of Nahshon, the son of Amminadab, the son of Ram, the son of Hezron, the son of Perez, the son of Judah, the son of Jacob, the son of Isaac, the son of Abraham, the son of Terah, the son of Nahor, the son of Serug, the son of Reu, the son of Peleg, the son of Eber, the son of Shelah, the son of Cainan, the son of Arphaxad, the son of Shem, the son of Noah, the son of Lamech, the son of Methuselah, the son of Enoch, the son of Jared, the son of Mahalalel, the son of Kenan, the son of Enosh, the son of Seth, the son of Adam, the son of God (Luke 3:23-38).*

As you can see from the above genealogical list, Jesus descended from David, Jesse, Judah, Jacob, Isaac, Abraham, and Shem. Next we will explore Matthew's genealogy, which covers Joseph's ancestral line. We will see that the same key names once again appear, but this time going no further back than Abraham:

> *This is the genealogy of Jesus the Messiah the son of*

David, the son of Abraham: Abraham was the father of Isaac, Isaac the father of Jacob, Jacob the father of Judah and his brothers, Judah the father of Perez and Zerah, whose mother was Tamar, Perez the father of Hezron, Hezron the father of Ram, Ram the father of Amminadab, Amminadab the father of Nahshon, Nahshon the father of Salmon, Salmon the father of Boaz, whose mother was Rahab, Boaz the father of Obed, whose mother was Ruth, Obed the father of Jesse, and Jesse the father of King David. David was the father of Solomon, whose mother had been Uriah's wife, Solomon the father of Rehoboam, Rehoboam the father of Abijah, Abijah the father of Asa, Asa the father of Jehoshaphat, Jehoshaphat the father of Jehoram, Jehoram the father of Uzziah, Uzziah the father of Jotham, Jotham the father of Ahaz, Ahaz the father of Hezekiah, Hezekiah the father of Manasseh, Manasseh the father of Amon, Amon the father of Josiah, and Josiah the father of Jeconiah and his brothers at the time of the exile to Babylon. After the exile to Babylon: Jeconiah was the father of Shealtiel, Shealtiel the father of Zerubbabel, Zerubbabel the father of Abihud, Abihud the father of Eliakim, Eliakim the father of Azor, Azor the father of Zadok, Zadok the father of Akim, Akim the father of Elihud, Elihud the father of Eleazar, Eleazar the father of Matthan, Matthan the father of Jacob, and Jacob the father of Joseph, the husband of Mary, and Mary was the mother of Jesus who is called the Messiah. Thus there were fourteen generations in all from Abraham to David, fourteen from David to the exile to Babylon, and fourteen from the exile to the Messiah (Matthew 1:1-17).

Throughout history the Jewish people have been noted for their attention to genealogical record-keeping. If there had been any contention regarding the ancestral lines of Jesus as recorded in both Matthew and Luke, the people of that time would have been quick to point out those discrepancies and effectually bury the case for Jesus' messianic claim, which did not happen.

The following probabilities concerning Jesus' descent from the following men have been proposed by Christian author Ralph Muncaster.[64] Abraham was one chance in 150 million, as based upon the estimates of the world's population of men at the time of Abraham. Isaac was one chance in two, since Abraham had only two sons. Jacob was one chance in two, since Isaac had only two sons. Judah was one chance in twelve, since Jacob had twelve sons. Jesse was one chance in thirty, since Judah had five sons, Perez had at least two sons, Hezron had three sons, Ram had at least one son, Amminadab had at least one son, Nahshon had at least one son, Salmon had at least one son, Boaz had at least one son, and Obed had at least one son. Mathematically, this renders 5 x 2 x 3 x 1 x 1 x 1 x 1 x 1 x 1 = 30. Finally, David was one chance in eight, since Jesse had eight sons.

When one multiplies the above probabilities (150,000,000 x 2 x 2 x 12 x 30 x 8 = 1,728,000,000,000), it becomes obvious that statistically the chances of Jesus fulfilling the messianic genealogy requirements recorded in the Old Testament were incredibly small, only one chance in 1.728 trillion – unless a supernatural explanation is offered, of course. Jesus clearly fulfilled the ancestral requirements for the messiah, as outlined in the Old Testament.

THE BIRTHPLACE OF CHRIST

According to the Old Testament, Messiah would be born in Bethlehem Ephrathah, and he would have origins "of old, from ancient times" (Micah 5:2), and there will be a very unusual and prominent "star" connected to his birth (Numbers 24:17). The fulfillment of this prophecy is seen in Matthew 2:1-2 and John 1:1-2, 14.

Matthew tells us that Jesus was born in Bethlehem Ephrathah, and that his birth was associated with an unusual "star" in the sky, while John tells us that Jesus – whom he calls the "Word" or *Logos* in Greek – had "origins of old," a

---

[64] Ralph Muncaster, *Evidence for Jesus* (Eugene, OR: Harvest House Publishers, 2004), 159. Actually, my calculation is more conservative than Muncaster's. Muncaster states that Jesse was one chance in 240, which makes the odds against Jesus being the messiah by lineage even greater.

poetic way of saying that he is God incarnated:

> *After Jesus was born in Bethlehem in Judea [Bethlehem Ephrathah], during the time of King Herod, Magi from the east came to Jerusalem and asked, "Where is the one who has been born king of the Jews? We saw his star when it rose and have come to worship him" (Matthew 2:1-2).*

> *In the beginning was the Word, and the Word was with God, and the Word was God. He was with God in the beginning...The Word became flesh and made his dwelling among us. We have seen his glory, the glory of the one and only Son, who came from the Father, full of grace and truth (John 1:1-2, 14).*

Matthew correctly identifies the birthplace of Jesus, as well as describing the "star" over the land of Judah that was connected with his birth. Additionally, John reveals that Jesus was present at the creation of the universe, so symbolically speaking Jesus had "origins of old, from ancient times" although in the literal sense of the term Jesus – as God incarnate – was actually without origin.

The following probability has been estimated for Messiah being born in Bethlehem Ephrathah: One or two chances in 100, since the estimated population of Bethlehem Ephrathah at the time of Christ was 2,000-4,200, while the estimated population of Palestine as a whole was 209,000. Some are quick to point out, however, that when considering the probability in terms of the world's population as a whole rather than just the entirety of Palestine, we have a probability of one chance in 100,000,000.[65] Regardless of which number one sides with, it is obvious that no one would have been expecting Messiah to come from the small village of Bethlehem Ephrathah had it not been foretold in Scripture.

"GOD WITH US"

According to the Old Testament, Messiah will be called Immanuel, which means "God with us." The prophet Isaiah wrote, "Therefore the Lord himself will give you a sign: The

---

[65] Ibid.

virgin will conceive and give birth to a son, and will call him Immanuel" (Isaiah 7:14). The fulfillment of this prophecy is seen in Matthew's Gospel:

> *All this took place to fulfill what the Lord had said through the prophet [Isaiah]: "The virgin will conceive and give birth to a son, and they will call him Immanuel" (Matthew 1:22-23).*

Forget about probabilities and "number crunching" on this one: The fact that God became flesh and made his dwelling among us (John 1:14) is an amazing prophecy that really defies statistics. It is claimed in the myths and legends of ancient times that the gods came into the world, but none of those stories match up to the biblical account of God the Son taking on flesh and making his (temporary) home with humanity. That God would enter the world as a vulnerable baby and grow up in a normal manner, and even more incredible that he would be a man of peace and not a warrior set on righting the injustices of the world through violence, is almost inconceivable. Yet that is the biblical view of Jesus.

It is very important to note that God the Son, Jesus Christ, was born of a virgin and not simply born of a "young woman," as some skeptics claim the Hebrew word for "virgin" should be most accurately translated. A few hundred years before the time of Christ, either 70 or 72 Jewish scholars got together in Alexandria, Egypt to translate the Old Testament from Hebrew into Greek, and they were convinced that the Hebrew word for "virgin" meant exactly that – a virgin, and not just a young woman – and they made certain that the word was properly understood in the Greek to mean a virgin. Young woman give birth to children all the time – there's nothing unusual or noteworthy there – but a true virgin giving birth to a child is, of course, a very supernatural occurrence. Since Jesus was sinless, he really had to be born of a virgin – since Jesus was supernaturally conceived he was not tainted by the fallen nature that all of the rest of us suffer from.

THE MIRACLES OF CHRIST

According to the Old Testament, Messiah will have the power to calm the sea (Psalm 107:29) and perform many other special miracles (Isaiah 35:4-6). The fulfillment of this prophecy is seen in Matthew 8:23-27 and 15:29-30:

> *Then he got into the boat and his disciples followed him. Suddenly a furious storm came up on the lake, so that the waves swept over the boat. But Jesus was sleeping. The disciples went and woke him, saying, "Lord, save us! We're going to drown!" He replied, "You of little faith, why are you so afraid?" Then he got up and rebuked the winds and the waves, and it was completely calm. The men were amazed and asked, "What kind of man is this? Even the winds and the waves obey him!" (Matthew 8:23-27).*

> *Jesus left there and went along the Sea of Galilee. Then he went up on a mountainside and sat down. Great crowds came to him, bringing the lame, the blind, the crippled, the mute and many others, and laid them at his feet; and he healed them (Matthew 15:29-30).*

What are the chances of these miracles being accomplished apart from divine intervention? Obviously zero, since only God can work true miracles.

TEACHING IN PARABLES

According to the Old Testament, Messiah will utilize parables in his teaching. The psalmist wrote, "My people, hear my teaching; listen to the words of my mouth. I will open my mouth with a parable; I will utter hidden things, things from of old..." (Psalm 78:1-2). The fulfillment of this prophecy is seen in Matthew's Gospel:

> *The disciples came to him and asked, "Why do you speak to the people in parables?" He replied, "Because the knowledge of the secrets of the kingdom of heaven has been given to you, but not to them. Whoever has will be given more, and they will have an abundance. Whoever does not have, even what they have will be taken from them. This is why I speak to them in parables: "Though seeing, they do not see; though hearing, they do not hear or understand" (Matthew 13:10-13).*

I personally do not want to assign a numerical probability to this prophecy, simply because it is not only very possible, but even likely that other religious teachers in the ancient world taught in a manner that somewhat resembled Jesus' parable form. This prophecy is merely one more piece of evidence in the overall case for the divine messianic status of Jesus.

THE BETRAYAL OF CHRIST

According to the Old Testament, Messiah will be betrayed by a friend for thirty pieces of silver:

> *I told them, "If you think it best, give me my pay; but if not, keep it." So they paid me thirty pieces of silver. And the LORD said to me, "Throw it to the potter" – the handsome price at which they valued me! So I took the thirty pieces of silver and threw them to the potter at the house of the LORD (Zechariah 11:12-13).*

The fulfillment of this prophecy is described by the Apostle Matthew:

> *Then one of the Twelve – the one called Judas Iscariot – went to the chief priests and asked, "What are you willing to give me if I deliver him over to you?" So they counted out for him thirty pieces of silver. From then on Judas watched for an opportunity to hand him over (Matthew 26:14-16).*

This prophecy has been assigned a probability of one chance in 50, a number which is fairly conservative.[66] However, one could just as reasonably assign a probability of one chance in 25 or even one chance in 100; there is definitely room for debate on this one. Let it simply be said that it is possible for a religious leader to be betrayed by one of his or her closest followers – Jesus is almost certainly not unique in this way – but the fact that Zechariah foretold of this betrayal of the Lord hundreds of years before the event happened, even mentioning the exact monetary value behind the betrayal, is quite intriguing.

---

[66] Grant Jeffrey, *Jesus: The Great Debate* (Toronto, Ontario, Canada: Frontier Research Publications, Inc., 1999), 233.

ISAIAH'S "SUFFERING SERVANT"

Messiah will be a sin offering, a "Passover lamb" who will fulfill several prophecies found in Isaiah 53. This is one of the most amazing passages of Scripture concerning the Messiah, Jesus Christ. Isaiah's Suffering Servant is of special interest to the Christian believer, as these verses were written over seven centuries before the birth of Christ, yet Jesus – and Jesus alone – fulfills this passage of Scripture perfectly.

The New Testament is clear that Christ bore the sins of humanity; compare this to Isaiah's revelation:

Surely he took up our pain and bore our suffering, yet we considered him punished by God, stricken by him, and afflicted (Isaiah 53:4).

This was to fulfill what was spoken through the prophet Isaiah: "He took up our infirmities and bore our diseases" (Matthew 8:17).

To further corroborate this point, one only needs to consider the next verse from Isaiah 53, and compare it to what the Apostle Peter wrote:

But he was pierced for our transgressions, he was crushed for our iniquities; the punishment that brought us peace was on him, and by his wounds we are healed (Isaiah 53:5).

He himself bore our sins in his body on the cross, so that we might die to sins and live for righteousness; by his wounds you have been healed (1 Peter 2:24).

The punishment that Christ endured on the cross was for the salvation of humanity, exactly as described by Isaiah. Christ truly suffered for fallen humanity:

We all, like sheep, have gone astray, each of us has turned to our own way; and the LORD has laid on him the iniquity of us all (Isaiah 53:6).

For you were like sheep going astray, but now you have returned to the Shepherd and Overseer of your souls (1 Peter 2:25).

The silence of Christ during his trial is mirrored in these passages:

> *He was oppressed and afflicted, yet he did not open his mouth; he was led like a lamb to the slaughter, and as a sheep before its shearers is silent, so he did not open his mouth (Isaiah 53:7).*

> *The chief priests accused him of many things. So again Pilate asked him, "Aren't you going to answer? See how many things they are accusing you of." But Jesus still made no reply, and Pilate was amazed (Mark 15:3-5).*

Christ was buried in the family tomb of a rich man, although Christ himself was not considered to be wealthy:

> *He was assigned a grave with the wicked, and with the rich in his death, though he had done no violence, nor was any deceit in his mouth (Isaiah 53:9).*

> *As evening approached, there came a rich man from Arimathea, named Joseph, who had himself become a disciple of Jesus. Going to Pilate, he asked for Jesus' body, and Pilate ordered that it be given to him. Joseph took the body, wrapped it in a clean linen cloth, and placed it in his own new tomb that he had cut out of the rock. He rolled a big stone in front of the entrance to the tomb and went away (Matthew 27:57-60).*

Christ would have been disposed of in the manner common for a criminal or outlaw of society if Joseph of Arimathea had not successfully requested that Jesus' body be entrusted to his care. Joseph, a wealthy man, had Christ's body placed in his own family tomb.

The New Testament makes it clear that Christ did not sin; his mission was truly that of a "Suffering Servant" who died for the sins of fallen humanity:

> *Yet it was the LORD's will to crush him and cause him to suffer, and though the LORD makes his life an offering for sin, he will see his offspring and prolong his days, and the will of the LORD will prosper in his hand (Isaiah 53:10).*

> Then Jesus came to them and said, "All authority in heaven and on earth has been given to me" (Matthew 28:18).

After Christ's death on the cross, he was resurrected from the dead. This resurrection is the hope of all believers:

> After he has suffered, he will see the light of life and be satisfied; by his knowledge my righteous servant will justify many, and he will bear their iniquities (Isaiah 53:11).

> But Christ has indeed been raised from the dead, the firstfruits of those who have fallen asleep (1 Corinthians 15:20).

> So Christ was sacrificed once to take away the sins of many; and he will appear a second time, not to bear sin, but to bring salvation to those who are waiting for him (Hebrews 9:28).

There is only one intercessor between God and humanity, the God-man Jesus Christ. Isaiah described Christ's work of intercession for fallen humanity:

> Therefore I will give him a portion among the great, and he will divide the spoils with the strong, because he poured out his life unto death, and was numbered with the transgressors. For he bore the sin of many, and made intercession for the transgressors (Isaiah 53:12).

> For there is one God and one mediator between God and mankind, the man Christ Jesus (1 Timothy 2:5).

This amazing passage from Isaiah is found in Jewish Bibles today, though many claim that it is left out of the weekly synagogue readings.[67] When people read Isaiah 53 without knowing which part of the Bible it comes from, they often wrongly assume it is from the New Testament. Isaiah clearly

---

[67] It is often claimed that Rabbi's do not include the Suffering Servant passage from Isaiah 52:13-53:12 during the weekly synagogue readings. True or not, most people who read the Suffering Servant passage from Isaiah come to the conclusion that it is Jesus that is being described in the text, despite the fact that Isaiah lived 700 years before Christ. This passage alone has been a powerful evangelistic tool for apologists.

foresaw the sufferings of Jesus to pay for the sins of a fallen world. Many modern rabbis say that the suffering described by Isaiah are those of the nation of Israel. However, most ancient rabbis said that the passage referred to Messiah's sufferings, not to those of the nation of Israel. This includes ancient rabbinical commentators from the Babylonian Talmud, Midrash Ruth Rabbah, Zohar, and even the great Jewish thinker Rabbi Moses Maimonides.

Isaiah 53 cannot refer to the nation of Israel, or any mere human being, but only to Jesus – who was, and is, fully God *and* fully man. This conclusion is based upon several points. First, the servant of Isaiah 53 is an innocent and guiltless sufferer, yet Israel is never described as sinless. Second, Isaiah said, "It pleased the LORD to bruise him." Has the awful treatment of the Jewish people really been God's pleasure, as is said of the Suffering Servant in Isaiah 53:10? Third, the person mentioned in this passage suffers silently and willingly. Yet all people, Israelites included, complain when they suffer. Only Christ, in the New Testament, goes to his death quietly and in full submission to God. Fourth, the figure described in Isaiah 53 suffers, dies, and rises again to atone for his people's sins. Isaiah 53 describes a sinless and perfect "sacrificial lamb" who takes upon himself the sins of others so that they might be forgiven. The terrible suffering of the Jewish people does not in any way atone for the sins of the world. Isaiah 53 speaks of one who suffers and dies in order to provide a legal payment for sin, so that others can be forgiven. This cannot be true of the Jewish people as a whole, or of any mere human being. Fifth, the prophet speaking is Isaiah himself, who says the sufferer was punished for "the transgression of my people" (verse eight). The people of Isaiah are Israel, therefore the sufferer of Isaiah 53 suffered for Israel, and therefore was not Israel itself. Sixth, the figure of Isaiah 53 dies and is buried, according to verses eight and nine. The people of Israel have never died as a whole. They may have come close during the Holocaust, but even then a significant number of the Jewish people survived. Seventh, if Isaiah 53 cannot refer to Israel, can the passage refer to Isaiah himself? Isaiah said he was a sinful man of unclean lips (6:5), therefore Isaiah could not die to atone for our sins. Nor could it have been Jeremiah or Moses. Isaiah, Jeremiah, and Moses were all prophets who gave us a glimpse of what Messiah would be like, but none fit the description of Isaiah 53, for all were sinners and fallen in nature. Beyond any doubt, Isaiah is referring to Jesus, the "Lamb of God who takes away the sins of the world" (John 1:29).

THE TORTURE ON THE CROSS

According to the Old Testament, Messiah's hands and feet will be pierced (Psalm 22:16), and he will thirst while being put to death (Psalm 69:20-21). Despite the horrific torture he will undergo, he will not have a single bone broken during his execution (Psalm 22:17). The fulfillment of this prophecy is seen in Matthew 27:32-56, Mark 15:21-41, Luke 23:26-49, and John 19:17-37.

As described in these New Testament passages, Jesus was crucified in the usual manner, which entailed nails being driven through the hands or wrists as well as the feet. Likewise, Jesus thirsted while on the cross, and yet for all of his suffering not one bone was broken.

Being that crucifixion was not devised as a means of torturous death until the sixth century BC, and not used specifically by the Romans until the fourth century BC,[68] it is very unlikely to have been so well described by the psalmist. David is considered to have authored all of the psalms in Book One (Chapters 1-41),[69] and David lived approximately a thousand years before Jesus. Even if this particular psalm were to be dated to 450 BC, the latest date for the psalms,[70] it is still half a century before the Romans began using crucifixion. Even then, why would anyone suspect that Messiah would undergo crucifixion?

---

[68] Ralph Muncaster, *Evidence for Jesus* (Eugene, OR: Harvest House Publishers, 2004), 179.
[69] Jim George, *The Bare Bones Bible Handbook* (Eugene, OR: Harvest House Publishers, 2006), 91.
[70] Ibid.

ADDITIONAL PROPHECIES

In addition to the prophecies described above, several other prophecies are used as part of a cumulative case for the deity of Christ. The prophecy of the "passing of the scepter" (Genesis 49:10) is of interest to the student of Bible prophecy. The Jews "scepter of control" was passed to the Romans when the Jews no longer had the right, under Roman rule, to stone to death blasphemers. This event happened in AD 11. In order for this prophecy to be fulfilled, the Messiah had to be born before the scepter was passed (AD 11), and the death of Messiah had to happen sometime after that event. Although the date of Jesus' birth is a point of contention among historians and biblical scholars, it is generally accepted that Jesus was born sometime between 7-2 BC, and his death on the cross is generally considered to have taken place sometime around AD 30-33.[71] Therefore, history fully supports that this prophecy was fulfilled by Jesus Christ.

Although maybe not the most convincing prophecy when taken on its own, the prophecy of being "called out of Egypt" is worth noting. Hosea wrote, "When Israel was a child, I loved him, and out of Egypt I called my son" (Hosea 11:1). Granted the prophet was referring to Israel the nation, nonetheless Jesus was also called out of Egypt from his brief journey there as a child in hiding (Matthew 2:13-23).

The prophecy of a king on a donkey was recorded in Zechariah 9:9 and fulfilled near the end of Christ's life (Matthew 21:1-11; Mark 11:1-11; Luke 19:28-38; John 12:12-16). Although it is conceivable that Jesus could have rigged this prophecy to conform to the writings of the prophet Zechariah – although that would have involved collusion on a grand scale – when put into the context of the fulfilled messianic prophecies as a whole it becomes one more significant piece of evidence in the "Prophetic Case for Christ."

The prophecy of the messenger who precedes the Messiah is also intriguing. Grant Jeffrey noted that, to his knowledge,

---

[71] Ralph Muncaster, *Evidence for Jesus* (Eugene, OR: Harvest House Publishers, 2004), 161-162.

no other king "was preceded by a messenger to herald his arrival."[72] Although some may protest that the religion known as Baha'i includes such a teaching, Jeffrey is correct since the "Bab" – the religious leader who preceded Baha'u'llah, the founder of Baha'i – actually claimed to be a major manifestation of God himself, not just a messenger preparing the way for a greater one to come. Regarding Jesus as Messiah, Isaiah revealed this prophecy (40:3), while Matthew recorded the fulfillment (3:1-3).

Although the list of prophecies examined in this work is not exhaustive by any means, the list is more than adequate to demonstrate that the Old Testament messianic prophecies were completely fulfilled in the person of Jesus Christ. The only potential obstacle remaining is to show that the accepted dates for the books of both the Old and New Testaments are correct. Since many skeptics are quick to argue that the messianic prophecies were rigged after the fact – in other words, the Old Testament messianic prophecies were recorded only after the corresponding fulfillment was described in the New Testament – it is imperative to address the lines of evidence which render the proper dates for the writings found in both testaments. Once it is demonstrated that several hundred years did, in fact, transpire between the Old Testament messianic prophecies and their New Testament fulfillment, it becomes apparent that the Bible is truly a collection of books originating from outside of time as we know it.

DATING THE BIBLE

Skeptics of Christianity charge that the fulfillment of Old Testament messianic prophecies in the New Testament occurred only because the Old Testament is not nearly as old as believers claim it is. According to these skeptics, the Old Testament prophecies of the coming messiah that are believed to have been fulfilled in the New Testament were, in fact, added into the various books of the Old Testament at a

---

[72] Grant Jeffrey, *Jesus: The Great Debate* (Toronto, Ontario, Canada: Frontier Research Publications, Inc., 1999), 231.

later time, namely the first century AD. However, this skeptical claim can easily be refuted upon examining the evidence for the almost complete immutability of the Old Testament throughout its history.

External verification of the traditionally accepted dating of the Old Testament comes from two major areas, the Dead Sea scrolls and the Septuagint. As it turns out, these two lines of evidence offer an impressive degree of support for the historical continuity of the Old Testament.

THE DEAD SEA SCROLLS

The Dead Sea scrolls, discovered in 1947 near Qumran on the northwest shore of the Dead Sea in Israel, have verified the reliability of the Old Testament. Every Old Testament book, with the exception of Esther, was found among the scrolls, either in its entirety or in part. The scrolls, written between 250 BC and AD 65, corroborate the Masoretic version of the Old Testament text; in fact, the two versions are nearly identical.[73]

A complete copy of Isaiah was discovered among the Dead Sea scrolls. Even though this copy was dated a thousand years earlier than the oldest manuscript previously known, it has proven to be word-for-word identical to the standard Hebrew Bible in more than ninety-five percent of the text. The remaining five percent variation consists mostly of very minor deviations in spelling, and none of these deviations carry any doctrinal changes whatsoever.

The Dead Sea scrolls prove that the biblical scribes took great care in going about their work of copying God's Word. These scribes knew they were handling the Word of God, so they carefully accounted for every letter, word, and line to ensure their accuracy. Even so, it is human nature to make mistakes, no matter how minor they might be. That is why we have some variants in the text. Nonetheless, overall we can have a high degree of confidence that the Old Testament which we possess today is that which God intended us to

---

[73] Ralph Muncaster, *Examine the Evidence* (Eugene, OR: Harvest House Publishers, 2004), 187-190.

have.

THE SEPTUAGINT

The Septuagint, which is the Greek version of the Old Testament that is dated to sometime between the second and third centuries BC, is important for two reasons. First, the Septuagint was the version of Scripture commonly available during the time of Jesus, and therefore is of special importance to Christians. Second, the Septuagint establishes that the messianic prophecies were foretold before the time of Jesus, so that no one can say the prophecies were rigged after the life of Christ.

The Septuagint was translated from Hebrew Scripture during the time of, or even slightly earlier than, the Dead Sea scrolls. Therefore, we may use the Septuagint to clarify matters of biblical doctrine and history. The Septuagint establishes the fulfillment of the messianic prophecies through Jesus, further strengthening the case for Christ's deity.

THE NEW TESTAMENT

The books of the New Testament are considered by most reliable scholars to have been written within the first century. Interestingly, the so-called "dating debate" within New Testament studies seems to be centered in the idea that some of the books were not written until the second century, which in this case spreads the gap between the Old and New Testaments even further but also allows for the likelihood that the eyewitnesses to Jesus' life and ministry would have all died by then, allowing the authors of the New Testament texts a chance to include questionable "facts" that fulfill the Old Testament messianic prophecies but were in reality not true. However, as mentioned the bulk of reliable scholars date the entirety of the New Testament within the first century, and in most cases within the lifetimes of many who witnessed Christ's ministry firsthand. In general the books that are assigned an original date in the second century or later are the Gnostic writings, which are clearly not orthodox Scripture and have no place in a study of fulfilled messianic prophecy.

WHAT I DISCOVERED

Some lines of evidence for Christianity are "offensive weapons," while others are more defensive in nature, such as science and archaeology which point us in the direction of Christianity while at the same time refuting skeptical accusations such as the belief that modern science has effectively buried the belief in God or that some specific person from the Bible never really existed. Fulfilled messianic prophecy is definitely an offensive weapon: It's not so much refuting a competing idea or worldview as it is proclaiming belief in Jesus Christ as Lord and Savior. This is the kind of rock-solid evidence that leads to conversions.

The Old Testament's messianic prophecies were completely fulfilled in the person of Jesus Christ, exactly as Christians have claimed since the time of Christ. Being that the accepted dates for both the Old and New Testaments are very well established, and reveal a time span of hundreds of years between them, the only way out for the skeptic who refuses to consider the possibility of divine guidance for Scripture is to assert that the prophecies were inserted into the Old Testament at a later date, after the time that the corresponding prophecies were fulfilled in the New Testament. However, there is no way that devout Jews would ever allow their holy scriptures to be tampered with. Religiously devout Jews were, and continue to be, zealous guardians of Scripture; the Jews are known as being the "People of the Book" for good reason. Likewise, devout Christians, especially the early Jewish Christians who maintained the utmost respect for the Jewish scriptures, would also have prevented this from happening. The evidence is clear: Fulfilled messianic prophecy is a fact that can only logically be attributed to the supernatural guidance of human history by God himself, despite the best efforts of skeptics to refute this line of evidence for Christianity. It is now clear that God is not aloof and disinterested in his creation, as deists claim. God, in fact, became one of us. Fulfilled messianic prophecy cannot be explained away by the skeptic, and as a result atheism, pantheism, and deism are left looking battered and wholly implausible at this point in the investigation of Christianity's truthfulness.

Chapter 5

THE JESUS OF HISTORY

According to many opponents of the Christian faith, the Jesus of history is nothing more than a conglomeration of earlier pagan myths that somehow, over time, manifested into the Christ of faith. In other words, the Jesus of history – if he even existed – is certainly not the Christ of faith worshiped by untold millions for the past two thousand years. Proponents of this idea attempt to place Jesus in the same category as King Arthur or Robin Hood: Men who they believe never really existed, but instead were devised either as a means of promoting moral character and chivalry, or were composite characters who represented the best traits of two or more real men from history.

THE JESUS MYTH HYPOTHESIS

In our modern age of skepticism it is not surprising that the Jesus myth hypothesis has been proposed, although it carries little weight among the majority of modern historians and scholars. The reason for this is that Jesus' existence as a real person in the historical record is just too overwhelming to deny:

> *The thesis that Jesus never existed has hovered around the fringes of research into the New Testament for centuries but [has] never been able to become an accepted theory. This is for good reason, as it is simply a bad hypothesis based on arguments from silence, special pleading and an awful lot of wishful thinking. It is ironic that atheists will buy into this idea and leave all their pretensions of critical thinking behind.*[74]

G.A. Wells was arguably the most prominent of the Jesus

---

[74] James Hannam, "Refuting the Myth that Jesus Never Existed." http://www.bede.org.uk/jesusmyth.htm

myth proponents in modern times.[75] Highly influential among skeptics of Christianity, Wells inspired atheist author and lecturer Dan Barker to widely promote this idea among both lay and academic audiences throughout America.[76] Barker has been very active on college and university campuses, and in that setting he has been able to promote the Jesus myth hypothesis much more effectively than many of the other skeptics of Christianity.

As with many controversial issues within modern theology, the idea of the Jesus myth hypothesis can, at least in part, be traced back to the Enlightenment, that simultaneously fascinating yet troubled time when all things sacred were called into question. A few radical French thinkers in the final years of the eighteenth century argued that Christ was based upon a combination of Persian and Babylonian mythology, and a century later there were many others who enjoyed great success in spreading this idea as well. During this time two German scholars from the History of Religions School, Wilhelm Bousset and Richard Reitzenstein, heavily promoted this belief, and certainly their status as scholars served to spread this idea.[77]

In the first half of the twentieth century the preeminent atheist Bertrand Russell doubted whether Christ ever existed at all, and confidently proclaimed that we cannot know anything for certain about Jesus. Just three years later Joseph Wheless claimed that documents were forged to make the imaginary person of Jesus seem not only historically real, but to also be the "Christ of faith."

The most recent publication promoting the theory comes from Timothy Freke and Peter Gandy. Their 1999 best-seller

---

[75] However, Wells does allow for the possibility that the "Jesus legend" is based upon an actual historical figure from first century Galilee, although this person should not be connected in any way with the figure of Christ as he appears in the Gospels.

[76] Dan Barker is a former pastor and evangelist who now writes, lectures, and debates from the atheist position.

[77] C. Foster Stanback, *The Resurrection: A Historical Analysis* (Spring, TX: Illumination Publishers International, 2008), 70.

The Jesus Mysteries, which was named Book of the Year by London's *Daily Telegraph*,[78] has enjoyed considerable success among the alternative religious crowd, which is composed mostly of religiously-oriented humanists and New Age mystics. Freke and Gandy have been highly critical of the traditional view of Christianity, instead heavily promoting a more generic, "spiritual" version of Christianity that is steeped in the pagan mystery religions. Additional resources promoting the Jesus myth hypothesis in recent times include Tom Harpur's *The Pagan Christ* and Robert M. Price's *Deconstructing Jesus* and *The Incredible Shrinking Son of Man*.

THE JESUS OF HISTORY

It has been noted that if Jesus was a mythical figure akin to King Arthur or Robin Hood, then the Jesus myth hypothesis fails to address two very important points.[79] First, why were tens of thousands of first century Christians willing to lose everything, including their lives, for a myth? It makes no sense that the Roman government would brutally persecute the peaceful followers of a non-historical, mythical figure. Second, why would Saul of Tarsus, who had been persecuting the followers of Christ, give up literally everything he had going for him – which was a lot, by Jewish standards of the day – to become a follower of Jesus himself? Obviously, there was something more going on than simple devotion to a new religious myth, of which the historicity of its main character was supposedly questionable. Something real, and unbelievably powerful in its ability to stir the souls of mankind, had really taken place.

Some proponents of the Jesus myth hypothesis argue that if Jesus had really existed, he would have appeared in the records of ancient Rome; Jesus is, after all, the most prominent figure in world history. As it turns out, there are scant

---

[78] Lee Strobel, *The Case for the Real Jesus* (Grand Rapids, MI: Zondervan, 2007), 158.
[79] Mark Eastman & Chuck Smith, *The Search for Messiah* (Fountain Valley, CA: Joy Publishing, 1996), 239.

few records that remain from the days of ancient Rome, save the writings of a few who were interested only in the hierarchy of the Roman ruling class:

> ...there are no surviving Roman records but only highly parochial Roman historians who had little interest in the comings and goings of minor cults and were far more concerned about Emperors and Kings. Jesus made a very small splash while he was alive and there was no reason for Roman historians to notice him.[80]

We must remember that much of Jesus' influence upon the world took place after his death and resurrection. The spread of Christianity gained massive momentum at Pentecost (Acts 2), but it took several years for Christ's followers to make a significant impact upon the Roman Empire as a whole, so whatever was written about Jesus from the pens of Roman historians took place well after Jesus' earthly life simply because it took some time to significantly impact the Roman Empire.

However, there are ancient secular and Jewish historians who recorded for us the reality of Jesus' earthly existence. These men generally opposed Christianity, although a few leaned closer to indifference and merely reported the facts with seemingly no ulterior motives in place. Either way, through their writings the existence of Jesus is confirmed. Following are some of these extra-biblical historians of old. It is important to realize that this is not a comprehensive list, but rather is an adequately sufficient survey for the purpose of establishing the point at hand. No single example offered should be considered as being wholly adequate to prove the historicity of Jesus, but rather all of the examples in this chapter combine to establish the historicity of Jesus.

FLAVIUS JOSEPHUS

Flavius Josephus, who was born Joseph ben Matthias in AD 37 and lived until approximately AD 100, was the son of

---

[80] James Hannam, "Refuting the Myth that Jesus Never Existed." http://www.bede.org.uk/jesusmyth.htm

a Jewish priest who eventually became a priest himself. As a member of the Pharisee's, Josephus was well-educated and intellectually capable. He was later recognized by Roman officials, who had captured him in AD 67 during the Jewish Revolt, as being a man of scholarly talent, and as a result he was utilized by Rome as a scribe and an interpreter. Roman officials gave him the name Flavius Josephus, under which he wrote his historical works.

Two passages from Josephus discuss Jesus of Nazareth. The first reference, which today is referred to as the *Testimonium Flavianum*, comes from Book 18 of *Antiquities*. It is as follows:

> *Now there was about this time Jesus, a wise man, if it be lawful to call him a man, for he was a doer of wonderful works, a teacher of such men as receive the truth with pleasure. He drew over to him both many of the Jews, and many of the Gentiles. He was the Christ, and when Pilate, at the suggestion of the principal men among us, had condemned him to the cross, those that loved him at the first did not forsake him; for he appeared to them alive again the third day; as the divine prophets had foretold these and ten thousand other wonderful things concerning him. And the tribe of Christians so named from him are not extinct at this day.*[81]

Needless to say, this passage is controversial simply because no non-Christian Jew such as Josephus would be inclined to write so positively about Jesus. Phrases such as, "He was the Christ," and "for he appeared to them alive again the third day" would not be attributed to someone who was not a Christian. Jesus mythologists are quick to say that these blatantly Christian passages were later inserted by believing scribes, in the attempt to spread the Gospel. However, Christopher Price notes that the majority of scholars have concluded that much of the *Testimonium Flavianum* is an authentic work of Josephus, and that even if Christian scribes

---

[81] Christopher Price, "A Thorough Review of the Testimonium Flavianum." http://www.bede.org.uk/Josephus.htm

later added a few lines to this passage – which admittedly does seem to be the case – "the partial validity of this one passage is enough to sink their [the Jesus mythologists] entire argument."[82] Apart from the phrases supporting the deity of Jesus, the fact of Jesus' historical reality is very obvious from this passage.

The tenth century Arabic version of the *Testimonium Flavianum* seems more in line with what a non-biased Jewish reporter might record for posterity:

> *At this time there was a wise man who was called Jesus. And his conduct was good, and he was known to be virtuous. And many people from among the Jews and the other nations became his disciples. Pilate condemned him to be crucified and to die. And those who had become his disciples did not abandon his discipleship. They reported that he had appeared to them after his crucifixion and that he was alive; accordingly, he was perhaps the Messiah concerning whom the prophets have recounted wonders.*[83]

This Arabic-to-English translation of the *Testimonium Flavianum* is more neutral concerning Christ's deity, but is certainly rock-solid in supporting the reality of the historical Jesus. That, of course, is the point of all this.

The second reference to Jesus by Josephus concerns the murder of James, the half-brother of Jesus, at the hands of Ananus, the Jewish High Priest:

> *But the younger Ananus who, as we said, received the high priesthood, was of a bold disposition and exceptionally daring; he followed the party of the Sadducees, who are severe in judgment above all the Jews, as we have already shown. As therefore Ananus was of such a disposition, he thought he had now a good opportunity, as Festus was now dead, and Albinus was still on the road; so he assembled a council of judges, and brought before it the brother of Jesus the so-called Christ, whose name was James, together with*

---

[82] Ibid.
[83] Alan Humm, "Josephus on Jesus."
http://www.jewishchristianlit.com/Topics/JewishJesus/josephus.html

some others, and having accused them as lawbreakers, he delivered them over to be stoned.[84]

In this passage, Josephus refers to Jesus as "the so-called Christ," which is not at all an unreasonable statement from an unbelieving Jew, but rather is merely a reporting of the facts. When these two passages are taken together, it becomes obvious that Josephus – a first-rate historian of the ancient Roman world – confirms the historicity of Jesus of Nazareth.

THALLUS & JULIUS AFRICANUS

Thallus was a Roman historian who wrote primarily around the middle of the first century, not long after the time of Jesus. Although none of Thallus' original writings have survived, Julius Africanus – an early Church Father who wrote in the first part of the third century – did have access to the writings of Thallus during his time, and it is in large part through Africanus that we are able to reference the earlier work of Thallus. Thallus, as relayed by Africanus, discussed the darkness that occurred during the time of Christ's crucifixion: "Now from the sixth hour until the ninth hour there was darkness over all the land."[85] This is an excellent extra-biblical corroboration of the event that three of the gospel writers record for us (Matthew 27:45; Mark 15:33; Luke 23:44-45). However, Thallus attempted to naturalistically explain away this darkness, although Africanus did not agree with his reasoning: "Thallus, in the third book of his history, explains away the darkness as an eclipse of the sun, unreasonably as it seems to me."[86]

There was a very good reason why Africanus denied Thallus' theory that an eclipse of the sun accounted for the darkness at Christ's crucifixion. Africanus, a learned man of his time, was aware that the crucifixion took place during the

---

[84] Christopher Price, "A Thorough Review of the Testimonium Flavianum." http://www.bede.org.uk/Josephus.htm
[85] Mark Eastman & Chuck Smith, *The Search for Messiah* (Fountain Valley, CA: Joy Publishing, 1996), 246.
[86] Ibid.

Passover, and Passover always occurs during a full moon – and therefore a solar eclipse could not have taken place. The darkness must be accounted for by some other means, which must have been from "beyond nature" as the only likely natural explanation for darkness during otherwise normally light hours is a solar eclipse, which lasts just a matter of minutes – certainly not three hours as described in Scripture.

Although Thallus attempted to explain away the darkness during Christ's crucifixion, it must be stressed that Thallus did not attempt to deny the historical reality of Jesus, his crucifixion, or the darkness that occurred during the crucifixion. Rather, he reported about this event as though it really happened, further establishing the historicity of Jesus.

PHLEGON & PHILOPON

Philopon was a sixth century secular historian who also discussed the darkness at the time of Christ's crucifixion, by building upon the second century writings of Phlegon: "...and about the darkness [at Christ's crucifixion]...Phlegon recalls it in his book *The Olympiads*."[87] Like Thallus, the unbelieving Phlegon also reports the facts concerning Jesus' historicity, including the darkness that occurred during the crucifixion.

CORNELIUS TACITUS

Cornelius Tacitus was born sometime between AD 52-55, and he eventually became a senator in the Roman government under the leadership of Emperor Vespasian. He was known for being a very reliable and fact-based historian, never exercising a desire to skew the facts in order to promote a good story.[88] Tacitus only wrote about events either within his lifetime, or at the most a few generations before him.[89] This was unlike many ancient historians, who often wrote about events which occurred many centuries before

---

[87] Ibid.
[88] Ibid.
[89] John Oakes, *Reasons for Belief* (Spring, TX: Illumination Publishers International, 2005), 62.

their time. In *Annals* (15.44), Tacitus records for us the following:

> But not all the relief that could come from man, not all the bounties that the prince could bestow, nor all the atonements which could be presented to the gods, availed to relieve Nero from the infamy of being believed to have ordered the Conflagration, the fire of Rome. Hence to suppress the rumor, he falsely charged with the guilt, and punished Christians, who were hated for their enormities. Christus, the founder of the name, was put to death by Pontius Pilate, procurator of Judea in the reign of Tiberius: but the pernicious superstition, repressed for a time broke out again, not only through Judea, where the mischief originated, but through the city of Rome also, where all things hideous and shameful from every part of the world find their center and become popular. Accordingly, an arrest was first made of all who pleaded guilty; then, upon their information, an immense multitude was convicted, not so much of the crime of firing the city, as of hatred against mankind.[90]

Eastman and Smith note that Tacitus' record of Jesus' profound influence upon the Roman Empire is rarely, if ever, called into question by historians and scholars, so reliable was his reputation as a historian.[91] Many biblical scholars have noted that Luke, the author of both the Gospel of Luke and Acts, was similar to Tacitus in that he also had an eye for great detail in his reporting of events.

MARA BAR-SERAPION

Sometime after the Roman destruction of the Jewish Temple in AD 70, the Syrian scholar and Stoic philosopher Mara Bar-Serapion wrote the following letter:

> What advantage did the Athenians gain from putting Socrates to death? Famine and plague came upon them as a

---

[90] James Patrick Holding, "The Testimony of Tacitus." http://www.tektonics.org/jesusexist/tacitus.html
[91] Mark Eastman & Chuck Smith, *The Search for Messiah* (Fountain Valley, CA: Joy Publishing, 1996), 249.

judgment for their crime. What advantage did the men of Samos gain from burning Pythagoras? In a moment their land was covered with sand. What advantage did the Jews gain from executing their wise King? It was just after that their Kingdom was abolished. God justly avenged these three wise men: the Athenians died of hunger; the Samians were overwhelmed by the sea; the Jews, ruined and driven from their land, live in complete dispersion. But Socrates did not die for good; he lived on in the teaching of Plato. Pythagoras did not die for good; he lived on in the statue of Hera. Nor did the wise King die for good; He lived on in the [Christian] teaching which He had given.[92]

This letter describes the "wise King," a title which clearly referred to Jesus. Although not a Christian believer, Bar-Serapion nonetheless refutes the idea that Jesus was a mythical figure who never really existed.[93]

LUCIAN OF SAMOSOTA

The Greek satirist Lucian, who was extremely harsh toward Christians,[94] wrote of Christ around AD 170.[95] The following is an excerpt from the writings of Lucian concerning Jesus: "The Christians, you know, worship a man to this day– the distinguished personage who introduced their novel rites, and was crucified on that account."[96] If Jesus had been merely a mythical figure who was nothing more than a conglomeration of previously known dying-and-rising gods from the pagan world, Lucian would not have written about him as if he had really existed at one time. A "distinguished personage" does not accurately describe a mythical figure,

---

[92] James Patrick Holding, "Secular References to Jesus: Mara Bar-Serapion." http://www.tektonics.org/jesusexist/serapion.html

[93] By placing Jesus in the same league as Socrates and Pythagoras, Bar-Serapion likely considered Jesus to have been a great teacher from earlier times, but not God in the flesh.

[94] John Oakes, *Reasons for Belief* (Spring, TX: Illumination Publishers International, 2005), 62.

[95] Mark Eastman & Chuck Smith, *The Search for Messiah* (Fountain Valley, CA: Joy Publishing, 1996), 250.

[96] Ibid.

but rather one who actually existed at some time in history.

THE BABYLONIAN TALMUD

The Babylonian Talmud is a collection of rabbinical commentaries which was compiled during AD 200-500. Part of the Babylonian Talmud referred to as Sanhedrin 43a contains a clear reference to Jesus, as well as the impact that he had made upon the Jewish people of his time:

> *It has been taught: On the Eve of the Passover, they hanged Yeshu [Jesus]. And an announcer went out in front of him, for forty days saying: "he is going to be stoned because he practiced sorcery and enticed and led Israel astray. Anyone who knows anything in his favor, let him come and plead in his behalf." But, not having found anything in his favor, they hanged him on the Eve of the Passover.*[97]

Clearly, this is a reference to Jesus, who in Hebrew was known as Yeshu or Yeshu'a. The forty day announcement period, which does not appear in the four Gospels, is certainly an interesting piece of information, whether it is truly accurate or not.

Eastman and Smith make an interesting point. According to Jewish law, it was illegal to enact capital punishment during the Eve of the Passover,[98] yet the Babylonian Talmud clearly states that Jesus was hanged (crucified) at that time. This passage incriminates the Jewish authorities, especially the High Priest who allowed this act of capital punishment during a forbidden time.

Some other interesting points from this passage need to be addressed. The writer referred to Jesus as having "practiced sorcery," which is a clear indication that Jesus' miracles could not be denied by the Jewish authorities, but rather had to be explained away in some other manner – namely, sorcery or demonic activity. Also, this passage states that Jesus had "led Israel astray," which reveals the division that Jesus

---

[97] Ibid.
[98] Ibid.

created among the people of Israel. Some would follow Jesus, recognizing him as Messiah, while others would scoff at his claims of deity. The writer of this passage went on to state that the rabbinical leaders of the day taught that Jesus had five disciples: Matti, Necki, Netsur, Burni, and Toda.[99] Although Jesus had formed a group of twelve apostles and, in fact, had many disciples or followers, the name Matti could easily be a reference to Matthew, one of the twelve apostles and a Gospel writer.[100]

MAIMONIDES

Maimonides, or Rambam as he was also known, was a thirteenth century rabbi who was highly revered among the Jewish people of the day. It was said that "there was never a greater man than Maimonides except Moses."[101] Maimonides wrote a fourteen volume work entitled the *Mishne Torah*, in which he referenced the person of Jesus many times, although never in a positive light. Following is a passage from Maimonides concerning Jesus' influence upon the world:

> *Jesus of Nazareth who aspired to be the Messiah and was executed by the court was also [alluded to] in Daniel's prophecies (Daniel 11:14) as "the vulgar [common] among your people shall exalt themselves in an attempt to fulfill the vision, but they shall stumble." Can there be a greater stumbling block than Christianity?*[102]

Maimonides establishes the historical existence of Jesus by referring to his execution by the court (Jewish authorities), his association with the Old Testament prophecies (Daniel), and the division that he created among the Jewish people when referring to Christianity as a "stumbling block." Maimonides almost certainly had the words of both Isaiah and Paul in mind when he wrote about Christianity as being

---

[99] Ibid.
[100] However, in all fairness Matthew was a common male name during the time of Jesus.
[101] Mark Eastman & Chuck Smith, *The Search for Messiah* (Fountain Valley, CA: Joy Publishing, 1996), 254.
[102] Ibid.

a stumbling block:

> He *[Jesus]* will be a holy place; for both Israel and Judah he will be a stone that causes people to stumble and a rock that makes them fall. And for the people of Jerusalem he will be a trap and a snare (Isaiah 8:14).

> Jews demand signs and Greeks look for wisdom, but we preach Christ crucified: a stumbling block to Jews and foolishness to Gentiles (1 Corinthians 1:22-23).

Of course, even today Jesus remains a stumbling block for the world as a whole. Some will believe, while others will scoff.

ADDITIONAL EXTRA-BIBLICAL REFERENCES

The Roman statesman Pliny the Younger, who began practicing law in AD 79 while only eighteen years of age, eventually served as the governor of Bithynia in Asia Minor. During this time he began to persecute Christians in his region for their supposed atrocities against the Roman state. In his letter to Emperor Trajan, Pliny inquired of how he should deal with Christians who would not recant of their faith. Although not specifically mentioning the person of Jesus, Pliny nonetheless offers support for the historicity of Jesus in that if Jesus had been a mythical figure along the lines of Dionysus or another seasonally dying-and-rising pagan god, then Pliny would have used that line of evidence against Christ's followers. However, Pliny noted the devotion that the Christians possessed, which was due to their following a real person from the historical record, rather than a mythical figure.

Caius Suetonius Tranquillus was a Roman historian who served as the private secretary of Emperor Hadrian. As the head of Rome, Hadrian was especially concerned over the rising spread of Christianity, and therefore he took the "Christian problem" quite seriously. Writing under the direction of Hadrian, Suetonius referred specifically to the followers of Christ, once again indirectly supporting the historicity of Jesus.

Finally, the *Gospel of Thomas*, although a Gnostic writing

which has no real theological significance for Bible-believing Christians, does serve to corroborate the historicity of Jesus. "While the Gospel of Thomas has no canonical theological value and is from a sect regarded as heretical, it does have historical value as a corroborative document [it establishes the historicity of Jesus] written by those familiar with the teachings of Jesus, near the time of Jesus."[103]

In summary, it is clear from both ancient secular and non-biblical Jewish writings that Jesus was a real person who lived in Judea during the first century. Although many skeptics have forcefully debated the deity of Jesus, they cannot offer any real support for the claim that Jesus never existed. In the next section we will examine the evidence which refutes the idea that Jesus was merely a conglomeration of various dying-and-rising gods of the ancient world.

FINDING THE REAL JESUS

As previously discussed, the claim has been made that Jesus is nothing more than an amalgamation of earlier dying-and-rising gods as well as men of renown from the ancient world. Upon a very superficial inspection, this skeptical claim may seem to hold some weight, but when a more thorough investigation is undertaken, each of the various examples offered by skeptics fall by the wayside, revealed to be nothing more than false claims offered with an ulterior motive in mind, namely to refute Christian theism at any cost.

Although not an exhaustive list of gods or heroes from which Jesus is supposedly copied, the following names[104] comprise the most commonly claimed figures: Zoroaster, Mithra, Krishna, Buddha, Horus, Osiris, Attis, and Dionysus. In this chapter only Zoroaster and Mithra will be addressed in point-by-point detail, and Krishna and Buddha will be refuted in terms of the inconsistency between Eastern theology

---

[103] Ralph Muncaster, *Examine the Evidence* (Eugene, OR: Harvest House Publishers, 2004), 209.
[104] James Patrick Holding, "Shattering the Christ Myth." http://www.tektonics.org/shattering.html

and traditional Christian doctrine. The other figures noted may be dismantled in a similar fashion.

ZOROASTER

Skeptics of Christianity claim that Zoroaster shares several similarities with Jesus.[105] These supposed similarities include Zoroaster being born of a virgin through an "immaculate conception." He was baptized in a river, and in his youth he astounded wise men with his great wisdom. He was tempted in the wilderness by the Devil, before beginning his ministry at the age of thirty. He baptized with water, fire, and "holy wind," and performed miraculous feats such as the casting out of demons and restoring the sight to a blind man. He taught about Heaven and Hell, and revealed many mysteries including resurrection, judgment, salvation, and the apocalypse. He was considered to be the "Word made flesh," although he was eventually slain. The religion he founded had a Eucharistic component, and he even had a sacred cup or "grail." Finally, his followers expect a "second coming" in the year 2341, when he will usher in a golden age for humanity.

After reading that list of comparisons, what's a Christian believer to think? At first glance, this list of claimed similarities seems incredibly daunting to the follower of Jesus. Is it possible that Jesus is nothing more than a later copy of Zoroaster? We must be careful to analyze this list using scholarly means, in order to determine three things. First, is it possible that some of these claimed similarities are merely that – *claimed* – and not really true? Second, if these claims are true could they be explained in a way that is both logical and plausible? Third, if a claimed similarity is true, does the claim hold any real weight? In other words, is it vague and therefore meaningless? It is important to discern the evidence, or lack thereof, and approach the subject with an open mind and a willingness to consider alternate explanations.

---

[105] James Patrick Holding, "Was the Story of Jesus Stolen from that of Zoroaster?" http://www.tektonics.org/copycat/zoroaster.html

Whether a Christian believer or a skeptic, one must always avoid wild, unfounded explanations as a means of appealing to any hypothesis.

It turns out that some of these similarities are actually true and are confirmed by way of scholarly literature, whereas other claims are way off the mark and "come from sources that are way, way too late – even as late as the tenth century."[106] Needless to say, this could very well indicate that Zoroaster was copied from Jesus, rather than the other way around.

The Avesta is the main source for the details of Zoroaster's life. This is a collection of sacred texts that Zoroastrians hold dearly, paralleling the Bible for Christians. The Avesta was put into written form in the fourth century AD, although there may be some dispute as to the date of the original writings. The major point, however, is that, "Some of the material probably comes from a time before the Christian era, but most of this is reckoned to be hymns and some basic information that was part of the oral tradition. The rest seems likely to have been added later, and for good reason."[107] The "good reason" was almost certainly for the purpose of retaining spiritual appeal in the light of Christianity's great success. James Patrick Holding comments on this:

> *The incorporation of certain motifs into the Zoroastrian tradition in the ninth century CE could indicate the conscious attempt of the [Zoroastrian] priesthood to exalt their prophet in the eyes of the faithful who may have been tempted to turn to other religions [namely, Christianity]. In other words, if we see a "Jesus-like" story in these texts, especially this late, we have a right to suspect borrowing – but in exactly the opposite way that critics suppose!*[108]

If the Zoroastrian priests of the era when Christianity first infiltrated Persia had become distraught over the success of the Christian evangelists, then maybe they were responsible

---

[106] Ibid.
[107] Ibid.
[108] Ibid.

(at least in part) for initiating the "copycat" hypothesis as a means of retaining their brethren. As a note of interest, Matthew, Thomas, and Jude (Thaddeus) are all associated by way of church tradition with the preaching of the Gospel in Persia, and would therefore have been at odds with the priests of Zoroaster.[109]

Before tackling the skeptical claims listed above, three points concerning the basic theology of both Zoroastrianism and Christianity must be mentioned. First, it should be noted that scholars are unclear as to whether or not Zoroaster was even a historical figure, let alone the time period into which he may have lived. Most sources place Zoroaster around 600 BC, although "one scholar has suggested a date as early as 1700 BC."[110] Therefore, it is possible that Zoroastrianism is a mythically-based religion, founded by a man who never even existed. After some research on this topic, however, I believe that Zoroaster was a real person, although his chronological status is definitely in question.

Second, Zoroastrianism does contain a concept that very closely resembles bodily resurrection, although it must be pointed out that this belief is most clearly described in the Zoroastrian texts that were written after the founding of Christianity. One must ask the question, "Did the Jews develop the concept of bodily resurrection during their Persian exile, or did the Persians instead assimilate this idea from the Jews, having been influenced by prominent Jewish theologians such as Ezekiel or Daniel?" There is no direct evidence either way, but one should not automatically assume that the Jews stole this idea from the Persians. Perhaps it was the other way around.

Third, the claim has been made that the Jewish idea of Sa-

---

[109] The "priests of Zoroaster" could possibly have been the magi, although the definitive identity of the magi from the birth account in Matthew 2:1-12 remains a matter of debate. Perhaps some of the magi were open to the overarching theme of the Christian faith, whereas others saw Christianity as being an "enemy" religion, a false offshoot of Judaism.
[110] James Patrick Holding, "Was the Story of Jesus Stolen from that of Zoroaster?" http://www.tektonics.org/copycat/zoroaster.html

tan is borrowed from Zoroastrianism. However, two points need to be made concerning this claim. The first point is that Satan appears in Job, which is a very early book of the Bible – some biblical scholars maintain that Job may have lived close to the time of Abraham, if not before – and in Job the clear teaching is that Satan is a created being who is completely subordinate to God. On the other hand, in Zoroastrianism the evil god is essentially a dualistic equal to the good god, which is completely off the mark from biblical teaching. The second point is that even though the Old Testament writers used some Persian words for civic matters, they did not use any Persian words for religious matters. This makes perfect sense, since the Jews were forced to live among the Persians for much of their exile, but nonetheless they retained their religious purity. Therefore, the Jews would not have based their concept of Satan upon the beliefs of some other culture. These are some very significant divides in what is supposed to be an otherwise extremely similar pair of religions.

It must be noted that no references are found within the Avesta which would substantiate seven of the previously mentioned claims.[111] These are (1) Zoroaster was born of a virgin, through an "immaculate conception" by a ray of divine reason; (2) Zoroaster was baptized in a river; (3) Zoroaster baptized with water, fire, and holy wind; (4) Zoroaster cast out demons and restored sight to a blind man; (5) Zoroaster had a sacred cup[112] similar to the Holy Grail of Christian lore; (6) Zoroastrianism had a Eucharistic component; (7) Zoroaster was the "Word made flesh." These claims clearly originated apart from the holy writings of this religion, almost certainly for the purpose of challenging the great success of Christianity from the first century onward.

What of the other claims? Is there any degree of truth

---

[111] Ibid.
[112] However, it should be noted that the "Holy Grail," which was the cup or chalice of Christ, is not a biblical concept but rather is based upon a legend that likely traces to the Medieval period.

found in the remaining claims, and do they have at least some literary substantiation? Yes, but even these claims are not as rock-solid as skeptics would have us believe. First, in his youth Zoroaster did astound wise men with his wisdom. At the age of seven, Zoroaster was placed under the care of a wise man, but he had disputes with several magi – the Persian word for the learned wise men of that kingdom – some of whom he attempted to refute. Zoroaster was clearly a child prodigy, as was Jesus, but in quite a different way. Jesus did not irritate and refute the learned scholars of his day, but rather astounded them with his great wisdom and insight. The fact that two religious founders were both spiritually and intellectually advanced at a young age is not really all that surprising.

Second, Zoroaster was, according to the literature, tempted in the wilderness by the Devil. After ten years (rather than forty days) of visionary experiences, a lesser demon was sent to deceive Zoroaster. Therefore, both the time frame and the identity of the demon are significantly different from that found in Christianity.

Third, Zoroaster did begin his ministry at the age of thirty, but two points concerning this matter must be made. The first point is that this belief "comes from the Pahlavi literature, which is post-Christian by several centuries,"[113] and the second point is that thirty is the age at which Iranian men come to "wisdom." It has been amusingly noted that "the ancients gave as much regard to the 'big three-oh' as we [do]."[114]

Fourth, Zoroaster did teach about Heaven and Hell, as well as other spiritual issues of great importance, but ultimately Zoroastrianism is a works-based religion regarding salvation and the afterlife. In the area of salvation, only the idea of bodily resurrection is passingly similar. The concept of substitutionary blood atonement for the sins of all humani-

---

[113] James Patrick Holding, "Was the Story of Jesus Stolen from that of Zoroaster?" http://www.tektonics.org/copycat/zoroaster.html
[114] Ibid.

ty is completely missing from Zoroastrianism, which is the key doctrine of salvation in Christianity.

Fifth, Zoroaster was slain, but his death had no significance concerning substitutionary atonement for the sins of humanity, as did Jesus' death. There are two completely different stories about Zoroaster's death.[115] In the first story, which is a later, post-Christian story, Zoroaster was struck by lightning. In the second story – which is the more generally accepted account – Zoroaster was killed at the age of seventy-seven in a temple by a priest. It may be that Zoroaster was killed, but this is not at all unusual for religious leaders throughout history.

Finally, the followers of Zoroaster do have a version of the apocalypse:

> *I have been able to confirm that this [apocalyptic account] is true to some extent: a return is expected in 2341 CE, to start a golden age; the details on age 30 I have found nowhere. Whether this future Deliverer would indeed be Zoroaster himself again is indeed something that has been interpreted, but later Zoroastrian texts think that the person will be of the line of Zoroaster, not Zoroaster himself.*[116]

Many, if not most, of the major world religions feature some type of apocalyptic scenario or at least address it if even briefly, so this supposed similarity is not surprising in the least. Most people, regardless of their religious beliefs, are intrigued by the question of how the world will end, and almost all religions take a stance on this issue.

After taking the time to explore this skeptical claim in some detail, it may be stated with great certainty that Zoroaster and Jesus are not one and the same figure with different names only. Instead, Zoroaster and Jesus are two religious founders with drastically different lives.

---

[115] Ibid.
[116] Ibid.

MITHRA

In the Roman Empire during the time of the early church, Mithraism was one of the greatest non-Jewish competitors of Christianity, although today few are even aware of this once prominent religion. Named in honor of Mithra, who was considered to be a savior figure, this mystery religion reached into the far corners of the empire and was quite popular among soldiers. But unlike Zoroastrianism, whose founder may very well have been a real figure in history, Mithraism was almost certainly based upon a mythical figure. Mythical or not, however, proponents of the Jesus myth hypothesis make several claims of similarity between Mithra and Jesus.[117] These are: (1) Mithra was born of a virgin on December 25th, no less in a cave, and his birth was attended by shepherds; (2) Mithra was considered a great traveling teacher and master; (3) Mithra's followers were promised immortality; (4) Mithra was buried in a tomb and rose again after three days; (5) Mithraism had a Eucharist or Lord's Supper; (6) Mithraic services were conducted by priests called "fathers" and the chief of the fathers – who was basically the pope, who lived in Rome – was called Pater Patratus.

How does each one of these claims hold up to the weight of evidential scrutiny? Let's begin with the birthdate for Mithra. Regarding the claimed birthdate of December 25th, it should first of all be noted that this widely-accepted day for Christ's birth is not based upon Scripture, but rather upon very old pagan traditions related to the festivals of Saturnalia and Sol Invictus. When Christianity became the state religion of the Roman Empire in AD 380, Christian believers adopted December 25th as a way to more easily assimilate the influx of pagan adherents into the church, in the sincere hope that they would eventually come to accept the one true God and

---

[117] James Patrick Holding, "Was the Story of Jesus Stolen from that of the Persian Deity Mithra?" http://www.tektonics.org/copycat/mithra.html

Savior, the Lord Jesus Christ.[118] So, in essence December 25th is not really an issue at all, because knowledgeable Christians typically don't believe that Christ was even born on this day.

Also on the subject of Mithra's birth, he "was not born of a virgin in a cave; he was born out of solid rock, which presumably left a cave behind – and I suppose technically the rock he was born out of could have been classified as a virgin!"[119] Timothy Paul Jones, an expert on early church history, verifies that Mithra was born from stone, leaving a cave behind him.[120] So there really was no virgin birth involved. Although shepherds do seem to have been in attendance at the birth of Mithra, this appears in Mithraic literature about a century after the New Testament was completed,[121] so if anyone is borrowing from someone else it would appear that Mithraism is the "copycat" religion.

Regarding the claim that Mithra was a great traveling teacher and master, there is no evidence of this in the literature, but even if there was, why should that be surprising? The founding figures of the great religions of the world are oftentimes described as having been great teachers of wisdom, traveling throughout their native lands and beyond, so this point is really insignificant.

Regarding the promise of immortality to his followers, it must be acknowledged that most religions offer some sort of plan for eternal life, otherwise what hope do they really have to offer their adherents? A religion without the promise of immortality is likely a religion with relatively few followers. Even religious humanism at least promises that both our

---

[118] Andrew McGowan, "How December 25th Became Christmas." https://www.biblicalarchaeology.org/daily/biblical-topics/new-testament/how-december-25-became-christmas/
[119] James Patrick Holding, "Was the Story of Jesus Stolen from that of the Persian Deity Mithra?" http://www.tektonics.org/copycat/mithra.html
[120] Timothy Paul Jones, *Conspiracies and the Cross* (Lake Mary, FL: Front Line, 2008), 107.
[121] James Patrick Holding, "Was the Story of Jesus Stolen from that of the Persian Deity Mithra?" http://www.tektonics.org/copycat/mithra.html

good deeds and our genes will live on in future generations, albeit this is not exactly most people's idea of immortality. However, regarding the claim that Mithra shed blood for his followers:

> *In practical terms, however, the only hard evidence of a "salvational" ideology is a piece of graffiti found in the Santa Prisca Mithraeum (a Mithraist "church" building, if you will), dated no earlier than 200 AD, that reads, 'And us, too, you saved by spilling the eternal blood.' Note that this refers to Mithra spilling the blood of the bull – not his own – and that (according to the modern Mithraic "astrological" interpretation) this does not mean "salvation" in a Christian sense (involving freedom from sin) but an ascent through levels of initiation into immortality.*[122]

Therefore, "shed blood" in Mithraism means something completely different than the shed blood involved in Christ's substitutionary atonement: "…Mithra himself never becomes the sacrifice."[123] Christian salvation is wholly different from Mithraic salvation, which is nothing more than spiritual progression through higher levels of enlightenment.

Regarding the claim that Mithra was buried in a tomb and then resurrected three days later, there seems to be no clear-cut references to this at all. As one expert on the subject has noted, "I see no references anywhere in the Mithraic studies literature to Mithra being buried, or even dying, for that matter and so of course no rising again and no "resurrection" to celebrate."[124] On the other hand, the resurrection of Christ is the most important event in human history, and in this regard Mithra simply does not compare to Jesus.

Regarding the claim that Mithraism has a Eucharist (Communion or Last Supper), it has been noted that:

> *The closest thing that Mithraism had to a "Last Supper"*

---

[122] Ibid.
[123] Timothy Paul Jones, *Conspiracies and the Cross* (Lake Mary, FL: Front Line, 2008), 108.
[124] James Patrick Holding, "Was the Story of Jesus Stolen from that of the Persian Deity Mithra?" http://www.tektonics.org/copycat/mithra.html

was the taking of staples (bread, water, wine and meat) by the Mithraic initiates, which was perhaps a celebration of the meal that Mithra had with the sun deity after slaying the bull. However, the meal of the initiates is usually seen as no more than a general fellowship meal of the sort that was practiced by groups all over the Roman world – from religious groups to funeral societies.[125]

Communion and religious community meals are not at all unusual, and many religious groups from this time in history would have followed this practice. The Epicureans were a philosophical group that in many ways functioned as a community-based religion similar to Christianity, and they partook in a community meal as well. However, a Mithraic communion-type meal of "body and blood" only goes back to the mid-second century,[126] which is a hundred plus years after the events written about in the four Gospels. Therefore, it once again seems that Mithraism borrowed from Christianity, and not vice versa.

Lastly, regarding the claim that Mithraic services were conducted by so-called "fathers," and that the chief of these fathers (Pater Patratus) was a sort of pope who always lived in Rome, it must be acknowledged that this is true. But is this really significant? The use of familial terms, such as father and Pater Patratus, is no surprise as familial terms are often used by different religious groups since they are most useful for expressing endearment. Therefore, this is not especially surprising – or necessarily significant, for that matter.

To conclude this section on the supposed similarities between Mithra and Jesus, it is obvious that when one examines the claims of the skeptics, there really is no legitimate basis for believing that Jesus was merely a re-telling of the story of Mithra. If anything, Mithraism borrowed elements of the Gospel in order to stem the tide of defeat that it was

---

[125] Ibid.
[126] Timothy Paul Jones, *Conspiracies and the Cross* (Lake Mary, FL: Front Line, 2008), 108.

experiencing at the hands of the ever-expanding Christian faith. When a religion has to incorporate elements of a more popular, and more convincing, religion into its system of theology in order to remain at least somewhat appealing, it is a sure bet that the religion will not be around much longer – which was the case with Mithraism. Although in a past era Mithraism and Christianity were opponents in the battle for the hearts and minds of people, Mithraism today is an essentially extinct religion. Groups such as the Julian Society, who are dedicated to the restoration of the pagan religions of the past, and the upper levels of Freemasonry, which is considered by many to be the "keepers of the ancient wisdom," have kept Mithraism alive to some extent, although certainly not in its exact original form.

KRISHNA & BUDDHA

Krishna is a prominent figure within Hinduism, although his historicity is a matter of debate, and the Buddha – originally Siddhartha Gautama, whose historicity is not a matter of serious debate – was the founder of the Buddhist religion. Both figures have been proposed by skeptics as being prototypes for the Christ myth. However, when one examines the basic doctrines of both Hinduism and Buddhism it becomes very clear that neither figure could have been an influence upon Christianity, as Christian theology is worlds apart from the beliefs that comprise these Eastern religions. If Jesus' teachings had been drawn from both of these Eastern sources, then we should expect Christian theology to be very similar, if not nearly identical, to both Hinduism and Buddhism. Nothing could be further from the truth, however.

It should be noted that there are several excellent resources that refute the idea that Krishna and Buddha served as the template for Jesus.[127] However, the fact that Eastern philosophy in general is so radically different from tradition-

---

[127] H. Wayne House, *The Jesus Who Never Lived* (Eugene, OR: Harvest House Publishers, 2008), 114-125. This resource may very well be the best point-by-point refutation of the idea that both Krishna and Buddha are the models for Jesus of Nazareth.

al biblical theology is more than sufficient to refute the idea that Jesus was copied from either Krishna or Buddha.

In many ways, Hinduism is the polar opposite of Christianity. If Christ was based in large part upon Krishna, then it would seem reasonable for the teachings of Christ to reflect Hindu theology, which is certainly not the case.128 Several points of conflict need to be addressed. First, although the exact number varies according to the sources examined, Hinduism boasts millions of gods, each being a manifestation of a particular characteristic of the impersonal god of monistic pantheism, who is known as Brahma in Hinduism. Therefore, Hinduism is a combination of pantheism, monism, and polytheism, and was already well-established centuries prior to the time of Christ.129 Throughout the New Testament God reveals the reality of Christian theism, not the impersonal god of pantheism-monism combined with polytheism. This is a major point of contention that alone refutes the idea that Christ was merely copied from Krishna.

Second, Hinduism generally allows for Jesus as being merely one of many incarnations of God. Other incarnations include (or at least might allow for) Krishna, Rama, Shiva, Vishnu, Buddha, Confucius, Lao Tsu, Moses, Muhammad, and so on. These incarnations are known as "avatars." The Bible, however, tells us that there has only been one divine incarnation, Jesus the Christ (John 1:1-3, 14), and Scripture denies the existence of other gods (Isaiah 44:6; John 5:44; 17:3; Romans 3:29-30; 1 Corinthians 8:4; Ephesians 4:4-6; 1 Timothy 2:5; James 2:19). This alone is a huge refutation of the idea that Jesus was merely copied from Krishna.

Third, Hinduism is very pluralistic, promoting the belief that "all paths lead to God." However, "Jesus answered, 'I

---

[128] There is, however, a wide-range of positions within the Hindu belief system, but in general Hindu's hold to a combination of pantheism-monism-polytheism and also embrace the concept of karma-reincarnation.

[129] Hinduism was originally a blend of animism and polytheism, but became pantheistic-monistic-polytheistic around 800-600 BC, well before the time of Christ.

am the way and the truth and the life. No one comes to the Father except through me'" (John 14:6). Certainly the Hindu idea of pluralism – that anyone who is obedient to his or her worldview or religion will be united to the divine when this earthly life is over – is in stark contrast to Christianity.

Fourth, reincarnation is a foundational teaching in Hinduism that is accepted by all of its followers. Once again, however, Scripture refutes this common belief: "Just as man is destined to die once, and after that to face judgment, so Christ was sacrificed once to take away the sins of many people; and he will appear a second time, not to bear sin, but to bring salvation to those who are waiting for him" (Hebrews 9:27-28). There is no place within the Christian worldview for the idea of reincarnation.

Certainly there are other theological disagreements as well, but the above four points are more than sufficient to point out the major discrepancies that exist between Hinduism (Krishna) and Christianity (Jesus), which should not exist if Jesus was based in large part upon the figure of Krishna.

Although there is a wide range of beliefs among Buddhists regarding the existence and nature of God, in general they hold to the belief that God is unimportant in achieving eternal life. Buddhism as a whole is functionally atheistic, although on an individual basis Buddhists may be atheistic, agnostic, pantheistic, or polytheistic. The Bible, however, reveals God's nature as three persons in one God, thereby refuting these non-Christian beliefs.

Additionally, since God's existence is unimportant in achieving eternal union with Brahma, Buddhism is works-based regarding salvation, which is ultimately tied into karma and reincarnation.[130] Although there will always be differences among practicing Buddhists regarding doctrinal issues, in general karma and reincarnation remains a key doctrine of this religion, and is therefore in opposition to the

---

[130] Despite being an attempt to reform Hinduism in several ways, Buddhism retained the Hindu concept of karma and reincarnation.

clear biblical teaching that all people die once and then face judgment (Hebrews 9:27-28). There is no near-endless cycle of "do-over's" in Christianity.

As with Hinduism, there are other theological differences between Buddhism and Christianity that could be addressed, but both of the above differences are more than sufficient to make the point that if Jesus was, at least in large part, based upon the historical character known to us as the Buddha, then we should expect to see major commonalities in the teachings of Buddha and Christ, which is not the case. It is obvious that Eastern theology, especially regarding both the existence and nature of God as well as salvation, is light years apart from traditional Christian doctrine. The only versions of Christianity that have any similarity to Eastern philosophy are the pseudo-Christian religions that attempt to blend East and West, namely Christian Science and Unity School of Christianity.

THE LIST GOES ON

The list of religious figures that supposedly served as the basis for Jesus is long indeed. In addition to those already mentioned, there is a long-list of characters which includes Adonis, Alcides, Romulus, and Tammuz. A detailed look at each and every character ever proposed as being a template for Jesus would be an incredibly long, not to mention redundant, undertaking. In the end, each and every one of these figures is demonstrated to be either (1) historically insignificant, if not blatantly mythological; (2) theologically incompatible with Christian doctrines; (3) well after the time of Christ and the writing of the New Testament, meaning that the figure in question, rather than Jesus, is the copycat.

THE EXPERTS WEIGH IN

The late Ronald Nash was an expert on the relationship between Christianity and the Greco-Roman religions that battled for worldview supremacy during the early days of the church. No stranger to the copycat idea, Nash noted several distinct differences between Jesus and the pagan gods from which Jesus was supposedly derived.[131] First, not one of the dying-and-rising savior gods ever died for someone else, and not one of them ever died as a substitutionary atonement for the sins of all humanity. The concept of the one true God becoming incarnate and undergoing a substitutionary death for the sins of all people who have ever lived is completely unique to Christianity. Second, Jesus died once to cover all the sins of humanity, whereas the pagan gods died and then re-animated on an ongoing basis, usually seasonally and most often in conjunction with the growing cycle of crops. Third, Jesus was a real person from the historical record, whereas the pagan gods were merely mythical figures. There is no way that these pagan gods could truly have risen from the dead when they never really lived in the first place. Fourth, Jesus died voluntarily, and his death was the most victorious moment in all of human history. This is in stark contrast to the pagan gods.

So convincing are these differences that Nash noted, "The tide of scholarly opinion has turned dramatically against attempts to make early Christianity dependent on the so-called dying and rising gods of Hellenistic paganism."[132] Needless to say, there are still proponents of the idea that are more than willing to keep this particular fire burning even today, despite the evidence against this hypothesis.

Nash summarized the most serious weaknesses of the Jesus myth hypothesis.[133] First, similarity does not prove dependence. Having said that, one must remember the four distinct differences between Christianity and the gods of Greco-Roman paganism as described above. Second, the alleged similarities are either exaggerated at best, or purely invented at worst. Third, Christian doctrine was fully developed, in written form no less, well before the end of the first century, whereas the Greco-Roman mystery religions were not fully

---

[131] John Ankerberg & John Weldon, *The Passion and the Empty Tomb* (Eugene, OR: Harvest House Publishers, 2005), 200.
[132] Ibid.
[133] Ibid.

developed until the second century, so it is more likely that the pagan religions borrowed from Christianity, and not vice versa. Additionally, Nash noted that it is unlikely that any real interaction between Christianity and the mystery religions took place before the third century. Fourth, the New Testament writers would never have dreamed of doing such a thing as borrowing ideas from polytheistic, nature-based pagan religions. None of the New Testament authors were even remotely close to advancing pagan theology in their writings. Christianity is exclusive in terms of recognizing only one Savior and Redeemer, whereas the pagan religions were (and are) syncretistic. Fifth, Christianity is historically-based, and can be shown to be true through a historical and archaeological analysis of the content of its literature, whereas the mystery religions of Greece and Rome were based upon mythical characters that we call "gods." Sixth, Christian doctrine has remained unchanged from the time of the original writings in the first century until this very day, whereas the mystery religions changed in order to suit their needs. For example, the Mithraic practice of taurobolium, which is bathing in a bull's blood for the purpose of spiritual cleansing, was initially believed to maintain its efficacy for twenty years. After twenty years one would need to do it again in order to remain spiritually clean. However, since Christians are promised eternal life through Christ's sacrificial atonement on the cross, a one-time event that did not require repeating, Mithraism changed from once every twenty years to one time only for the taurobolium. It is obvious that Mithraism needed to change in order to keep up with the appeal of Christianity.

Apologist and early church historian Timothy Paul Jones notes that the Jesus myth hypothesis actually involves three points.[134] First is the questionable historicity of Jesus, which was addressed earlier in this chapter. Second is the supposed pagan parallels to Christianity, which has formed the bulk of

---

[134] Timothy Paul Jones, *Conspiracies and the Cross* (Lake Mary, FL: Front Line, 2008), 103.

this chapter. Third is the claim that the earliest Christians were not at all concerned with an earthly Jesus, but rather viewed Jesus as being a mythical composite character that merely represented theological and moral values in human form. Since the previous two points have already been thoroughly addressed, let us briefly look at this last point.

According to Jesus myth proponents Timothy Freke and Peter Gandy, the Apostle Paul believed that Jesus was merely a mythical composite figure,[135] representative of the new theological and moral teachings of Christianity. In other words, Christ was the King Arthur or Robin Hood of Paul's time. However, a basic knowledge of Paul's New Testament writings clearly reveals that this was not the case. Galatians 1:17-19, which discusses Paul's encounter with Christ's brother James, makes no sense if Jesus was mythical. Why would a mythical being have a physical, flesh-and-blood brother? Additionally, Paul reveals that Jesus was born physically: "But when the set time had fully come, God sent his Son, born of a woman, born under the law" (Galatians 4:4). Finally, Paul clearly pointed out Jesus' physicality in his first epistle to the church in Corinth, a passage which has become known as Easter's earliest creed:

> For what I received I passed on to you as of first importance: that Christ died for our sins according to the Scriptures, that he was buried, that he was raised on the third day according to the Scriptures, and that he appeared to Cephas, and then to the Twelve. After that, he appeared to more than five hundred of the brothers and sisters at the same time, most of whom are still living, though some have fallen asleep. Then he appeared to James, then to all the apostles (1 Corinthians 15:3-7).

This passage of Scripture makes no sense if a mythical Jesus is being discussed. Mythical, imaginary figures do not die, undergo burial, and then resurrect, and they certainly do not appear before hundreds of people at one time.

Freke and Gandy have declared that it was not until the

---

[135] Ibid.

time of Justin Martyr, in the mid-second century, that Jesus became literally human, and not just a mythical composite figure.[136] However, Paul refuted this idea long before Justin.[137]

Michael Licona, one of the most accomplished experts on the subject of the evidence for Christ's resurrection, is quick to remind us that the Jesus myth hypothesis, no matter how convincingly it may be stated, does not in any way negate the incredible evidence for Jesus' resurrection.[138] Licona also points out that T.N.D. Mettinger, a member of the Royal Academy of Letters, History, and Antiquities of Stockholm, undertook an extensive examination of the copycat hypothesis and arrived at the conclusion that "the consensus among modern scholars – nearly universal – is that there were no dying and rising gods that preceded Christianity. They all post-dated the first century."[139] This is, of course, merely a reiteration of the conclusion arrived at by Nash and other experts on the subject.

Foster Stanback, an accomplished scholar who has written extensively on Christ's resurrection, notes that the various figures claimed to be the basis for Jesus can be classified in one of two categories. In the first category the gods return each year to a certain place without really having died in the first place, and in the second category the gods die but do not return from the dead.[140] He makes it a point of noting that, "There is no unambiguous instance in the history of religions of a dying and rising deity."[141]

When one considers how opposed the Jews of Jesus' time were to pagan practices and beliefs, it becomes clear that

---

[136] Ibid.
[137] Justin Martyr lived from approximately AD 100-165, while the Apostle Paul died in Rome c. AD 67.
[138] Lee Strobel, *The Case for the Real Jesus* (Grand Rapids, MI: Zondervan, 2007), 160.
[139] Ibid.
[140] C. Foster Stanback, *The Resurrection: A Historical Analysis* (Spring, TX: Illumination Publishers International, 2008), 72.
[141] Ibid.

none of the earliest Christians – who were predominately Jewish – would have a desire to create another false religion based upon a nature deity. The devout Jews of the time were thoroughly convinced of the belief in one God, so why would they be interested in developing a new pagan cult that borrowed from the polytheism that they had always opposed? This makes no sense.

The incarnation, mission, death, resurrection, and ascension of Christ are all unique among the religions of the world, whether ancient or modern. The dual nature of Christ is totally unlike anything described in the pagan religions. Christ was fully God, yet at the same time fully man. Christ was not 50% God and 50% man, unlike many of the children of pagan mythology who had a divine father and an earthly mother. The dual nature of Christ is a concept that we today are unable to fully wrap our minds around; how much more so this would have been for the pagans of the New Testament era and during the time of the early church. Christ's mission – which was to die a substitutionary death for the sins of all humanity – was also a foreign concept to these early pagans, and the concept of a bodily resurrection was completely against the grain of Greco-Roman thought. Finally, Christ's ascension back into the realm of Heaven, as opposed to the idea of journeying to the underworld, from whence he would return at the completion of another growing season, was also completely illogical to the Greco-Roman mind. It is clear that Jesus was not an amalgamation of various pagan gods, but something new and different – and, this time, something true.

WHAT I DISCOVERED

The proponents of the Jesus myth hypothesis have been quick to promote the idea that (1) Jesus never really existed, but instead (2) he was merely a fictional character who was nothing more than an amalgamation of previously known gods, heroes, or religious founders from the ancient pagan world. However, I found the opposite to be the case. Jesus was a real person from the historical record, and Jesus was not mythologized into godhood, nor was his legend based upon the stories of previously known characters, fictional or real. The evidence that Jesus was, and is, who the Bible proclaims him to be is simply much too strong to accommodate these poorly substantiated beliefs from the skeptical world.

Despite the objections of skeptics, the "Case for Christ" stands up to the test of evidences. Many in the world of atheism, pantheism, and deism may promote these beliefs as being fact, yet the evidence says otherwise. The disbelieving world may choose not to believe in the deity of Jesus, but that goes against many powerful lines of evidence in favor of the biblical worldview.

Chapter 6

THE CHRIST OF FAITH

In this chapter we will examine how the Jesus of history and the Christ of faith are one and the same. Much of this chapter revolves around the evidence for the reliability and authority of Holy Scripture. If it can be demonstrated that the Bible is a reliable source of information concerning God, man, and the divine plan for human history, then we can know for certain that Jesus is God, because Scripture clearly reveals this to us.

RELIABILITY OF THE NEW TESTAMENT

The number of surviving New Testament documents, whether complete, partial, or fragmentary, is amazing: 5,700 copies in Greek, 8,000-10,000 documents in Latin, 8,000 documents in Armenian, Ethiopic, and Slavic, and approximately 1,000 documents in various other languages. This adds up to approximately 23,000-25,000 surviving manuscripts. Since the New Testament was originally written in Greek, we can reasonably compare the 5,700 Greek documents that we have to other important works from the ancient world. Homer's *Iliad* has the greatest number of surviving copies outside of the New Testament, but comes in a distant second when compared to the Greek scriptures: Only 643 surviving copies. This is a large number of copies when compared to the other works of antiquity, but it nonetheless pales in comparison to the New Testament. Other ancient writings, by author, include Demosthenes (200 surviving copies), Tacitus (twenty surviving copies), Livy (twenty surviving copies), Caesar (ten surviving copies), Herodotus (eight surviving copies), Thucydides (eight surviving copies), Plato (seven surviving copies), Pliny Secundus (seven surviving copies), and Aristotle (five surviving copies). Compared to the huge number of surviving New Testament manuscripts, these non-biblical writings are a mere fraction at best. This large number of surviving manuscripts for the New Testament allows scholars to compare many documents of the same books so as to determine the level of consistency regarding what is written. As it turns out, the New Testament is extremely consistent.[142]

The timeframe between the date of the actual historical events being described and the date of the original writings, as well as the date of the original writings and the date of the earliest surviving copies, is very minimal for the New Testament when compared to other writings from the ancient world. It can be said that the New Testament is by far the best historical work of antiquity in terms of dating. The death and resurrection of Christ took place approximately AD 30-33, and there is evidence that James was written as early as AD 38. That's only five to eight years between the life of Christ and James' writing. The other books of the New Testament were written within the first century, and many of them in the sixties and seventies. (In fact, a very good case can be made for the New Testament having been completed before AD 70, which we will look at shortly.) Compare this very minimal time span to other works from the ancient world in terms of the number of years from the historical events being described to the date of the original manuscripts: Homer (400 years), Livy (400 years), Pliny Secundus (750 years), Caesar (1,000 years), Tacitus (1,000 years), Plato (1,200 years), Thucydides (1,300 years), Herodotus (1,300 years), Demosthenes (1,300 years), and Aristotle (1,400 years).

Some fragments of Mark's Gospel that were recently found in Egypt have been tentatively dated as early as AD 45, which is amazingly close to the beginning of the church era as recorded in Acts 2.[143] The New Testament was written

---

[142] Ralph Muncaster, *Examine the Evidence* (Eugene, OR: Harvest House Publishers, 2004), 198-201.
[143] John Oakes, *Reasons for Belief* (Spring, TX: Illumination Publishers International, 2005), 148.

down while many of the eyewitnesses of Jesus' miracles were still alive, and therefore they would have been able to refute the Gospels – but they did not, because they knew what they had seen with their own eyes.

The New Testament manuscripts are definitely primary sources, something which the other works of antiquity cannot boast. John Mark utilized Peter as his primary source of reference, and John Mark himself was an early follower of Christ. Luke is considered to be a meticulous historian who also lived out many of the events described in Acts, and Matthew, John, and Paul, as apostles of Christ, were definitely primary sources as well. On the other hand, even though Josephus, Tacitus, and most of the other ancient historians were excellent scholars by most accounts, they had to rely upon resources outside of their own firsthand experiences. They were recording what they believed to be true as based upon sources they believed to be credible.

Overall, the believer can state with great confidence that the New Testament contains all the traits of a historically authentic document, even though the original writings were penned on perishable material that did not last long – and they were surely read repeatedly by the early followers of Christ, which also hastened their demise. Fortunately for us, they were meticulously copied by people who took Scripture seriously. The New Testament is really the only literary source with such a high-level of internal and external corroborating evidence.[144]

LUKE: A FIRST-RATE SCHOLAR

Skeptics of Christianity have been quick to criticize the biblical authors, referring to them as uneducated, simple-minded men who lived in a pre-scientific culture over-run by superstition. However, nothing could be further from the truth. Paul was a highly-educated Pharisee who came from

---

[144] Chad V. Meister, *Building Belief: Constructing Faith from the Ground Up* (Grand Rapids, MI: Baker Books, 2006), 127-155; Ralph Muncaster, *Examine the Evidence* (Eugene, OR: Harvest House Publishers, 2004), 197-206.

Tarsus, one of the preeminent cities of the Roman world in terms of higher education and the place which offered the best schools of philosophy and rhetoric.[145] Likewise, Luke was a physician and a highly-meticulous historian who was incredibly accurate when recording place names, civic titles, and other details that only one who had been there could know.

Luke refers to Lysanias being the tetrarch of Abilene in about AD 27 (Luke 3:1). Critical scholars made the point that Lysanias was not a tetrarch, but instead the ruler of Chalcis approximately fifty years earlier. However, an inscription was later found which demonstrated that Luke was exactly right, and the skeptics had been too quick to criticize Luke.

Another example is Luke's reference to *politarchs* in the city of Thessalonica (Acts 17:6), which is translated as "city officials" in the New International Version of the Bible. Critics maintained that Luke was in error because no evidence of the term *politarch* had been found in any ancient Roman documents. However, an inscription from a first century arch was later found which demonstrated Luke's accuracy in this matter. *Politarch* was a real title after all.

George Konig discusses the supposed contradiction of Luke and Mark:

> ...the gospel of Luke states that Jesus was walking into Jericho when He healed the blind man Bartimaeus, while Mark says He was coming out of Jericho. McRay explained, "It only appears to be a contradiction when you think in contemporary terms, in which cities are built to stay put. But that wasn't necessarily the case long ago. Jericho was in at least four different locations as much as a quarter of a mile apart in ancient times. The city was destroyed and resettled near another water supply or a new road or nearer a

---

[145] John McRay, *Archaeology and the New Testament* (Grand Rapids, MI: Baker Academic, 1991), 234-235. Tarsus was known for having the best schools of Stoic philosophy. When Paul encountered the Stoic philosophers in Athens (Acts 17:16-34), he was likely very well-versed in their belief system.

mountain or whatever. The point is, you can be coming out of one site where Jericho existed and be going into another one, like moving from one part of suburban Chicago to another part of suburban Chicago." Mark and Luke are both right, Jesus could have been going out of one area of Jericho and into another at the same time.[146]

One prominent archaeologist carefully examined Luke's references to 32 countries, 54 cities, and nine islands, and did not find a single mistake. Luke was, without doubt, a truly first-rate historian.[147]

The implications of Luke's historical accuracy is this: Since he was so incredibly meticulous in all that he wrote regarding history, geography, civic titles, and so forth, we should also reasonably expect that Luke was meticulous in the area of theological matters as well. Of course, this is a problem for skeptics for the simple reason that Luke boldly proclaimed that the Jesus of history is also the Christ of faith. Why would someone from the ancient world write a fictionalized account of a uniquely dying-and-rising (one time, not seasonally) Savior-God and then insert incredibly precise historical details into the account? This simply does not make sense.

INNOCENT UNTIL PROVEN GUILTY

From a legal perspective, a written document should be considered both legitimate and truthful unless proven otherwise; "innocent until proven guilty" applies to literary sources as well as to people. Most skeptics will assume the stance that the Bible is simply Hebrew mythology and not historically factual, but this is only because many skeptics do not know how to read the Bible as literature. The Bible is a literary work, among other things, but unfortunately many skeptics tend toward reading certain ideas into the Bible rather than simply letting the Bible speak for itself. This happens in large part because skeptics assume a straight-forward

---

[146] George Konig, "A Tribute to Luke, and his Accuracy as a Historian." http://www.konig.org/wc112.htm
[147] Ibid.

reading of the text in a modern English translation, foregoing the rules of literary genre and ignoring the cultural considerations of the ancient Near East. Perhaps most importantly, their worldview presuppositions frame their viewpoint. It really does take the work of the Holy Spirit in order to truly "see the light of the glory of Christ" (2 Corinthians 4:4).

Ultimately, even though Scripture is truly the Word of God (2 Timothy 3:16-17), it takes the illumination of the Holy Spirit in order for one to get past the idea that the Bible is simply outdated Hebrew superstition (1 Corinthians 2:14). Meditate on these words from the Apostle Paul:

> *For the message of the cross is foolishness to those who are perishing, but to us who are being saved it is the power of God. For it is written: "I will destroy the wisdom of the wise; the intelligence of the intelligent I will frustrate." Where is the wise person? Where is the teacher of the law? Where is the philosopher of this age? Has not God made foolish the wisdom of the world? For since in the wisdom of God the world through its wisdom did not know him, God was pleased through the foolishness of what was preached to save those who believe. Jews demand signs and Greeks look for wisdom, but we preach Christ crucified: a stumbling block to Jews and foolishness to Gentiles, but to those whom God has called, both Jews and Greeks, Christ the power of God and the wisdom of God. For the foolishness of God is wiser than human wisdom, and the weakness of God is stronger than human strength (1 Corinthians 1:18-25).*

The New Testament, and especially the four Gospels, is *prima facie*[148] evidence for both the historical Jesus and the Christ of faith – who, by the way, happen to be one and the same – but the non-Christian world will not recognize this. That is why believers must be "ready with an answer" and willing to gently and respectfully engage those who are not Christian believers (1 Peter 3:15).

---

[148] *Prima facie* is a Latin term meaning "accepted as correct until proven otherwise," and in the context of the Bible refers to the truthfulness found in Scripture – a truthfulness that stands up to the test of good scholarship.

THE CASE FOR A PRE-AD 70 COMPLETION

Most conservative, and even some not-so-conservative, Bible scholars claim that the original writings that make up the New Testament were completed near the end of the first century. However, nowhere does the New Testament mention the destruction of Jerusalem and the complete devastation of the Jewish Temple in AD 70 at the hands of the Romans. Perhaps this is an indicator that we should seriously consider the idea that the entire New Testament was completed before that time. If that is the case, then the time between the events being described and the original writings of the New Testament is amazingly short, far better than any of the other surviving works of antiquity can claim. That means that the original copies of the New Testament books were written within the lifetimes of many of the eyewitnesses to Jesus' ministry, as well as the beginning of the church at Pentecost (Acts 2).

There are some very interesting lines of evidence for a pre-AD 70 date for Revelation, which is by almost all accounts the final book to be written in the New Testament. Regarding Revelation's status as the final book of Scripture, the last chapter contains this dire warning regarding the addition or subtraction of God's holy words:

> *I warn everyone who hears the words of the prophecy of this scroll: If anyone adds anything to them, God will add to that person the plagues described in this scroll. And if anyone takes words away from this scroll of prophecy, God will take away from that person any share in the tree of life and in the Holy City, which are described in this scroll (Revelation 22:18-19).*

Admittedly John is describing the "words of the prophecy of *this* scroll" or the book of Revelation specifically, but note how well the final sentences conclude Scripture as a whole: "He who testifies to these things says, "Yes, I am coming soon." Amen. Come, Lord Jesus. The grace of the Lord Jesus be with God's people. Amen" (Revelation 22:20-21). Certainly these final words of Scripture apply to the entirety of the Bible.

If a case can be made for a pre-AD 70 date for Revelation, and Revelation was the final book to be penned, then the New Testament as a whole was written very early, and the historical reliability of the New Testament is boosted tremendously. There are five primary lines of evidence behind an early date for Revelation. First, the inscription to the Syriac version of the book contains the following quote: "The Revelation which God made to John the evangelist, in the Island of Patmos, to which he was banished by Nero Caesar." This would place the book before AD 68, which was the year Nero died, unless John wrote this book quite some time after he arrived on the island. However, Revelation 1:11 states that John was supposed to write down the visions that he had, and then send this in letter form to the seven churches in Asia Minor that are mentioned in the text. Surely John would not have procrastinated that long in completing this divinely-ordered task.

Second, there was a very small window of time when only seven churches existed in Asia Minor, and that was the early sixties of the first century. Paul established nine churches in Asia Minor, but Revelation only discusses seven churches. The reason for this is that Colossae, Hierapolis, and Laodicea were destroyed by an earthquake in AD 61, but only Laodicea was rebuilt immediately afterward. This left only seven churches in Asia Minor prior to the beginning of the Roman-Jewish War, when the Temple was destroyed by the Romans. This lines up exactly with the book of Revelation.

Third, the Church of Philadelphia was told by Christ, "Since you have kept my command to endure patiently, I will also keep you from the hour of trial that is going to come on the whole world to test the inhabitants of the earth" (Revelation 3:10). Some who propose an early date for Revelation claim that the "hour of trial" was the first wave of widespread, violent persecution, which is considered to have begun under the kingship of Nero, who died in AD 68.

Fourth, the book itself may have been written when Herod's Temple was still standing: "I was given a reed like a measuring rod and was told, "Go and measure the temple of God and the altar, with its worshipers. But exclude the outer court; do not measure it, because it has been given to the Gentiles. They will trample on the holy city for 42 months" (Revelation 11:1-2). Although late-daters' of Revelation claim that the temple being described is a future Holy Temple of God, those who insist on an early date are adamant that there is not one verse in the entire Bible which speaks of a rebuilt third temple.

Fifth, Luke proclaimed that the disciples would witness the destruction of the Jewish Temple (Luke 21:20). Some take "disciples" to mean the twelve apostles. However, it is clear that many of them did not even come close to surviving until the time of the Jewish Temple's destruction in AD 70. Please keep in mind that the dates of death for the twelve apostles are very approximate, as are the places where they lived and died after Christ's command to spread the Gospel worldwide. According to tradition, Peter died in AD 64, so could not have witnessed the destruction of the Jewish Temple. Andrew died in AD 70, and may have witnessed the event if he had been in Jerusalem, but according to tradition he had been gone from the area for a number of years. James, the brother of John, was the first apostle to die, in AD 44-45, which was well before the event under consideration. John, who cared for Mary after the Crucifixion, is considered to have lived into the nineties and could have witnessed the event if he had been in Jerusalem. According to tradition, however, he was almost certainly in Ephesus. Philip died in AD 54, well before the event. Bartholomew died in AD 70, but according to tradition he was in the area of Armenia, not Jerusalem. Matthew died sometime between AD 60-70 while in Ethiopia. Thomas died in AD 70, but had been in India for years. James the Less is believed to have died in AD 63, seven years before the event under consideration. Simon the Zealot died in AD 74, but had been widely traveled for several years before the destruction of the Jewish Temple, having gone to Egypt, Cyrene, Mauritania, Britain, Libya, and

Persia. Judas Thaddeus died in AD 72, but had been in Mesopotamia for quite some time before the event under consideration. Lastly, as we know from Scripture (Matthew 27:5; Acts 1:18) Judas Iscariot died very shortly after the arrest of Jesus, approximately four decades before the destruction of the Jewish Temple. Clearly, only a few of the twelve apostles could have witnessed the destruction of Jerusalem and the Jewish Temple, but even then some very strong traditions have them living well beyond Jerusalem in AD 70. However, if "disciples" simply means followers of Christ, then certainly many of the eyewitnesses to Christ's ministry could have witnessed the destruction of the Jewish Temple.[149]

There may be other indicators for a pre-AD 70 date as well, but the above lines of reasoning seem adequate to provide a good case for this proposition. Needless to say, not everyone is sold on an early date for Revelation, but as shown a case can be made for this position and, if it turns out to seem quite reasonable, Christian believers can be confident that their source book is historically reliable. That, in turn, helps us to have confidence in what Scripture says regarding Jesus Christ and all matters spiritual.

JEWISH MESSIANIC EXPECTATIONS

The list of messianic claimants in the first century was quite long, but what is most amazing is that the number of messianic claimants during this century greatly eclipsed all other centuries before and after; in fact, no other century even came close. Therefore, it seems certain that there had to be a reason for it, and the reason is that the Jews were expecting Messiah sometime in the first century, and the reason could only be due to an Old Testament prophecy pointing them to that specific period of time.

Of course, many first century Jews did come to the realization that Messiah had come exactly as foretold, in the per-

---

[149] Michael Patton, "What Happened to the Twelve Apostles?" http://www.credohouse.org/blog/what-happened-to-the-twelve-apostles-how-do-their-deaths-prove-easter

son of Jesus of Nazareth. Jesus fulfilled the Old Testament prophecies exactly, plus many of them had seen firsthand the miracles performed by Christ. However, many Jews could not accept Messiah as being a lowly carpenter from Galilee who preached a message of love and peace. They were expecting – make that *demanding* – a warrior who would right the wrongs of their oppressors, despite the description of the Suffering Servant in Isaiah 53. In other words, many of the Jews intentionally missed Messiah.

After the destruction of the Jewish Temple in AD 70, Judaism changed dramatically. Prior to this event, Judaism was centered in the temple sacrificial system, but afterward Judaism became rabbinical as the sacrificial system was necessarily abandoned, since sacrifices could only be performed in the Temple – which no longer existed. One might wonder why they did not attempt to build a much less elaborate temple elsewhere, and resume the sacrificial system.

Likely the Jews feared that the Romans would once again squash that project, regardless of where it was built, and no one could blame them. Plus, they believed that their temple could only be constructed at one place, Mount Moriah, or not at all. These are surely reasons why the Jews did not rebuild a smaller-but-adequate temple elsewhere, but another reason surely existed as well. The Jews suffered a devastating blow to their psyche, and their worldview was left in pieces. This happened for three reasons. First, the Old Testament messianic prophecies pointed them in the direction of the one true Messiah arriving in the first century. They had seen false messiah's come and go, and each one of them likely weakened their hopes, if even just slightly each time, but when added up this took a toll on their faith in the coming Messiah. Second, when the Temple was destroyed, and Messiah had not yet come (although in reality he had) the Jewish belief in Messiah became uncertain for many of them. Third, Judaism was in the process of a huge division, with many Jews accepting Christ as Messiah while many other Jews despised the new Christian sect. Although some Jews were certain that Jesus had been just another false claimant to the title of Messiah, many others were proclaiming that their Jewish brothers and sisters had missed Messiah altogether. Not only were the pagan temples beginning to feel the effect of Christianity by the time of the Temple's demise in AD 70, but so were the synagogues. Both institutions were shrinking in numbers as their one-time followers had become Christians, seemingly overnight.

Why did the first century Jews expect Messiah during their time? Even the magi from the East, who were either Hebraic in origin or at the very least had been influenced by the Hebrews through Daniel and others, knew to be on the look-out for the signs of his coming. Certainly at the top of the list of important messianic prophecies, primarily because it provided a timeframe for Messiah's coming, is the prophecy of the "Seventy Sevens" from Daniel:

> *(Gabriel speaking to Daniel) Seventy "sevens" are decreed for your people and your holy city to finish transgression, to put an end to sin, to atone for wickedness, to bring in everlasting righteousness, to seal up vision and prophecy and to anoint the Most Holy Place. Know and understand this: From the time the word goes out to restore and rebuild Jerusalem until the Anointed One, the ruler, comes, there will be seven "sevens," and sixty-two "sevens." It will be rebuilt with streets and a trench, but in times of trouble. After the sixty-two "sevens," the Anointed One will be put to death and will have nothing. The people of the ruler who will come will destroy the city and the sanctuary. The end will come like a flood: War will continue until the end, and desolations have been decreed. He will confirm a covenant with many for one "seven." In the middle of the "seven" he will put an end to sacrifice and offering. And at the temple he will set up an abomination that causes desolation, until the end that is decreed is poured out on him (Daniel 9:24-27).*

This prophecy renders an exact date by which to start our calculations regarding the "sevens." It turns out that Jesus was the only messianic claimant that could possibly have fulfilled this amazing prophecy.

Since this prophecy is the only one that allows us to determine when Messiah was to be expected, we need to look at other scriptural references in order to determine the start date for the countdown to Messiah:

> In the month of Nisan in the twentieth year of King Artaxerxes, when wine was brought for him, I took the wine and gave it to the king. I had not been sad in his presence before, so the king asked me, "Why does your face look so sad when you are not ill? This can be nothing but sadness of heart." I was very much afraid, but I said to the king, "May the king live forever! Why should my face not look sad when the city where my ancestors are buried lies in ruins, and its gates have been destroyed by fire?" The king said to me, "What is it you want?" Then I prayed to the God of heaven, and I answered the king, "If it pleases the king and if your servant has found favor in his sight, let him send me to the city in Judah where my ancestors are buried so that I can rebuild it." Then the king, with the queen sitting beside him, asked me, "How long will your journey take, and when will you get back?" It pleased the king to send me; so I set a time (Nehemiah 2:1-6).

The above date has been calculated to be between February 27th and March 28th, 444 BC. Regarding the seven "sevens" and sixty-two "sevens," in mathematical terms this comes out to (7 x 7) + (62 x 7) or 49 + 434 = 483 years. Tacking this number of years onto 444 BC, we come to AD 39, which is six years beyond AD 33, the year that is commonly believed to have been when Christ was crucified.[150] However, our modern, Western understanding of a year is based on the 365-day Gregorian calendar, which the Jews did not abide by. The Jews, like other cultures in the ancient Near East, utilized a 360-day lunar calendar. Therefore, if we modify the math to account for this difference, we arrive at the following timeframe: 483 x 360 = 173,880 days, and 173,880 days = 476 years and 25 days on our modern calendar (365.24219879-day conversion). 476 years and 25 days

---

[150] However, AD 30 is also a strong possibility for being the year of Christ's crucifixion.

from February 27th to March 28th of 444 BC brings us to the month of the Jewish Passover in AD 33, when Jesus was entering Jerusalem for his final week.[151] Scripture accounts for the whereabouts of only one messianic claimant at that time, one who also happened to be recognized as the King of Israel:

> Six days before the Passover, Jesus came to Bethany, where Lazarus lived, whom Jesus had raised from the dead...The next day the great crowd that had come for the festival heard that Jesus was on his way to Jerusalem. They took palm branches and went out to meet him, shouting, "Hosanna! Blessed is he who comes in the name of the Lord! Blessed is the king of Israel!" (John 12:1, 12-13).

Daniel called the coming Messiah the "Anointed One" and the "ruler," which the Apostle John confirmed over five centuries later. That is amazing, and that is why the priests and all those who studied Scripture diligently were expecting Messiah at that time.

Jesus was the only messianic claimant that fulfilled that prophecy perfectly, and many of the people obviously knew it (John 12:12-13). The followers of Christ had to be devastated when he was crucified just a few days later. Although many were convinced that Messiah would be a warrior-priest who would right the wrongs of their Roman oppressors, they neglected to grasp the full impact of Daniel's words centuries earlier: "After the sixty-two "sevens," the Anointed One will be put to death..." (Daniel 9:26a). Why was Christ put to death? As a sacrificial atonement for the sins of humanity:

> For even the Son of Man did not come to be served, but to serve, and to give his life as a ransom for many (Mark 10:45).

> For God so loved the world that he gave his one and only Son, that whoever believes in him shall not perish but have eternal life (John 3:16).

---

[151] Although, once again, not every biblical scholar holds to the AD 33 date for Christ's crucifixion.

For we know that our old self was crucified with him so that the body ruled by sin might be done away with, that we should no longer be slaves to sin – because anyone who has died has been set free from sin (Romans 6:6-7).

RELIABLE EYEWITNESSES OF CHRIST

There are several reasons why we should take the accounts of the eyewitnesses seriously. First, the eyewitnesses never attempt to refute the miraculous works of Jesus. They simply could not do so, as they saw these miracles take place before their very eyes, and there is no way that dozens, and even hundreds, of people could disbelieve what they saw (1 Corinthians 15:6). For those who refused to acknowledge the divine nature and messianic status of Jesus, they had to explain the miracles in some other way, which usually meant attributing them to the demonic realm. Even the religious leaders of the day who opposed Jesus could not outright deny the miracles of Christ. Amazingly, when Jesus raised Lazarus from the dead, there were some who even then refused to believe in Jesus as Messiah:

Therefore many of the Jews who had come to visit Mary, and had seen what Jesus did, believed in him. But some of them went to the Pharisees and told them what Jesus had done. Then the chief priests and the Pharisees called a meeting of the Sanhedrin. "What are we accomplishing?" they asked. "Here is this man performing many signs. If we let him go on like this, everyone will believe in him, and then the Romans will come and take away both our temple and our nation." Then one of them, named Caiaphas, who was high priest that year, spoke up, "You know nothing at all! You do not realize that it is better for you that one man die for the people than that the whole nation perish." He did not say this on his own, but as high priest that year he prophesied that Jesus would die for the Jewish nation, and not only for that nation but also for the scattered children of God, to bring them together and make them one. So from that day on they plotted to take his life (John 11:45-53).

Fortunately for mankind, Jesus did die upon the cross as a

substitutionary blood atonement for the sins of all people, but this was not the death for Jesus that Caiaphas had in mind. Caiaphas knew that Christ was innocent of the slanderous accusations made against him, but yet he could not accept Jesus as Messiah. Caiaphas could do only one thing: Kill Jesus.

Second, the sheer number of the eyewitnesses to Christ's resurrection is very impressive: Over 500 people at one time (1 Corinthians 15:6). When Paul wrote this letter to the church in Corinth in or around the year AD 55, he stated that many of these eyewitnesses were still alive. Therefore, with so many eyewitness testimonies to be taken into consideration, there is no way that any of the skeptics of the time could have seriously refuted Paul's claim that Christ had been resurrected from the dead. It is unreasonable to believe that over 500 people can simultaneously hallucinate about an event such as seeing the risen Christ. Additionally, smaller groups such as the apostles saw the risen Christ:

> *While they were still talking about this, Jesus himself stood among them and said to them, "Peace be with you." They were startled and frightened, thinking they saw a ghost. He said to them, "Why are you troubled, and why do doubts rise in your minds? Look at my hands and my feet. It is I myself! Touch me and see; a ghost does not have flesh and bones, as you see I have." When he had said this, he showed them his hands and feet. And while they still did not believe it because of joy and amazement, he asked them, "Do you have anything here to eat?" They gave him a piece of broiled fish, and he took it and ate it in their presence (Luke 24:36-43).*

Interestingly, after the ascension of Jesus, the sightings – whether in large or small numbers – stopped. This is exactly what we would expect if Jesus was, in fact, ascended back into Heaven.

Third, the recorded fact that women were the first eyewitnesses to the empty tomb demonstrates that the Gospels are historically accurate, because if the Gospel accounts of the empty tomb had been made up, no historian or Gospel writer from that time period and culture would have used women for witnesses. Women were, unfortunately, second-class citizens in this time and place, and their testimony was not even allowed in court. The New Testament records that the risen Christ appeared to Mary Magdalene and other women before any men had encountered the empty tomb. The apostles did not believe Mary Magdalene when she told them the tomb was empty, as even the apostles were a product of their culture and upbringing. The Gospels recorded this fact simply because that was how the event took place. The Gospel writers were especially careful historians, and as previously noted Luke's reputation as a first-class historian with an incredible eye for detail is not seriously called into question today.

Fourth, the apostles underwent a courageous conversion from cowards to bold witnesses for Christ. After the crucifixion, and before witnessing the empty tomb, the apostles hid behind locked doors, assuming that they would be the next victims of the combined wrath of the Jewish leaders and the Roman hierarchy. After witnessing the risen Christ, however, they went from scared to brave in an instant. It takes a major event to cause that kind of change, and Christ's resurrection was truly the most incredible event in all of history. Christ appeared to the apostles after his death, despite their being enclosed within a locked room (demonstrating his interdimensional post-resurrection nature). After witnessing the risen Christ, the apostles were no longer afraid of what would happen to them, because they knew the truth of the risen Christ who saves souls. A favorite encounter involves the great skeptic of the time, Thomas:

> Now Thomas (also known as Didymus), one of the Twelve, was not with the disciples when Jesus came. So the other disciples told him, "We have seen the Lord!" But he said to them, "Unless I see the nail marks in his hands and put my finger where the nails were, and put my hand into his side, I will not believe." A week later his disciples were in the house again, and Thomas was with them. Though the doors were locked, Jesus came and stood among them and said, "Peace be with you!" Then he said to Thomas, "Put

your finger here; see my hands. Reach out your hand and put it into my side. Stop doubting and believe." Thomas said to him, "My Lord and my God!" Then Jesus told him, "Because you have seen me, you have believed; blessed are those who have not seen and yet have believed" (John 20:24-29).

After this encounter, Thomas became a bold evangelist for the risen Christ, having traditionally been associated with evangelistic success in both Persia and India. According to tradition, while in the latter country he was killed by an enraged Hindu priest because of his great success in turning multitudes away from Hinduism and to Christ. Thomas was only one of many Christian leaders who suffered martyrdom in the early church.

Fifth, the changed lives of not only the apostles but of the many eyewitnesses to Christ's resurrection lends great credibility to Christ's claim of deity. Jesus' brother James was openly skeptical that Jesus was Messiah during his brother's three-year ministry. Having witnessed the risen Jesus (1 Corinthians 15:7), James became a follower of Christ and eventually led the church in Jerusalem. Like so many others, he was later martyred for his faith. The number of similar eyewitnesses is near-countless. With so many eyewitnesses, it should not be surprising that the early church quickly spread throughout the Roman Empire and beyond, even "to the ends of the earth."

Sixth, as previously discussed Luke was an especially impressive historian. Whenever Luke recorded details for us in either his Gospel or in Acts, it can be shown that he was always correct, as confirmed through geography, archaeology, and non-biblical historical corroboration. As a physician (Colossians 4:14), Luke was certainly a well-educated man who was intellectually capable, with an obvious eye for detail.

Finally, the divine origin, infallibility, and reliability of Scripture gives us great confidence that whatever it has to say on any matter is true: "All Scripture is God-breathed and is useful for teaching, rebuking, correcting and training in righteousness, so that the servant of God may be thoroughly equipped for every good work" (2 Timothy 3:16-17). The reliability of Scripture is backed up by internal consistency, external verification through both non-biblical literary sources and archaeology, scientific insights centuries and even millennia ahead of modern corroboration, fulfilled prophecy, and so on. When Scripture discusses Christ, we can have great confidence that what it says about him is true.

JESUS AMONG THE RELIGIONS

In general, no other founders of the major world religions claimed to be God, yet that is exactly what Christ claimed for himself (John 5:18; 10:30). Abraham and the early prophets of Judaism would never have dreamed of claiming to be God incarnate, but rather they wrote of a future time when God would redeem humanity from its sins – the Redeemer first promised in the *protoevangelium* (Genesis 3:15). Siddhartha Gautama, better known as the Buddha, was functionally atheistic regarding God's existence, teaching that God was not necessary for spiritual enlightenment. Confucius was unsure about God's existence. If anyone would have suggested to Muhammad that he was God in the flesh, he most likely would have separated their head from their torso. Even the founders of the American-born pseudo-Christian groups, such as Mormonism, Christian Science, Jehovah's Witnesses, Unity School of Christianity, and so forth, denied divinity in any way.

The major exception to this was Baha'u'llah. He claimed to be the ninth, and final, incarnation of God. According to Bahai'i, previous incarnations of God include Abraham, Krishna, Moses, Zoroaster, Buddha, Christ, Muhammad, and the Bab.[152] Nonetheless, Baha'u'llah did not have the evidence to back up the claim of divinity. Baha'u'llah did not perform miracles, he did not resurrect himself back to life, and he did not fulfill previously foretold prophecies concern-

---

[152] It should be noted, however, that this list varies among the followers of Bahai'i.

ing both his deity and mission to save the world. Christ, on the other hand, did all of these things. Ultimately, every one of the founders or significant contributors to a major world religion is dead and has remained dead. Jesus, on the other hand, also died, yet unlike the others he remained dead for only three days before resurrecting back to life.

Regarding morality, Jesus is worlds apart from everyone else in human history. Jesus is the only person, except for Adam and Eve prior to the fall of mankind (Genesis 3), to have lived a sinless life, having been free of the fallen nature that everyone else possesses from birth. Muhammad was a warrior who took what he wanted, and lived anything but a sinless life. Buddha left behind his young wife and child in order to find his spiritual path, shirking that major responsibility. The Old Testament patriarchs Abraham, Isaac, and Jacob, as well as David and Solomon in later times, were religious leaders that failed miserably in key areas of life. Closer to our time, Mormonism's founder Joseph Smith lived anything but a moral life. No one lived the moral life that Jesus did, and no one offered humanity the awesome moral teachings that Christ did, such as the Sermon on the Mount (Matthew 5-7).

It has been said many times that all of the major world religions are close to each other when it comes to the topic of morality, and it is true that most offer some version of positive ethics – with the exception of some of the occult religions which are extremely hedonistic in nature. But Jesus' teachings go well beyond the usual mentality of the major world religions, instead prompting us as Christian believers to "turn the other cheek" and offer more to our fellow human beings than we are comfortable giving. Jesus taught, and demonstrated, true mercy and grace.

Regarding salvation, only Christ claimed to be a propitiatory blood sacrifice for the sins of all humanity, and he backed up his mission of salvation with his miracles as well as his fulfillment of Old Testament prophecies. No one else could do that, and no other major world religious leader claimed to do the same. Jesus claimed to not just be a wise sage who could show one how to attain "enlightenment" as did Buddha, but instead Jesus actually claimed to be the only way to eternal salvation (John 14:6). All of the other world religions are works-based, stating that one must do this and that in order to even have a shot at entering into Heaven, but Jesus did the work of salvation for us. We just have to make the free will choice of accepting his gift of eternal life (Revelation 3:20).

Many of the founders and the early leaders of the pseudo-Christian groups in particular lived lives of excess, demonstrating their ulterior motives by their examples. However, Jesus lived a life of poverty, being concerned only about spiritual and moral matters. Although Buddha shared this similarity with Christ, he failed in other ways.

Finally, no other name under Heaven has the power to halt the forces of evil that Jesus' name commands. When rebuking evil spirits, one would be a fool for invoking the name of Buddha or Confucius; those names carry no authority over the fallen spiritual dimension. Christ, however, does (Luke 4:31-37).

WHAT I DISCOVERED

In this chapter we have explored how the Jesus of history is more than just that: Jesus is God incarnate, the Creator of the universe and the Redeemer of fallen humanity. The Christ of faith is the object of worship for Christian believers, and Christ alone is the way to eternal life. Therefore, Jesus is more than just a man – although he certainly was, and is, that as well – and Jesus is even more than just a great prophet or religious leader. Since Jesus is God incarnate he deserves not only our full attention, but also our complete worship as well.

I started my journey as a skeptic, then I became a seeker of truth, and finally I became a follower of the risen Christ. It wasn't always easy, and it certainly wasn't quick. I went from being a person who liked Jesus but was turned off by Christianity to being an open-minded creationist who just wasn't quite ready for the whole "Jesus thing." But I kept at it, and eventually I came to the conclusion that Jesus is who the pages of the Bible claims that he is. Although I didn't exactly enter into the Christian faith "kicking and screaming" as the great apologist C.S. Lewis did decades earlier, I didn't exactly dance my way into the Christian fold, either. Some people, especially those who have hit rock bottom in life and have nowhere to go but up, tend to have dramatic conversion experiences that make for wonderful testimonies, but I didn't have that. God set me on a different path. Instead, my journey to Christ was focused on the search for truth, and it was very methodical and thorough, but nonetheless the end of the search lead me to the same place as the person with the dramatic conversion experience. Perhaps it can be said that, in the end, that is all that really matters.

Chapter 7

FAITH & REASON

As a seeker of spiritual truth in my mid-to-late twenties, I encountered a number of people who held to diverse views regarding the relationship between faith and reason. One man in particular, a Pentecostal pastor with a heart for helping everyone in need, freely admitted to knowing absolutely nothing about Christian evidences. For this man, faith in Christ – and faith alone, quite apart from any rational evidences for the existence of God or Jesus' deity – was all that mattered to him. On the other hand, another professing Christian of acquaintance seemed quite convinced that his faith was so well grounded in reason that he seemed to possess every answer to every question that has troubled Christian believers for centuries. Still another person confused matters by stating that neither faith nor reason could be trusted. For this man, absolutely nothing could be known for certain, either by faith or by reason. To a young seeker of truth, none of these views seemed realistic. With so many diverse views regarding the relationship between faith and reason, how should one approach this vitally important issue?

AN UNNECESSARY CONFLICT

Some Christians have the idea that faith and reason are in constant conflict, divided by an unbridgeable chasm, while other Christians maintain that either faith alone or reason alone is sufficient in trusting one's beliefs. In reality, both faith and reason work together seamlessly in order to help us know about God and spiritual matters. Therefore, faith and reason are not locked in a state of perpetual battle, as both are necessary for a successful Christian walk.

Nonetheless, there are too many Christians who perceive a conflict between these two ways of knowing about God and all things spiritual. On the one hand, we are supposed to have faith. The Apostle Paul clearly tells us that "the righteous will live by faith" (Romans 1:17; Galatians 3:11), and we are supposed to trust fully in God and not lean on our own understanding (Proverbs 3:5). It seems that we are supposed to trust God regardless of whether or not his words make perfect sense to us, and even when certain things go beyond ordinary logic.

On the other hand, God tells us to use the intellectual gift of reason (Isaiah 1:18). We are to have good reasons for what we believe about God and spiritual matters, and we are to be ready at all times to share those reasons with other people (1 Peter 3:15). We must attempt to show unbelievers that our belief in God, Jesus, and Scripture is reasonable, justified, and can be logically defended.

We must ask ourselves if it is faith or reason that is the basis for our belief in God and how we answer the big questions of life. Are we supposed to rely primarily upon our intellect, or should we accept the teachings of Scripture without any regard to logic and reasoning?

This apparent conflict troubles many people, yet when both faith and reason are properly defined in their biblical context all perceived conflicts dissolve. As it turns out, we are to have good reasons for what we believe, yet we must also live by faith.

FAITH & REASON DEFINED

Many people define faith as believing in things that do not seem real, or even believing in things that seem to go against logic and reason. There is no doubt that this is what many people, both Christian believers and unbelievers alike, have in mind when they think of the word faith. Unfortunately, some believers even go so far as to pride themselves in their "blind faith." I have had more than a few people confront me with the statement, "Forget about reasons to believe, just have faith and take every word of Scripture literally." I know one man who, in an evangelistic encounter, told an unbeliever to forget about reason and simply embrace a blind faith in

Christ. However, the Bible does not promote a belief in this type of unexamined faith.

A far better definition of faith is a firm belief in something for which there is no conclusive, irrefutable proof from science, logic, or history. This definition does not deny that science, logic, or history can offer solid evidence for the Christian faith, but rather it states that the evidences offered – no matter how convincing they may be – still fall short of being conclusive or irrefutable. After all, if the evidences from science, logic, and history were conclusive and irrefutable, there would be no debate regarding the existence of God and the veracity of Christian truth claims.[153]

Reason, on the other hand, may be defined as the power of the mind to think, understand, and form judgments by the process of logical deduction. In modern society reason is generally considered to be more reliable, and certainly far less subjective, than is faith. Only in the past few decades or so, with the rise of postmodern (relativistic) thinking, has reason itself been called into question. Nonetheless, most people still consider reason to be more reliable and objective than faith, which is widely considered to be open to any number of personal interpretations.

Therefore, the question that professional and lay theologians alike struggle with is, "Which should we consider more reliable, faith or reason, when it comes to knowing truth?" Or is it possible that faith and reason are more equal than many have previously considered? Perhaps faith and reason are two distinct, yet equally valid, ways to spiritual knowledge. Throughout the centuries Christians have been divided on this matter, and various positions have arisen over time.

---

[153] Of course, even in the face of irrefutable evidence there would still be some people who would refuse to believe in the Christian worldview for emotional-spiritual reasons. The act of believing always contains a strong volitional component.

FAITH & REASON: DIFFERENT VIEWS

There are four possibilities regarding the relationship between faith and reason. First there is faith minus reason, which in philosophical terms is known as fideism. Fideism is derived from the Latin term *fides*, meaning "faith." Therefore, fideism is that philosophical position which maintains that one knows God and spiritual matters purely through faith.

Second, there is reason minus faith, which in philosophical terms is known as rationalism. Rationalism is that position founded upon the belief that unless one can "prove" something by pure logic or reason, then it is not true – or certainly not worth knowing about.

Third, there is the position that neither faith nor reason is a valid means of knowing about God, or anything else, for that matter. This is known as the postmodern position, which is marked by the prevailing attitude that no one can know anything with any certainty.

Finally, there is the classical approach to understanding God, Christ, and all things both temporal and eternal. This combination of faith plus reason utilizes our God-given gift of reasoning while at the same time putting our full trust (faith) in God's revelation through Scripture.

Needless to say, within each of these positions there are degrees of commitment to each view. Not every fideist is completely opposed to logical evidences, and not every rationalist rejects faith in God completely. Likewise, some postmodernists are closer to recognizing absolute truth than are others in their camp, and even within the biblical Christian approach there are some who elevate faith over reason or reason over faith, no matter how minimal that elevation may be. In other words, it is not always possible to pin every person nice and neatly into one of these four categories.

FIDEISM

As mentioned, fideism is derived from *fides*, the Latin word for faith. Fideism is that position which elevates faith far above reason. For some fideists that even means stressing faith to the point of holding reason in contempt. The fideist motto is, "I believe it, and that settles it." For the fideist, religious belief is not subject to logic and reasoning; religious belief is purely a matter of faith in God. Although there are many well-known examples of Christian fideists throughout the past 2,000 years, the early Church Father Tertullian, the Reformation giant Martin Luther, the extraordinary French scholar Blaise Pascal, the Christian existentialist Soren Kierkegaard, and the neo-orthodox theologian Karl Barth are usually offered as being the five most prominent fideists in Christian history. I would argue, however, that each of these men acknowledged that reason plays a role at times, and some were more open to logic and reasoning than were others.

TERTULLIAN

Quintus Septimius Florens Tertullianus, or more simply Tertullian (AD 160-220), is often referred to as the earliest proponent of the "pure faith" approach to knowing God. Tertullian said that what made Christianity so trustworthy for him is that it is not based upon reasoning, but rather it is based upon a supernatural worldview which in many ways runs counter to reason, echoing the vast chasm between the infinite God and finite people. For Tertullian, as for countless millions since his time, the truth of Christianity can only be explained by divine revelation, with human reasoning contributing very little. With that in mind, however, Tertullian was nonetheless very well-read and theologically astute, and he did utilize logic and reasoning when it was necessary to do so. For Tertullian, faith trumped – but did not completely erase – logic and reasoning.

Although Tertullian was not opposed to using logic and reasoning when the situation demanded it – he was, after all, a lawyer by training who most certainly possessed critical thinking skills – he nonetheless rejected the idea that one could mix Christian doctrines with Greco-Roman philosophy, unlike his predecessor Justin Martyr who was the first of the great apologists to live after the time of the Apostle Paul. (Justin Martyr was well-known for his synthesis of Christian theology and ancient Greek ideas.) Tertullian feared that pagan philosophy, if used incorrectly, could distort the message of Christ. Along this line, he is perhaps best known for his declaration, "What has Jerusalem to do with Athens, the Church with the Academy, the Christian with the heretic?" Tertullian was impressing upon his readers that there should be no attempt to integrate the doctrines of the Christian faith with the ideas of the pagan philosophers. Jerusalem, the home of revealed religion, can have no ideological relationship with Athens, the city known for giving rise to Greco-Roman philosophy, nor can the Church cooperate with Plato's Academy, as the Christian and the pagan are light years apart in their worldview. For Tertullian, Christianity and philosophy simply do not mix, and any attempt at synthesizing the two would result in nothing less than the watering down of Christian doctrine.

MARTIN LUTHER

The approach of "faith far above reasoning" was given special attention by many of the key Protestant reformers. Both Martin Luther (1483-1546) and John Calvin (1509-1564) stressed faith over reason, with Luther being far more dedicated to the faith-only approach. Calvin (fortunately) combined faith with at least a few reason-based evidences in his approach to theology. Theologians Kenneth Boa and Robert Bowman, Jr. note that fideism is most deeply-rooted in Lutheranism, and this is directly related to Luther's approach of faith far above reason. Although Boa and Bowman do not go so far as to formally label Luther a fideist, they nonetheless stress that the modern roots of fideism may be found in Luther.[154]

Luther maintained that the fallen nature of humanity was so severely debilitating that the rational mind on its own was

---

[154] Kenneth D. Boa & Robert M. Bowman, Jr., *Faith Has Its Reasons* (Colorado Springs, CO: Paternoster, 2005), 340.

simply incapable of knowing anything with certainty about God and his will. This is not dissimilar from what Augustine taught, which is not surprising as Luther was trained in the theology of Augustine. According to Luther all people must rely solely upon faith in God alone. Luther did, however, hold the belief that reason was sufficient for temporal affairs, or what he termed "matters of the kingdom of earth" (natural phenomena). However, when it came to eternal issues, or what he termed "matters of the kingdom of heaven" (supernatural phenomena), reasoning is absolutely incompetent. In fact, Luther took it a step further and proclaimed that reason is an enemy of God, actually being counter-productive in terms of knowing God and grasping spiritual matters.

Luther was convinced that, other than establishing a very general belief in God, natural theology[155] was quite useless as it offered no real knowledge concerning God's will and plan of salvation. The plan of salvation is simply beyond reason, proclaimed Luther, and therefore reason is unable to guide a person to the necessary knowledge required for salvation. For Luther, the Gospel must be heard, and accepted, on faith alone. Further, Luther held that any attempt to defend the Gospel through logic and reasoning would only succeed in subverting it: "Let us not be anxious: the Gospel needs not our help; it is sufficiently strong of itself. God alone commends it."[156] Had I been born in Germany during Luther's time, he probably wouldn't want to hang out with an apologist like me! Luther clearly fit into the traditional, even anti-intellectual, form of fideism.

BLAISE PASCAL

Blaise Pascal (1623-1662), a devout Roman Catholic who was the most extraordinary French scholar of the seventeenth century, excelled in mathematics, physics, and philosophy.

---

[155] Natural theology is that area of study devoted to understanding God's existence through both creation and the inherent moral compass embedded within every person (Romans 1:20; 2:14-15).
[156] Kenneth D. Boa & Robert M. Bowman, Jr., *Faith Has Its Reasons* (Colorado Springs, CO: Paternoster, 2005), 342.

Pascal pointed out the inadequacy of the usual arguments for God, being convinced that the "infinitely incomprehensible being" cannot be known through finite, comprehensible arguments. The most that these philosophical arguments could do was to establish the existence of the so-called "god of the philosophers," who is essentially the vague god of deism and certainly not the one true God revealed in Scripture. This is most extraordinary, since Pascal had been influenced by the rationalism of both Galileo and Rene Descartes. However, Pascal cannot accurately be called a traditional fideist since he adhered to three sources of belief: Reason, custom (church tradition), and inspiration. Being that reason was one of his major sources of religious knowledge, it seems that he was eclectic enough in his approach to theology that he combined faith with at least some use of Christian evidences.

However, Pascal was adamant that reason alone cannot determine the existence or non-existence of God. For Pascal, faith was rational, even in the absence of "rational proof" in a practical sense. In other words, for Pascal believing in God serves a practical purpose, whether or not there is solid rational evidence to back-up the claims of those who believe in God. "Pascal's Wager" is the idea that in the absence of proof for God's existence, it is better to side with God than with atheism, because the person who believes in God has everything to gain and nothing to lose, whereas the person who chooses atheism has everything to lose and nothing to gain. Remaining agnostic, in Pascal's opinion, was tantamount to choosing atheism, for not choosing to believe either way is equivalent to accepting atheism.

Although faith was of prime importance for Pascal, we may say that he exemplified a much more rational form of fideism, allowing a foot in the door for logic and critical thinking. His approach to understanding God and the claims of Christianity stressed faith, but not at the complete contempt of reason, as was the case with Luther.

SOREN KIERKEGAARD

Soren Kierkegaard (1813-1855) is known to history for

his proclamation that faith is characterized by a passionate commitment to God independent of reasoning, requiring a "leap of faith" as some have termed it.[157] For Kierkegaard, any reliance upon reason was not only unnecessary, but more importantly it would ruin the almost mystical reliance on "faith in matters unseen." For Kierkegaard, a truly genuine faith is not one that is established upon the basis of reason, but rather it transcends reason and attempts to understand God purely through a commitment of the will.

Kierkegaard held that each person can choose one of three lifestyles: (1) The aesthetic life, which is the life of pleasure; (2) the ethical life, which is lived in accordance to duty, laws, and decision-making; (3) the religious life, which is lived in service to God. Kierkegaard taught that one must make an intellectual decision to leave behind the hedonism of the aesthetic life in order to progress to the socially-responsible ethical life; it is reason which allows one to progress from the first stage to the second stage. However, one cannot further progress from there to the religious life by mere thought or reflection, as was possible before. Kierkegaard's famous "leap of faith" is necessary to get from the ethical to the religious life.[158] As an illustration of the religious life, Kierkegaard relied upon the example of Abraham. Although Abraham was a man of high moral standards who would not normally take an innocent life, he nonetheless went beyond his ethical standard to a life of complete obedience to God's commands. Abraham's willingness to sacrifice Isaac required a passionate "leap of faith." Until this life-changing event, Abraham – despite being a man of deep reverence for God – had not truly progressed beyond the ethical life.

Kierkegaard is much closer to the pure fideism of Luther

---

[157] It should be noted that Kierkegaard himself may never have used the phrase "leap of faith." Nonetheless, the phrase does properly express Kierkegaard's attitude regarding Christian conversion.

[158] R.C. Sproul, *The Consequences of Ideas* (Wheaton, IL: Crossway Books, 2000), 152.

than to the integration of faith and reason, as practiced by Tertullian and (especially) Pascal. This is interesting, as Kierkegaard always features in introductory philosophy courses, yet unlike the typical philosopher he lived out his spiritual life through faith rather than reason.

KARL BARTH

Karl Barth (1886-1968) is considered by many to have been the single most influential Christian theologian of the twentieth century. Barth stressed Scripture over natural theology, and faith over reasoning.

Barth heavily promoted the position of "faith seeking understanding" in which a person who has already accepted Christianity as being true then seeks to articulate a rational understanding of its core doctrines. In other words, apologetics is predominately for the Christian believer, not for the seeker or (especially) the skeptic. For Barth, faith guided the intellect and not vice-versa. Barth maintained that any attempt to begin with the intellect, as in natural theology, will never bring one to a true faith.[159]

For Barth, it was possible to know God only by faith. By faith alone we know with certainty that God exists, and by faith alone we know how God has reconciled us to him through Christ's sacrifice upon the cross. We cannot reason our way into this knowledge. This revelation from God comes directly from Christ through the Holy Spirit, and only indirectly from Scripture itself. Christ *personally* reveals himself to humanity, rather than *intellectually* revealing himself through written words.

Unfortunately, Barth's theology is marred by two key points. First, he leaned heavily toward universalism,[160]

---

[159] Peter May, "Karl Barth and Natural Theology?" https://www.bethinking.org/is-christianity-true/karl-barth-and-natural-theology

[160] However, it would be inaccurate to label Barth as being a dyed-in-the-wool universalist. Rather, many scholars have noted that he tended toward that belief, rather than proclaiming himself to be a staunch universalist.

which essentially makes apologetics an unnecessary endeavor. Second, he had no real use for apologetics, other than its use by Christian believers for the encouragement of their spiritual growth. Therefore, apologetics played no significant role is his writings. Like Luther, Barth held to a very traditional view of fideism.

A CRITIQUE OF FIDEISM

Unfortunately for the traditional fideist position, faith without reason produces an unreasonable faith. Although it is true that reason does not produce faith, it does support faith – and sometimes that makes all the difference when it comes to both strengthening the faith of a Christian believer as well as arming that person with the ability to address the questions, concerns, and challenges posed by both seekers and skeptics. As Christian believers, each of us must be ready to examine all things carefully and hold firmly to that which is good (1 Thessalonians 5:21). Since the fideist generally maintains an "I believe it, and that settles it" attitude, this often results in a failure to thoroughly examine doctrinal and evidential issues.

The emotionally-based appeal of fideism requires almost no preparation in the area of apologetics. The fideist focuses solely on personal testimony, the quoting of Scripture, and why the Christian faith has been a source of strength and hope for him or her personally. On the other hand, evidence-based apologetics – which the fideist generally avoids – requires doing some homework. Many unbelievers throughout the past two millennia have been unwilling to consider the existence of God and the deity of Christ until confronted by a challenge to examine the evidence for Christianity. Many people have converted to a saving faith in Christ not because they were seeking an emotional uplift, but because they were persuaded by the evidence. Jesus commands us to "love the Lord your God with all your heart, with all your soul, with all your mind, and with all your strength" (Mark 12:30). People are easily able to love the Lord with all their heart and soul through the process of introspection, but they must examine and thoughtfully consider the evidences for the faith in order to love God with all of their minds. Fideists are generally not as prepared to supply answers to those seeking well-grounded evidences for the faith. Just simply believing in Christ for the sake of believing is not an adequate incentive for many seekers. It certainly was not for me, so many years ago.

Finally, since faith is oftentimes considered to require a "leap," how do we know which faith to leap for? There are many faiths in the world today, such as the Jewish faith, the Muslim faith, the Hindu faith, the Mormon faith, and so on. It should be obvious that not all of these religious traditions can lead to God, as many of them completely contradict the others. We need reasons for choosing which faith to leap for, and those reasons must be *reasonable*. Therefore, reason is both significant and necessary to faith.

RATIONALISM

Rationalism maintains that in order to believe in anything, it must be possible to prove that thing by means of evidence and reasoning. In other words, rational thinking is of supreme importance to belief, and the ability to engage in logic and critical thinking is authoritative. The motto of rationalism is, "I understand in order that I might believe." Some rationalists are adamant that it is always wrong to believe in anything without sufficient evidence. This certainly opposes the fideist position that faith in and of itself is an adequate means of knowing truth.

Rationalism began during the Enlightenment of the seventeenth and eighteenth centuries, under the influence of many philosophers and scientists. Perhaps most notable among these great thinkers were Francis Bacon, Rene Descartes, John Locke, and Immanuel Kant, although others both before and after them played key roles in rationalist thinking as well. This Age of Reason was that time in history when European culture first began to replace God's Word with man's ideas. Although at first most of the Enlightenment thinkers maintained a general belief in the Creator, the Age of Reason would eventually lead modern society in the direction of naturalism.

THE ENLIGHTENMENT THINKERS

The Enlightenment elevated reason to the place of supreme authority for determining truth, and gave rise to many interesting thinkers. Rene Descartes (1596–1650), the founder of rationalism,[161] and John Locke (1632–1704), the founder of empiricism,[162] sought to use reason to defend the Christian faith. Unfortunately, several others used reason to discard both scriptural and ecclesiastical authority. Ironically, these materialists often relied heavily on the writings of Descartes and Locke in order to do so.

THE CHRISTIAN DEISTS

It was during the Enlightenment that deism arose, and this worldview quickly spread to the American colonies and eventually became influential among some of the key leaders of the Revolutionary War. Deism emphasizes logic and reasoning to the point where there is no place for faith. Although deists believe in God as the Creator only – not accepting the Trinity, the deity of Jesus, or the authority of the Bible – some deists, such as Thomas Jefferson (1743-1826) and Benjamin Franklin (1706-1790), combined the traditional views of deism with a strong appreciation for the moral teachings of Christ. Known as "Christian deists," they were pure rationalists who maintained the belief that we know God only through reason. For them, Christ was merely a great moral teacher of the ancient world, not God incarnate who came to save the world. However, a few of the Christian deists were known to pray, something that a pure deist would

---

[161] Rationalism is the belief that opinions and actions should be based on reason and verifiable knowledge, rather than on faith and emotions. For the rationalist, the reasoning mind is the supreme source for knowing about anything.

[162] Empiricism is the belief that all knowledge is derived from sensory experience. For the empiricist, sensory experience and the evidences that are derived from them is the supreme source for knowing about anything.

never consider doing. Therefore, we may say that, although they were committed to reason over faith, the Christian deists may have retained an element of faith, albeit to a very limited degree.

A CRITIQUE OF RATIONALISM

The author of Hebrews makes it clear that without faith, it is impossible to please God (Hebrews 11:6). Reason alone simply cannot produce faith. Reason may *support* faith, but it cannot *produce* faith.

Additionally, there are some truths that are known only through God's revelation in the written word. Perhaps the best example of this is God's triune nature. The natural world can point us in the direction of a Creator (Romans 1:20), but it cannot point us in the direction of God's triune nature. For that, we need God's self-revelation in Scripture.

Finally, rationalism fails to take into account the difference between the rational, thinking mind and the emotional-volitional will. There are many examples in our modern culture of people who have acknowledged the evidence for God in general, and even Christianity in particular, but nonetheless they choose not to act positively upon that evidence and instead remain comfortably settled in their unbelief. Just because there may be good evidences for believing in something – and Christianity has many credible, and even incredible, evidences in its favor – that does not mean that everyone will choose to accept those evidences and embrace the faith.

POSTMODERNISM

The term "postmodernism" is often discussed in Christian circles today, but in my experience believers neglect to define the term itself. Postmodernism generally refers to the tendency to accept different worldviews as all being of equal worth and validity. For a long time, the world has entertained many different "stories" regarding nature and ultimate reality. Atheism has its story, pantheism a different story, Christianity a still different story, and so on. With postmodernism no one story can have any more credibility than any other; all stories are equally valid and equally worthy.

Postmodernism is primarily defined by an attitude of subjectivity in moral, religious, and philosophical matters. Therefore, postmodernism is essentially synonymous with relativism.

It is commonly held that before postmodern thinking developed, people were concerned with rational, evidence-based reasons for knowing what is true. Postmodernism, on the other hand, maintains that much of what we think might be true is derived at through personal feelings and what seems to "work" for us. Yet interestingly enough, even many postmodern thinkers today are reluctant to give much credit to emotions, finding them to be untrustworthy as well. It seems that for many postmodern thinkers, neither faith nor reason offers a reliable means of knowing anything for sure. Therefore, in postmodernism it is ultimately pragmatism (what works) that decides truth – and even then truth may be constantly changing.

Two of the most influential postmodern thinkers were Jean-Francois Lyotard (1924-1998) and Jacques Derrida (1930-2004). The motto of postmodernism is often summed up in the phrase, "True for you, but not necessarily true for me."

A CRITIQUE OF POSTMODERNISM

The major problem with postmodern relativism is this: If all things are relative, then there is nothing which can be said to be absolutely true between individuals. It then becomes impossible to adequately function as a society when no one is certain of anything. If all moral views are equally valid, then do we really have the right to punish anyone? Our judicial system requires moral absolutes. In order to say that something is wrong, we must first have a standard by which we weigh right and wrong in order to make a judgment. If that standard of right and wrong is relative, then it is really no standard at all. In relativism, the standards of right and wrong are based upon social norms. Therefore, as society changes, the norms of right and wrong also change. This makes it impossible to consistently judge people for their supposed offenses against others.

The Law of Non-Contradiction is a major problem for postmodern thinking. The Law of Non-Contradiction states that two or more opposing statements cannot be simultaneously true. For example, Christ either is, or is not, God. Both statements cannot be simultaneously true. One can say that, "Christ is God for you, but not God for me." However, that statement is a matter of personal religious choice. What the person is really saying is, "I do not want Christ to be God for myself, but he can be whatever you want him to be." Whether or not one accepts Christ as God is not the same as the fact of Christ's deity. Personal opinion is not a rebuttal of the objective evidences which positively establish the deity of Christ.

A major contention of postmodern relativists is that people with varying viewpoints on a certain topic merely perceive different aspects of the same reality. In other words, they may only be aware of part of the reality, and not the reality in its entirety. The parable of the elephant and the six blind men of India may be used to illustrate this point. In this parable, the first blind man felt the elephant's side, and came to the conclusion that the elephant was a wall. The second blind man felt the elephant's tusk, and concluded that what he was feeling was a very large spear. The third blind man felt the trunk of the elephant, and decided that he was encountering a large snake. The fourth blind man felt the leg of the elephant, and was certain that he was feeling a tree trunk. The fifth blind man felt the elephant's ear, and decided that he was handling a fan. Finally, the sixth blind man felt the tail of the elephant, and concluded that he was holding a rope. According to postmodern relativists, this parable is supposed to teach us that our perception of reality is usually incomplete, and therefore we are unable to make absolute statements regarding the nature of ultimate reality. Absolutists, on the other hand, remind us that regardless of how any of the six blind men perceived the elephant, the fact remains that they were nonetheless encountering an elephant. In a spiritual context the lesson is this: God is God, regardless of how we perceive him. The Christian does not deny that we have an incomplete view of God, even in the face of God's self-revelation in Scripture (Isaiah 55:8-9; 1 Corinthians 13:12). However, there is much that we can know about God through his self-revelation. Scripture may not tell us every detail about God, but it is more than sufficient for us to know about – and to just plain know – the one true God.

BIBLICAL CHRISTIANITY

The classical approach in Christian thinking has always been to combine faith with reason. In Athens, Paul reasoned with the Greek philosophers in order to proclaim the Gospel to them (Acts 17:16-34), yet Paul was clearly a man of great faith (1 Timothy 1:12). The Greeks generally placed a very high emphasis upon reasoning, and Paul was able to meet them where they stood. Paul did not shy away from logic and reasoning, but rather he utilized it as a necessary tool for evangelism. Therefore, we can say that Paul combined great faith in Christ and his Word with the ability of the human mind to reason toward truth.

In the second century, Flavius Justinus – better known to the world as Justin Martyr (AD 100-165) – further developed the role of reasoning in order to both proclaim and defend the faith. Justin had converted to Christianity after a lengthy exploration of Greek philosophy, and even after his conversion he remained rooted in philosophy, a touchy subject for some of his fellow believers who viewed philosophy as being the enemy of divine revelation. Justin was convinced that the pagan philosophers had, at least in part, discovered some truths regarding the one true God of the universe, and this partial knowledge of God could serve as a connection point with Christianity. Justin was the first example outside of the New Testament of a dedicated Christian thinker who attempted to share the faith with unbelievers by first establishing a common ground or connection point based in logic and reasoning. Despite his emphasis upon rational thought, however, Justin was a man of great faith who considered the Bible to be his authoritative source of knowledge about God and spiritual matters: "Our doctrines [Christian beliefs] are greater than all human teaching [Greco-Roman philosophy]." We may safely say that Justin continued the positive relationship between faith and reason that was begun earlier with the Apostle Paul.

Neither Paul nor Justin shied away from using the logic and critical thinking skills associated with Greco-Roman philosophy, but rather they utilized these techniques as a way to forge a common point of interest with their unbelieving acquaintances. For Paul and Justin, even the pagan world knew some truths about the one true God, however limited that knowledge may have been, and they took advantage of those truths and built upon them with the Christian worldview. Both recognized that all truth comes from God, and therefore the one true God may be recognized to some degree by all people (Acts 17:28; Romans 2:14-15).

AUGUSTINE & ANSELM: A REASONED FAITH

Aurelius Augustinus, or more simply Augustine (AD 354-430), is considered by many to be the greatest theologian of the first one thousand years of the Church Age. Augustine always emphasized the ability of the mind to engage in logic and reasoning. Augustine was convinced that Christianity is a well-reasoned faith, and not just a matter of the "heart" or emotions. "Augustine was the sort of person who would not send his heart to a place where his head could not also go. In order for him to commit his life to Christianity, certain intellectual questions had to be resolved."[163] However, despite his emphasis upon reasoning, he was noted for his motto, "I believe, so that I may understand," demonstrating his strong commitment to the role of faith. For Augustine, the fall of Adam had so profoundly affected the human intellect that,

---

[163] Steve Wilkens, *Good Ideas from Questionable Christians and Outright Pagans* (Downers Grove, IL: InterVarsity Press, 2004), 118.

apart from the grace of God which changes both heart and mind, no one could begin to truly grasp the tenets of the Christian faith. Therefore, in order to understand the doctrines expounded in Scripture, one must first experience a true Christian conversion that allows for the renewal of the mind. Then, and only then, can one begin to understand the often difficult teachings associated with the biblical worldview.

The Medieval era saw the rise of another great Christian thinker who thoroughly embraced Augustine's position of faith seeking understanding. Despite his reason-heavy theology,[164] Anselm of Canterbury (1033-1109) always stressed the role of faith. Like his hero Augustine, he adhered to the "believe first, then understand later" philosophy of knowing God and spiritual truth. Anselm shared Augustine's view that in order to truly grasp the important concepts of the faith one must first believe in order to possess the clarity of mind that allows for understanding. Needless to say, this position runs counter to modern thinking, which maintains that in order to believe in something one must first examine the evidence both for and against the thing under consideration and then make an educated decision based upon what seems reasonable. For both Augustine and Anselm, proper reasoning concerning spiritual truth is an illusion unless one's mind is first clarified through Christian conversion. Only at that point can the man or woman of faith begin to truly understand what God has revealed in Scripture.

It should be noted that both Augustine and Anselm were highly intelligent and incredibly gifted scholars who exercised logic and reasoning in their examination of theological matters. Despite their position of "faith seeking understanding" they were nowhere close to being traditional fideists who maintained faith in Christ and Scripture apart from rational evidences. For Augustine and Anselm, the prerequisite to knowing spiritual truth was the saving faith that illuminat-

---

[164] Anselm is credited with developing the ontological argument for God's existence.

ed one's thoughts, but that in no way removed reasoning from the picture.

AQUINAS & NATURAL THEOLOGY

Thomas Aquinas (1225-1274) is considered to be the champion of logic and reasoning in the Medieval era, being known for his development of rational "arguments" or lines of evidence that demonstrate the existence of God.[165] Aquinas held the view that in order to possess a basic belief in God's existence and to be able to obtain knowledge of natural phenomena, we must first understand why we believe. However, Aquinas never held the view that reason alone could sustain Christian belief. Although reason-based evidence for God has a place in Christianity, it can never on its own produce an adequate knowledge of God. For Aquinas, Scripture and church tradition must be joined to logic and reasoning in order to have a truly robust, well-grounded faith.

Unlike Augustine, Aquinas believed that Adam's fall did not alter the intellectual abilities of people; critical thinking skills were essentially unhampered by the fall of humanity. Therefore, in Aquinas' view people could utilize logic and reasoning to great avail, but logic and reasoning applied only to natural matters – which, for Aquinas, also included a general belief in the existence of God (natural theology). When

---

[165] Aquinas' "five proofs" are (1) the proof from motion; (2) the proof from efficient cause; (3) the proof from necessary being; (4) the proof from degrees of perfection; (5) the proof from order in the universe. In the proof from motion, Aquinas taught that whatever is moved must be moved by some prior actuality, but without an infinite regress of movers. Therefore, a "Prime Mover" must exist. God is the eternal, uncaused Prime Mover who set everything in motion. The proof from efficient cause is essentially the evidence from cause-and-effect. The proof from necessary being is the idea that no being greater than God can be imagined – therefore, God exists. The proof from degrees of perfection is similar to the evidence from morality. Borrowing heavily from Augustine for this proof, Aquinas argued that it is impossible to have a relative comparison of anything without an absolute with which it can be compared, and that absolute is the perfection found only in God. Finally, the proof from order in the universe is essentially the same as the evidence from design.

it came to distinctly Christian doctrines, as opposed to a general belief in God, Aquinas was quick to admit that Scripture was absolutely necessary in order to begin to understand the mysteries of Christianity. For example, Aquinas would have been comfortable maintaining that God's existence could be known through a critical analysis of the lines of evidence which he proposed in his works, but in order to know that God is a triune being one must rely upon God's revealed words in Scripture. Reasoning about nature will never lead one to the conclusion that God exists in the form of a triune being. Therefore, we may say that the divide between Augustine and Aquinas was not as wide as many have maintained. As with the great theologians both before and after them, Augustine and Aquinas combined faith with reason in their pursuit of knowing God, although each had a different view of Adam's fall as it pertained to the abilities of the human mind to grasp things both natural and supernatural.

BALANCE IS KEY

Most Christian thinkers were careful to balance logic and reasoning with faith in Christ and Scripture. Some, like Luther and Kierkegaard, may have emphasized faith far above reason, while others may have been reason-heavy in their approach to understanding God and the natural order (Christian deists), but nonetheless all of the great Christian thinkers knew that they needed the combination of reason, scriptural authority, and faith in the risen Christ in order to truly know God and begin to understand those things of spiritual significance. After the time of the Reformation the Christian world began to see significant imbalances between faith and reason, with the overly rational approach of the Enlightenment thinkers and the "pure faith" approach of Luther, Kierkegaard, and much later Barth. To complicate matters further, today we have the attitude of postmodern skepticism, which calls into question the usefulness of both faith and reason. After examining the history of the debate between faith and reason, it is no wonder that many Christians today are confused about the proper relationship between these two ways of knowing God and spiritual truth.

BIBLICAL FAITH

The Bible itself describes what faith is. Hebrews 11:1 tells us that faith is the substance of things hoped for, the evidence of things not seen. Biblical faith is not "blind faith" but rather it is a strongly warranted confidence. The phrase "hoped for" does not imply a mere wishful thinking as in, "I sure hope there's no more snow this winter." (Seriously, I hope there's no more snow this winter. It's actually snowing as I'm typing these words!) Rather, the Greek word used indicates a confident expectation, the kind of confidence we have when we have a good reason to believe something.

Biblically, faith is having confidence in something you have not experienced with your senses. For example, when we believe that God will keep a promise, this constitutes faith because we are yet to experience God keeping that particular promise, but nonetheless we have a good reason for believing this as God has demonstrated over and over again that he keeps his promises. This is demonstrated in both Scripture and the lives of individuals even today.

BIBLICAL REASON

Reason is a divine gift that allows us to draw conclusions and inferences from the information we have at our disposal, such as God's revelation in Scripture as well as the God-given ability to deduce facts. Reason is an essential part of Christianity. In fact, God tells us to reason (Isaiah 1:18; Acts 17:17).

No one could directly know that they are saved apart from using reason. The Bible states, "If you declare with your mouth, 'Jesus is Lord,' and believe in your heart that God raised him from the dead, you will be saved" (Romans 10:9). If we have genuinely acknowledged that Jesus is Lord, and we believe that God raised him from the dead, then we are saved. We must use logical reasoning in order to come to this conclusion. This is the kind of reasoning God wants us to engage in, since we are reasoning from Scripture.

Unfortunately, people tend to either treat reason as being the ultimate source of knowing spiritual truth, in which case reason replaces Scripture (Christian deism), or they put reason aside, considering it to be irrelevant if not downright counterproductive to one's faith (traditional fideism). Neither is a healthy approach to knowing God and spiritual truth. Every sincere Christian believer should recognize the inherent danger of relying solely on reason, as opposed to a healthy reliance upon God's revelation in Scripture. It is absolutely certain that there are some things that people can never understand by the intellect alone, such as God's triune nature and Christ's atoning sacrifice upon the cross. However, Scripture is clear that reasoning, though likely flawed to some degree through the effects of Adam's fall, is nonetheless a proper means of knowing things both natural and supernatural, temporal and eternal. Both 1 Peter 3:15 and Isaiah 1:18 offer biblical support for this belief.

Since God is rational (Romans 16:27) we are also rational (Ephesians 5:1), as we are made in God's image (Genesis 1:26-27). We are commanded to seek wisdom and understanding (Proverbs 4:5-7), since God wants us to use the mind he has given us, but he also wants us to use our minds properly – which is ultimately for his glory.

There is a place in Christianity for believing by faith. In fact, we are commanded throughout Scripture to believe by faith (Job 13:15; Matthew 9:22; 15:28; 21:21-22; John 11:25-26; Acts 6:5; 11:22-24; 14:9-10; 15:8-9; Romans 1:16-17; 4:16-25; 2 Corinthians 5:6-7; Ephesians 2:8-9; 6:16; Colossians 1:5-6; 2 Timothy 1:12-14; Hebrews 10:35-39; 11:6, 24-27). However, we are also commanded to use reasoning. Paul tells us that no one may be excused for failing to believe in the existence of the Creator for the simple reason that God's fingerprints are all over his creation: "For since the creation of the world God's invisible qualities – his eternal power and divine nature – have been clearly seen, being understood from what has been made, so that people are without excuse" (Romans 1:20). Recognizing God's power and glory requires us to use our God-given reasoning and senses, and it simultaneously strengthens one's faith.

FAITH IS NECESSARY FOR REASON

The Christian believer understands that reasoning reflects God, since God exhibits this quality and we are made in his image. The unbeliever, however, cannot account for the laws of logic and the ability to reason in this same way, since unbelievers do not accept the Christian worldview. For those who hold to atheism and molecules-to-man evolution, our thoughts can be nothing more than random chemical reactions in the brain, so in that naturalistic worldview we really should not trust our thoughts, no matter how logical they may seem to be, because ultimately there is nothing logical about random chemical reactions in the brain.

Since reason would be impossible without the laws of logic, which ultimately derive from the Christian worldview, we have a very good reason for our faith. Without faith we could not reason properly. Therefore, it turns out that Augustine and Anselm were correct in their assertion that in order to truly begin to understand anything, be it natural or supernatural, we must first have the clarity of thought that comes through spiritual regeneration in Christ (1 Corinthians 2:12-14). Aquinas was correct as well, in that knowing about purely spiritual matters requires God's revelation. Much later in history Blaise Pascal would also maintain that in order to know God with our mind, we must first believe God with our heart and soul – a matter that the Apostle Matthew wrote about sixteen centuries earlier (Matthew 22:37).

WHAT I DISCOVERED

During my days as a skeptic I believed that one had faith or one had reason, but never both at the same time. For me, faith and reason were mutually exclusive. It was incredibly enlightening to discover that faith and reason are complimentary ways of knowing about – and just simply knowing – God. As a skeptic I prided myself on being a man of reason, and as a seeker I admired many Christians who I considered to be people of faith, but it was only after I became a follower of Christ that I came to the realization that one could be both a person of reason and a person of faith at the same time. Although more than a few of my skeptical friends would question my "man of reason" status (there may be some truth in that!), I can proudly say that I'm now a man of faith who enjoys searching for reasonable answers to the big questions of life.

Both faith and reason are vital elements in knowing God and recognizing the authority of Scripture. We need faith in order to properly employ reason, and we need reason in order to make sense of our faith. Whether or not one believes that Adam's fall thoroughly corrupted human reasoning, we can say with certainty that regarding purely spiritual matters – such as the Trinity or Christ's dual nature – we must rely on God's direct revelation in Scripture, while the general belief in God seems to be discernible through rational thought alone (Romans 1:20). Although the debate regarding the relationship between faith and reason has persisted throughout the centuries, we can say that both faith in God's special revelation must be joined to logic and reasoning in order to provide one with the faith of a mature believer who is equipped to take the message of Christ to a fallen world.

Chapter 8

WHEN WORLDVIEWS COLLIDE: PAUL IN ATHENS

Scripture contains numerous examples of apologetics in action. One of the earliest, and arguably still the greatest, of all apologists was the Apostle Paul. The record of Paul at the Areopagus in Athens, which was the hotbed of philosophical thought and debate throughout the Greco-Roman world during his time, serves as the best example of apologetics for the purpose of evangelism across worldviews.

Greece was the birthplace of Western philosophy, giving rise to Socrates, Plato, Aristotle, and numerous other thinkers both before and after them. Like cities in Western society today, Athens was a place of religious pluralism, and Paul clearly offered the Gospel to a diverse group of people, not only among the intellectual elite in the Areopagus but also among those in the synagogue and in the marketplace of the city, giving him ample opportunity to share the Gospel during his time in that city. Although the entirety of Acts is a study in Christian evangelism and apologetics, the account of Paul in Athens is especially impressive. Paul shared his faith in Christ with a group of people who prided themselves on their intellectual prowess, yet his heartfelt desire was always to see the lost accept God's free gift of salvation.

Paul's speech at the Areopagus, one of only two speeches before a pagan audience that was recorded by Luke in Acts,[166] is considered to be "the exemplary meeting between Jerusalem and Athens."[167] Paul's speech truly serves as the connection point in the battle between Judeo-Christian revelation and Greek rationalism, a battle which continues to this very day.

---

[166] The other speech being found in Acts 14:15-17.
[167] Ron Vince, "At the Areopagus (Acts 17:22-31): Pauline Apologetics and Lucan Rhetoric." http://www.mcmaster.ca/mjtm/4-5.htm

Since it is imperative that we demonstrate the living power of the Christian message while sharing our faith with others, it is crucial to "always be ready with an answer" (1 Peter 3:15) to the questions posed by seekers and skeptics alike. "Athenian philosophers" are alive and well today, and they deserve a rational-yet-biblical response from Christian believers, for Christ himself commanded us to take the message of the Gospel throughout the world (Matthew 28:16-20; Mark 16:14-18), and that includes those who are skeptical and maintain vastly different views regarding God, man, and nature. Unfortunately, many Christians today are not prepared to engage the seeking and the skeptical of our world. That's why books like this one have been written.

PAUL'S DISTRESS

Paul encountered a culture much different from what he was accustomed to in Jerusalem. The devoutly Jewish worldview would not allow for a preponderance of idols, let alone *any* idols, yet this was exactly what Paul encountered in Athens. "While Paul was waiting for them in Athens, he was greatly distressed to see that the city was full of idols" (Acts 17:16). Athens was truly packed with idols. "There was a temple of Ares, a temple of Hephaistos, an altar to Zeus, and statues for the various emperors that were worshiped. There were thirteen small altars dedicated to Augustus alone."[168] Paul was not the only person of antiquity to remark on the idolatry present in Athens. The historians Strabo, Livy, Josephus, and Pausanias also remarked on the abundance of statues, and Athenian religiosity in general, that took Paul by surprise. Paul was surely saddened by this grand display of idolatry, especially if he had read the inscription under Emperor Claudius' statue which described

---

[168] Alida Leni Sewell, "Paul at Athens: An Examination of His Areopagus Address in the Light of its Historical and Philosophical Background." http://www.freewebs.com/reformationalphilosophy?Sewell/Acts17.pdf

him as the Roman "savior and benefactor."[169]

Although Athens was steeped in pagan idolatry, Paul not only contained the obvious displeasure that he must have felt, but he even went one step further and used that idolatry as a stepping stone into his discourse on the biblical worldview. As evangelists today, Christian believers must also find points of contact (points of interest) with unbelievers that allow us to enter into dialogue with them, capturing their interest long enough to make a proper presentation of the Gospel.[170]

PAUL'S METHOD OF EVANGELISM

Paul encountered a diverse population of listeners, both educated and uneducated, in the synagogue and in the marketplace. "So he reasoned in the synagogue with both Jews and God-fearing Greeks, as well as in the marketplace day by day with those who happened to be there" (Acts 17:17). Since the Jews and the God-fearing Greeks were already grounded in theism, there was no reason to present evidence for the existence of a personal Creator-God to them. Therefore, Paul would have begun with the evidence for the deity of Christ: The miracles, the resurrection, and Christ's fulfillment of Old Testament prophecy were certainly foundational lines of evidence in Paul's "Case for Christ." For the Jews and the God-fearing Greeks, Paul relied heavily upon Hebrew Scripture when making the case for Jesus as Messiah.

---

[169] Ibid.

[170] "Points of contact" or "points of interest" should not be confused with "common ground," as the biblical worldview has very little in common with the secular worldview in terms of areas where both agree. However, points of contact may include topics or questions that both believers and unbelievers alike find intriguing, such as the issue of origins. Even though Genesis 1:1 is worlds apart from the naturalistic view of origins, the question of how the world began is nonetheless a topic that both groups find fascinating and worth investigating, and therefore it is a potential point of contact.

PAUL'S USE OF PHILOSOPHY

Fortunately for the Athenian philosophers that heard Paul's presentation of the Gospel, and for those of us today who can read Luke's brief account of it, Paul was both highly-educated and rhetorically-able to state his case among the best minds of that particular time and place. Even though many of us who read this passage in Acts may be inclined to think that Paul was "out of his league," that was not the case at all.

Before Paul was known as the Apostle Paul, he was first known as Saul of Tarsus, revealing to us the city of his birth (Acts 22:3). Tarsus was well-known in antiquity as being a major center of education, especially in philosophy in general and Stoic philosophy in particular.[171] In fact, Tarsus was one of three major cities known for the study of philosophy and rhetoric, the other two being Athens and Alexandria. Yet it was commonly held that Tarsus surpassed even Athens and Alexandria in this regard.[172] As a Roman citizen (Acts 22:22-29), Paul may very well have been privileged enough to have taken advantage of some of these educational opportunities and may have known far more about the Epicurean and Stoic philosophies than we realize. Perhaps this extensive education was part of God's plan to have Paul become the apostle to the Gentiles (Romans 11:13).[173]

When Paul wandered through the marketplace, he would have encountered a religiously diverse population, with some formally trained in philosophy. Almost all of the Athenians were unfamiliar with Christianity, therefore Paul had to be ready with an answer at all times (1 Peter 3:15). Fortunately, he almost certainly knew about worldviews other than Christian theism.

---

[171] John McRay, *Archaeology and the New Testament* (Grand Rapids, MI: Baker Academic, 1991), 234.
[172] J. Daryl Charles, "Engaging the (Neo) Pagan Mind: Paul's Encounter with Athenian Culture as a Model for Cultural Apologetics (Acts 17:16-34)." https://www.biblicalstudies.org.uk/pdf/athenian+charles.pdf
[173] Ibid.

CONFRONTING THE PHILOSOPHERS

In Athens, Paul found himself in the birthplace of philosophy, although the city was a shadow of its former glory: "Athens had become little more than a provincial city within the Roman empire, having lost much of its former glory and importance."[174] Whether or not Paul was familiar with the various philosophies beforehand, he definitely encountered them in a direct way during his time in Athens:

> *A group of Epicurean and Stoic philosophers began to debate with him. Some of them asked, "What is this babbler trying to say?" Others remarked, "He seems to be advocating foreign gods." They said this because Paul was preaching the good news about Jesus and the resurrection (Acts 17:18).*

The term "babbler" means "an intellectual plagiarist,"[175] therefore Paul was not held in high esteem by everyone in attendance. To better understand the concept of competing worldviews in the context of evangelism, it is important to examine the belief systems of both the Epicurean and Stoic philosophers, as more than a few analogies may be made between these ancient schools of philosophy and some modern religious ideas.

The Epicureans

The Epicurean philosophy, which was founded by the Greek thinker Epicurus in the fourth century BC, sought to establish a system of thinking that was more religious in nature, rather than purely logical-rational. In fact, Epicurus provided his followers with the opportunity to engage in a religious-type fellowship with other like-minded adherents.

Epicurus founded his philosophy upon the atomic theory of Democritus, another great thinker who lived a century earlier. Atomic theory states that the universe consists of atoms

---

[174] Alister E. McGrath, *Mere Apologetics* (Grand Rapids, MI: Baker Books, 2012), 63.
[175] Douglas Groothuis, *Christian Apologetics: A Comprehensive Case for Biblical Faith* (Downers Grove, IL: IVP Academic, 2011), 35.

which are eternal and constantly forming new combinations, giving rise to new forms over time. These new combinations of atoms are due to chance, in which atoms fall through infinite space and blindly interact with one another. This is sort of a "cosmic" version of naturalistic evolution. According to the Epicureans, even the gods and the soul within each human being are ultimately constructed of atoms.[176] Therefore, for the Epicurean matter is what constituted ultimate reality.

Epicureans considered the gods to be insignificant, as they were unconcerned with the affairs of men.[177] As a result, the Epicureans were essentially a strange combination of atheism and a polytheistic version of deism.[178] This philosophy is, in some ways, similar to many forms of Buddhism, which, interestingly enough, may have already made its way to the Mediterranean world by the time of Paul. Many Buddhist practitioners are functionally atheistic, maintaining that the existence of God is of no concern regarding the achievement of "spiritual enlightenment" since the only person who can save oneself is one's own self. Yet many of these same Buddhists believe in the existence of a vast array of spirit beings who may assist humanity in its pursuit of "nirvana," which is the Eastern version of Paradise. Therefore, if Epicureans have a modern counterpart, it's Buddhism – although Buddhism is certainly anything but modern.

The Epicureans held to a view of reality that is light years apart from the truth of Christian theism, in which the one true Creator of everything visible and invisible (Colossians 1:16) is intimately concerned for the well-being of his creation, even to the point of ultimate sacrifice for it (John 3:16). In order to proclaim the biblical worldview to this group of

---

[176] Ibid.
[177] Rick Wade, "The World of the Apostle Paul." http://www.leaderu.com/orgs/probe/docs/apospaul.html
[178] Epicureanism is atheistic in that only the material universe exists, and it is poly-deistic in that the many gods (*poly* meaning "many") were "out there somewhere," aloof and unconcerned with the affairs of men. Of course, this is much different than the usual Greek idea of the gods being intimately concerned with the affairs of men and women.

serious thinkers, Paul will first need to lay the foundation of creation out of nothing.

The Stoics

Unlike the Epicureans, the Stoics were pantheists[179] who regarded God as being the "Word-soul."[180] The Word-soul is the *Logos*, which is the Greek term used by John to describe the incarnate Christ (John 1:1-3). The Stoics held the *Logos* to be the rational discernment principle not only of the universe – the "Mind" inherent in the fabric of the cosmos – but also the rational, reasoning mind within every human being, which is an extension of the greater "Mind." Needless to say, the Stoics sought to live by reasoning.

Although the Stoics shared with Paul a belief in the Creator, their Creator was worlds apart from the Creator declared by Paul. The god of pantheism is nothing more than the embodiment of the laws of nature, and the Stoics, like all pantheists, confused the creation with the Creator (Romans 1:25). Paul, representing the one true God of the universe, proclaimed the God who is distinct from the universe, and who created everything from nothing.

Stoicism has modern philosophical connections to many of the Eastern religions as well as New Age spirituality in the West, and their postmodern, relativistic attitude to religious faith presents a daunting task to the modern Christian. As with the Epicurean philosophers, Paul will need to first share creation out of nothing before laying the foundation of the

---

[179] James Sire, *Why Good Arguments Often Fail* (Downers Grove, IL: InterVarsity Press, 2006), 134-137. It should be noted that some scholars classify the Stoics as panentheists, rather than pantheists. Whereas pantheists declare that God and the universe are exactly one and the same – confusing the creation with the Creator (Romans 1:25) – panentheists view the material universe as being the "body" of God, while the Divine Mind of God (*Logos* in Greek) is the principle of rational order and logic that extends beyond the material universe.

[180] Alida Leni Sewell, "Paul at Athens: An Examination of His Areopagus Address in the Light of its Historical and Philosophical Background." http://www.freewebs.com/reformationalphilosophy/Sewell/Acts17.pdf

redemptive message of Christ, which his audience most likely knows very little, if anything, about.

PAUL AND THE BIBLICAL WORLDVIEW

Both groups of philosophers would have needed a crash course in creation-sin-redemption before they could contemplate the truth of Christ. Unlike Peter in his speech at Pentecost (Acts 2:14-41), Paul first had to establish the case for the existence of a personal Creator-God who is distinct from the universe, and intimately concerned for the affairs of human beings. In doing this, he effectively refuted the scientific materialism, polytheistic deism, and pantheism that collectively formed the philosophical background of the Athenian philosophers. Could Paul do this using Scripture, or would he need to address this elite crowd in a manner that relied more upon general revelation? Paul first emphasized general revelation, while later working biblical doctrines into his presentation as he shared the more direct Christian beliefs of sin and redemption near the end of his speech.

CREATION EVANGELISM

Without the foundation of the one true Creator, non-Christians of all stripes can never really understand the Gospel:

> *A gospel without the message of the Creator, and the origin of sin and death, is a gospel* without the foundational knowledge *that is necessary to understand the rest of the gospel. Without this information – who then is Jesus Christ? Why did He need to die? Where did sin come from? Why can we say that all have sinned? Why do we die?*[181]

As noted above, one can never grasp the basic tenets of Christianity, such as the origin of sin and death, the need for redemption, and the restoration of all things, without first coming to know God as the transcendent Creator of every-

---

[181] Ken Ham, "Evangelism for the New Millenium." https://www.answersingenesis.org/gospel/evangelism-for-the-new-millennium/

thing. With that foundation in place, which is built upon the early chapters of Genesis, one can then begin to see the need for Christ. Paul realizes this, and begins his Areopagus presentation "in the beginning," exactly where it needs to start.

PAUL AT THE "UNIVERSITY"

At the Areopagus, Paul encountered scholars who were very experienced in debate:

> *Then they took him and brought him to a meeting of the Areopagus, where they said to him, "May we know what this new teaching is that you are presenting? You are bringing some strange ideas to our ears, and we would like to know what they mean." (All the Athenians and the foreigners who lived there spent their time doing nothing but talking about and listening to the latest ideas) (Acts 17:19-21).*

In the Areopagus Paul would have encountered a diversity of worldviews, as he had previously found in the marketplace, but this time the individuals were more educated than the general populace, and they were experienced at listening to, and debating with, speakers from a variety of backgrounds. Perhaps we might think of this situation in which Paul found himself as being comparable to a modern-day Christian presenting the good news of Christ to a group of philosophy majors who were already well-read in their field of study. Like Christians today, Paul had to be aware of the different worldviews present, and he needed to be ready to handle these worldviews effectively. He needed to be ready to deliver logically-sound and scripturally-based answers to those who were listening to his presentation, just as we do today.

PAUL'S GOSPEL PRESENTATION

Although Paul's presentation of the Gospel to the learned elite is truly one of the greatest examples of apologetics recorded in all of Scripture, it is likely that Luke gave us only a summary of Paul's presentation to these Athenian philosophers.[182] Following is commentary on each of the verses in this passage of Scripture, in the context of evangelism in an opposing worldview framework.

INTRODUCTION TO THE ATHENIAN PHILOSOPHERS

It is well understood by public speakers that "first impressions mean everything." Paul, as an experienced speaker regarding religious matters, certainly knew the value in putting his best foot forward. Luke records for our benefit Paul's introductory remarks:

> Paul then stood up in the meeting of the Areopagus and said: "People of Athens! I see that in every way you are very religious. For as I walked around and looked carefully at your objects of worship, I even found an altar with this inscription: to an unknown god. So you are ignorant of the very thing you worship – and this is what I am going to proclaim to you" (Acts 17:22-23).

Paul was almost certainly not insulting those present in the Areopagus, and we can assume that he always strove to proclaim the Gospel with respect. Peter urged all followers of Christ to share their faith "with gentleness and respect" (1 Peter 3:15), and Paul certainly would have spoken with respect for his audience as well. Paul did not alienate and drive away his listeners before he had a chance to proclaim the good news of Christ to them, but instead capitalized on their shared interest in spiritual matters when he noted that they were "very religious." This was not a slam against their religious pluralism, but rather it was Paul's way of connecting with their intense interest in all things spiritual. The Greek term *deisidaimonesterous* may not only be translated "very religious" or "extremely religious," but also as "somewhat superstitious,"[183] rendering the term somewhere between "re-

---

[182] Alida Leni Sewell, "Paul at Athens: An Examination of His Areopagus Address in the Light of its Historical and Philosophical Background." http://www.freewebs.com/reformationalphilosophy/Sewell/Acts17.pdf
[183] Ron Vince, "At the Areopagus (Acts 17:22-31): Pauline Apologetics and Lucan Rhetoric." http://www.mcmaster.ca/mjtm/4-5.htm

ligious" and "superstitious." Although "superstitious" carries negative connotations today, we may assume that Paul would not want to offend his listeners so close to the beginning of his presentation, before he had a chance to truly connect with them. Then again, we must acknowledge that the term "superstitious" may not have been such a pejorative term to the Athenians of Paul's time as it is to us today. Paul then captures the interest of his audience by stating that he is going to proclaim to them the identity of their "unknown god," who is, according to Paul, the God of the Bible. Paul makes this connection for the benefit of his non-Christian audience.

PAUL'S APPEAL TO CREATION

Paul, knowing that his audience is confused regarding origins, begins with creation. "The God who made the world and everything in it is the Lord of heaven and earth and does not live in temples built by human hands" (Acts 17:24). Creation is often an ideal starting point when engaging those of non-Christian worldviews, and Paul's audience in particular necessitated that he begin with this basic foundation. "The Epicureans would deny that God, or the gods, created the universe. The Stoics would believe in a Creator, but not a transcendent one. Their beliefs were pantheistic."[184] Therefore, beginning at creation was foundational to Paul's strategy for sharing the message of Christ with this academically-elite audience. Before they could even begin to grasp the concept of Christ as the resurrected Redeemer of fallen humanity, these philosophers first needed to understand the concept of a personal Creator-God. "An appeal to God as creator thus becomes a channel for introducing the theme of redemption in Christ."[185]

There is a very strong connection between Romans 1 and

---

[184] Alida Leni Sewell, "Paul at Athens: An Examination of His Areopagus Address in the Light of its Historical and Philosophical Background." http://www.freewebs.com/reformationalphilosophy/Sewell/Acts17.pdf

[185] Alister E. McGrath, *Mere Apologetics* (Grand Rapids, MI: Baker Books, 2012), 64.

Acts 17: Both chapters have "the function of pointing to human accountability."[186] Even though the Athenians have not yet heard of Christ, and find the concept of sin atonement to be strange, they nonetheless do possess the ability to understand that nature is not an accident (Romans 1:20) and they also have a moral conscience that pervades their thought lives, if not their actions (Romans 2:14-15). Therefore, Paul is able to lay the foundation of Christianity with creation and the inherent moral accountability of all people, knowing that his audience will be able to understand these issues and, hopefully, as a result grasp the more difficult Christian concepts later in his speech.

Athens boasted many grand temples, most dedicated to a Greek god or goddess, but Paul informed his listeners that God is not confined to buildings built by human hands. This idea was foreign to the Greek mind, however, as they were steeped in a polytheism that dedicated numerous temples to the gods as places for them to reside. Paul, as a Jewish Christian, recognizes that temples are constructed out of respect and worship of God, but do not *contain* God in any way. Even Solomon, the builder of the first great Jewish temple, declared that the temple could not contain the Creator (1 Kings 8:27), something that Stephen reiterated as well (Acts 7:48).

In opposition to the gods of Greece, Paul makes it clear that the one true God of the universe does not need to be served like a proud emperor. "And he is not served by human hands, as if he needed anything. Rather, he himself gives everyone life and breath and everything else" (Acts 17:25). God is independent and does not require anything from humanity for his existence. Certainly God is pleased when humanity offers true worship, but God does not *need* this worship for his existence, for God alone is self-existent. In comparison, the Greek gods thrived on human worship.

---

[186] J. Daryl Charles, "Engaging the (Neo) Pagan Mind: Paul's Encounter with Athenian Culture as a Model for Cultural Apologetics (Acts 17:16-34)." https://www.biblicalstudies.org.uk/pdf/athenian+charles.pdf

By stating that God "gives life and breath and everything else," Paul was stressing God's role not only as Creator, but as Sustainer of everything. This is a concept that was foreign to the Epicureans, with their polytheistic version of deism. The Stoics were much more comfortable with the idea of a god who sustains the creation, but their sense of creationism was purely pantheistic – the universe itself, and everything in it, merely emanated from the impersonal god of pantheism. Paul is using "creation apologetics" in an attempt to persuade his listeners to consider the worldview that he is espousing.

Paul then stresses the sovereignty of God in human history. "From one man he made all the nations, that they should inhabit the whole earth; and he marked out their appointed times in history and the boundaries of their lands" (Acts 17:26). Although the Jews and Christians of the time would have thought of Adam when Paul referred to the "one man" from which all others are descended, the idea of a single man as the progenitor of the human race was a foreign concept to the Greeks, who viewed people as being the physical offspring of a variety of gods who came to the earth in the distant past. Additionally, the notion that there is a sole, supreme Creator-God who watches over our lives, and even places us in the exact time and place that we should live, was a radical idea for the Greeks, whose worldview emphasized chance.

By proclaiming the unity of the human race, Paul implies that all people are equal, at least in the sense that all people are created in the image of God (Genesis 1:27). This was a major stumbling block for the Greeks, as they thought of themselves as being superior to other people groups, perhaps on account of their great accomplishments in philosophy and civics. Both groups of philosophers tended to attract the learned elites of their culture, so this was likely shocking to hear from Paul. However, unity and equality are a major message of Pauline theology (Galatians 3:28). Paul must firmly establish this point if he is to be successful at presenting the Gospel. It may be that many of those in attendance who scoffed at Paul did so because of this difficult teaching.

The various worldviews represented in the Areopagus on this day would have come into serious conflict with Paul's Christian theism.

THE GOD WHO PURSUES US

Paul then addresses humanity's need for God. "God did this so that they would seek him and perhaps reach out for him and find him, though he is not far from any one of us" (Acts 17:27). Perhaps Paul is stressing the free will component of salvation, pointing out to his audience that humans must play some part, however extensive or limited that may be, in "reaching out" to God. Once again, the Athenians would have found this to be a difficult concept to grasp. "In the minds of the Athenians, this immanence [of God] had more to do with a pantheistic closeness rather than a relational closeness such as can be experienced by becoming children of God."[187]

ESTABLISHING A CONNECTION POINT

Paul finds a cultural connection point with his audience by quoting from two of their own beloved poets. "'For in him we live and move and have our being.' As some of your own poets have said, 'We are his offspring'" (Acts 17:28). The first quote that Paul references – "For in him we live and move and have our being" – is from Epimenides, and is Paul's reminder that because God is the Creator and Sustainer of everything, we are never far from God. "We are his offspring," the second quote from Aratus, reminds Paul's listeners that it is erroneous to conceive of God as being anything other than personal. Material idols and altars housed in temples can never do justice to the one true God of the universe, who seeks a personal relationship with people. We are God's offspring, and therefore we are Created in God's own image (Genesis 1:27). To conceive of God as being distant

---

[187] Alida Leni Sewell, "Paul at Athens: An Examination of His Areopagus Address in the Light of its Historical and Philosophical Background."
http://www.freewebs.com/reformationalphilosophy/Sewell/Acts17.pdf

and aloof, as the Epicureans would have, or as being a Divine Flame (Force), as the Stoics did, is to commit a massive error. God is personal, and Paul wanted to forcefully drive home this foundational tenet of the biblical worldview.

Paul is not trying to "Christianize" these poets, but he does utilize the Athenian's familiarity with their writings to stress that God is the Creator and Sustainer of humanity in a very personal way for them. Sometimes an appeal to a common interest can lighten the stress of a worldview confrontation and put the non-Christian at ease. However, it must be noted that a point of common interest is not the same as common ground, since there is little, if any, theological common ground between the biblical and the non-biblical worldviews, and there is definitely no "neutral" ground whatsoever (Matthew 12:30; Romans 8:7; James 4:4).

THE NEED FOR REPENTANCE

Although it is a touchy subject in our modern society of religious skepticism, Paul does not omit the need for repentance in this encounter:

Therefore since we are God's offspring, we should not think that the divine being is like gold or silver or stone – an image made by human design and skill. In the past God overlooked such ignorance, but now he commands all people everywhere to repent (Acts 17:29-30).

Paul addresses the problem of idol worship head-on, yet he skillfully does so by tying this matter together with the Athenian poet's declaration that we are God's offspring. Paul bluntly points out that idol worship was committed out of ignorance in the past, but now all people must repent and enter into a correct relationship with God. That statement had to bruise more than a few egos, but repentance is an issue which cannot be skirted beyond a certain point – and Paul is at that point in his Gospel address. This is likely when he was beginning to lose the close-minded and hardhearted among his audience. This is always a potential problem when sharing the Christian faith across worldviews. Sometimes the initial proclamation of the Gospel may be too much for a non-Christian to absorb in one encounter.

THE NEED FOR THE REDEEMER

After having laid the foundation for the biblical worldview and the need for repentance, Paul then emphatically states his audience's need for Christ, the one and only Redeemer of fallen humanity. "For he has set a day when he will judge the world with justice by the man he has appointed. He has given proof of this to everyone by raising him from the dead" (Acts 17:31). The Jewish-Christian tradition speaks very strongly of a coming Judgment Day predetermined by God himself, in which the Messiah or "anointed one" will judge the entirety of human history. Divine judgment is often a bitter pill to swallow, so this was surely a difficult concept for Paul's Greek audience.

Some have pointed out a possible deficiency in Paul's Athenian presentation of the Gospel: Paul does not explain why and how Jesus had to live and die in the first place. But did Paul really fail to thoroughly explain the Christian message? Paul's Athenian address was almost certainly an edited version of what was actually said, rather than a complete word-for-word account of his presentation. In the Areopagus, the crowd would have insisted upon a complete presentation of any new idea, and there would have been an exchange between Paul and his audience, to give them a chance to thoroughly understand this new idea being presented.

Paul's presentation of the Gospel at Athens moves "from the nature of the true God to our responsibility as those beings who are morally answerable to him, and finally to the need for particular salvation through a human Judge who has risen from the dead."[188] Therefore, Paul addressed the foundational issues of God and creation, morality and ethics, salvation and the afterlife, and the end-times, in that order. This

---

[188] R.K. McGregor Wright, "Paul's Purpose at Athens and the Problem of 'Common Ground.'" http://www.vantil.info/articles/rkmw_ppaa.pdf

was surely no accident. Paul had a plan concerning his formal presentation of the Christian message, and he did not falter.

RESPONSE & REACTION

As is almost always the case, evangelistic encounters will end with both skepticism and conversion:

> *When they heard about the resurrection of the dead, some of them sneered, but others said, "We want to hear you again on this subject." At that, Paul left the Council. Some of the people became followers of Paul and believed. Among them was Dionysius, a member of the Areopagus, also a woman named Damaris, and a number of others (Acts 17:32-34).*

Two interesting points should be mentioned concerning these final verses. First, although the Greeks were concerned with the immortality of the soul, they vehemently denied bodily resurrection. This idea would have simultaneously bothered and intrigued these thinkers, as the physical body was generally considered to be the "prison house of the soul," and death was the only way to release the soul from that bondage. The Epicureans held that life ended with death, so bodily resurrection was an absurd notion for them (as was spiritual resurrection), while the pantheistic Stoics were doubtless confounded by Paul's teaching on Christian resurrection as well. Although they likely understood the concept of a transcendent Creator, this distinctly Christian concept of bodily resurrection would have been shocking to these philosophers.

Second, one criticism often leveled at Paul's speech in Athens is that it omitted the cross from the message. Once again, we must remember that what Luke recorded for our benefit is without doubt not the complete speech actually given:

> *Acts only gives us a summary of Paul's speech; he would have spoken far longer than the written text permits. So, we can be sure that Paul explained the full meaning of Jesus'*

life, death and resurrection.[189]

Perhaps it is possible that, due to difficulties that Paul may have encountered with these philosophers, he could have been significantly interrupted before he could expound upon the meaning of the cross. It can be said with great certainty, however, that if Paul had opened his speech with the message of the cross – and thereby omitted the reason for, and the necessity of, the cross – he likely would have been met with much more confusion and sheer skepticism than he was.

PAUL'S APPROACH IN ATHENS

In Athens Paul utilized a three-step approach to sharing his faith across worldviews.[190] First, Paul initially sought to contrast the Hellenistic worldview with that of Scripture. Rather than seeking neutral ground – which Scripture informs us does not exist – Paul tells his audience point blank, and in no uncertain terms, that the two worldviews are in stark contrast to one another. Essentially, Paul is preparing them to make a choice: Accept the biblical worldview, or continue on the path of falsehood. The situation is no different today.

Second, Paul drives home the point that every person must either align with God's will, or continue to be opposed to it. "The issue is sin and this can only be addressed by changing one's mind about the ultimate ethical reference-point, which is God in Christ as Judge."[191] Paul was warning his audience that they can accept Christ now, as Judge and Savior, or come face-to-face with Christ after this life – as Judge only. Once again, the situation is no different today.

Lastly, Paul laid out the chronology of the biblical worldview for his listeners. The Creator of everything became a man, who defeated sin and death through his sacrifi-

---

[189] Douglas Groothuis, *Christian Apologetics: A Comprehensive Case for Biblical Faith* (Downers Grove, IL: IVP Academic, 2011), 36-37.
[190] R.K. McGregor Wright, "Paul's Purpose at Athens and the Problem of 'Common Ground.'" http://www.vantil.info/articles/rkmw_ppaa.pdf
[191] Ibid.

cial atonement for this fallen world, and he will judge the world that he loves so much. This is light years apart from any version of the Greek worldview. In this regard, the Seven C's helps to make sense of the world we live in.[192] The Seven C's are, in order, (1) Creation, (2) Curse, (3) Catastrophe, (4) Confusion, (5) Christ, (6) Cross, and (7) Consummation, and each of these events from history tells the story of why Christ is the only true Savior of the world. The "Case for a Creator" is a great way to begin sharing the faith with both seekers and skeptics, as it solidifies the foundation for belief in the one true God of the universe. However, as magnificent as the creation is, it is apparent that not all is well with the world, and this is due to the effects of God's curse upon the world at the time of the rebellion, which directs us to the need for the cure: Christ. (Both the catastrophe of Noah's Flood and the scattering of people groups at Babel due to the confusion of language can be worked into a conversation with a seeker or skeptic, depending upon how interested he or she may be in the early history of the world. Both events help to further solidify the accuracy of the beginning chapters of Genesis.) Christ's atoning for the sins of the world upon the cross is what has reconciled fallen humanity to the holy God who is revealed throughout Scripture. Finally, God will fashion a new heaven and a new earth one day, which we cannot even begin to imagine. This will be a world in which there is no pain or death, and everyone in his or her right mind will want to be a part of it – and hence the need for salvation through Christ. Although Paul would not have used the Seven C's in the exact same manner as would a modern apologist, he essentially did employ this evangelistic technique in Athens as he began with creation and then moved into the need for Christ's gift of salvation, covering repentance and judgment along the way. Since we almost certainly do not have the complete message spoken to the Areopagus, it is possible that Paul addressed many, if not all,

---

[192] Ken Ham & Stacia McKeever, "Seven C's of History." https://answersingenesis.org/bible-history/seven-cs-of-history/

of the Seven C's.

Ultimately, the motivation for Paul in his Areopagus address was to see the pagan elites come to a saving relationship with the one true God of the universe. This was not merely an academic exercise in comparative philosophy, pitting the biblical and Greek worldviews against each other. Granted, very few in the time of the very early church could have engaged the Greek philosophers as effectively as Paul did.[193] He possessed the ultimate combination of innate intelligence and philosophical-religious education, yet ultimately it was the pastoral side of Paul – his heart for the lost – that shown the brightest in Athens. Paul's greatest apologetic tool was his love for people, not the impressive intellectual gifts that God had bestowed upon him. We all would do well to follow his shining example.

No matter what one believes about Paul's approach and content regarding this speech, there will always be some speculation involved, and we can never successfully argue a point that is lacking in evidence. In the end, the speech that we have is what we have, and Paul's Athenian address serves as the primary example of how to witness before an audience of well-educated non-Christians, both seekers and skeptics. This formal presentation of the Gospel by Paul, as recorded by Luke for our great benefit, is truly "evangelism across worldviews."

HOW OTHERS MIGHT HAVE DONE

How would some later Christian philosophers have done if they had been in Paul's place at the Areopagus? Although we can say with confidence that not all of them would have approached the Athenian crowd in the same way, let's examine how two of them – Soren Kierkegaard and Augustine – might have done. Kierkegaard, the early nineteenth century Christian existentialist, represents the mystical approach to sharing the Gospel, elevating faith far above reason. Kierke-

---

[193] Although Stephen, Apollos, and even Sergius Paulus would have been very effective apologists to the educated Gentiles of their day.

gaard would have approached this educated Athenian crowd with one primary goal in mind: Let them know that God is infinitely beyond human logic and reasoning, and can only be truly known through a total emotional and spiritual commitment to the Lord. He might even have borrowed a phrase from his philosophical predecessor Blaise Pascal: "The heart has its reasons of which reason knows nothing." Kierkegaard would bypass the logical deductions that the Greeks thrived on, and if there were a question and answer session after the formal presentation he would insist that everyone present make a leap of faith and accept Christ without regard to those sticky questions that sometimes act as stumbling blocks to the faith.

But how would this approach to evangelism have worked on the philosophical elites of Athens in the first century? Probably not so well. Athens was the birthplace of Western philosophy, and although there had been a long tradition of recognizing the place of emotions and intuitions within the Greek worldview, as a culture they thrived on logic and reasoning, and they would have wanted to engage with Kierkegaard on this level. Therefore, the Athenians would have been disappointed that their guest presenter was less than enthusiastic about diving into the intricacies of an apologetic conversation.

However, many today are quick to point out that we live in a postmodern culture where logic and reasoning is not the supreme source of knowing about anything, so maybe Kierkegaard's approach to sharing the faith would work just fine in our day. However, I'm convinced that, regardless of the current state of religious relativism that dominates Western society, there are still many people who need answers to the questions that block their path to salvation in Christ – and Kierkegaard's approach simply does not go there.

Augustine is generally considered to be the greatest Christian philosopher and theologian of the first millennium of the church age, if not the greatest mind since the Apostle Paul himself. Augustine would have been troubled by the Athenian philosophers' reliance upon the authority of man's words

– namely, their various schools of philosophy – rather than God's supremely authoritative words in Scripture, which they did not know. I suspect that Augustine would have spent the entirety of the evening prior to his formal presentation praying for God's Spirit to open the hearts and minds of those who would be in attendance the next day, for without this supernatural act of grace not one of his listeners could even begin to fathom the deep riches of the Christian message. Augustine would have insisted that his audience first accept Christ as their Lord and Savior, so that the deep questions of the spiritual life would have a chance of being answered satisfactorily. Augustine's motto was "faith seeking understanding," which is the opposite of how the world today thinks. Despite this approach to sharing the faith, however, Augustine would have fully engaged the crowd in the rational evidences for the faith, and they would have been richly blessed by it, for Augustine was no stranger to traditional apologetics. Augustine would have constantly prayed for the salvation of his listeners, all the while alternating between encouraging the Athenians to believe in order to understand and supplying them with rational evidences for the faith. Like Paul, Augustine almost certainly would have been successful in Athens.

CAN WE BE LIKE PAUL?

The account of Paul in Athens, as found in Acts 17:16-34, is truly a template for sharing the message of Christian salvation with people who adhere to non-Christian worldviews. Paul sharing his faith with the philosophers at the Areopagus would be no different from a preeminent Christian philosopher today speaking before a college or university crowd composed of both atheists (Epicureans) and "New Age" mystics (Stoics). Rather than assuming that the audience has a clue as to what Christianity is really all about, this modern evangelist would take the time to first drive home the point that the Creator of the heavens and the earth is the one supreme God over all of reality, far beyond yet intimately concerned for his creation. He or she would then work through the effects of Adam's fall to the need for repentance and salvation in the only one who can serve as the mediator between sinful man and the holy God: Jesus Christ. In short, this modern-day Paul would begin where we should all begin when sharing the faith with an unbeliever – at the beginning – and then he or she must thoroughly explain why the world, and every individual person who has ever lived in it, is in the condition that we observe today. Lastly, the most important point of all – the need for Christ – concludes the message of Christian hope.

Although not every believer would share the Gospel the same way, we should always be mindful of the fact that the unregenerate mind is incapable of truly understanding spiritual matters,[194] so we must constantly appeal to the grace of God in this matter and, while always being ready to give an answer (1 Peter 3:15), we must be constantly aware of the limitations of fallen man. Rather than focusing on one or even a few lines of evidence for the Christian faith, we must always demonstrate that only the Christian worldview in its entirety best explains the reality of the world we live in. In short, the "Case for Christ" is a comprehensive one, never leaning too heavily on any one evidence by itself. Evangelism always takes place at the level of worldview, not at the level of individual evidences.

So, when it comes to sharing our faith with others, can we be like Paul in Athens? The short answer is, Why not? Paul has already provided us with an approach that works. It may just take a little bit of practice on our part.

---

[194] Although it can be said with great certainty that every Christian believer who has ever lived has had at least one nagging question that always remained baffling!

Chapter 9

ONE LAST CHALLENGE TO THE FAITH

At this point, a brief review of the preceding eight chapters is in order. In chapter one we examined the beliefs behind the four most prominent worldviews today, those four being Christian theism, atheism, pantheism, and deism. If you ask ten theologians to name the most prominent worldviews today, you'll likely get ten different lists, but I'm convinced that every religion or philosophy can ultimately fit under the umbrella of one of these four worldviews. If Christians are going to take the message of Christ to the world (Matthew 28:16-20), it is best that they are first armed with at least a little knowledge concerning the beliefs of non-Christians. A theologically capable Christian can make a better case for his or her faith.

In chapter two we examined philosophical and scientific evidences that point us toward the existence of a personal Creator-God, namely the evidences from cause-and-effect, design, and the powerful correlation between science and Scripture. Not every one of these evidences will be convincing for everyone, of course. For example, James Sire has noted that the evidence from cause-and-effect has not been particularly useful for him,[195] whereas I became convinced of the existence of God (which later led to an acceptance of Christ as Lord and Savior) in large part because of this particular line of evidence. At the conclusion of chapter two it may be argued that, at the very least, a substantial case was made for the existence of a personal Creator-God, thereby refuting the atheistic and pantheistic worldviews, and seriously challenging the deistic position as well.

In chapter three we examined evidences for the God of the Bible that are based on the human experience, such as the

---

[195] James Sire, *Apologetics Beyond Reason* (Downers Grove, IL: IVP Academic, 2014), 17.

evidence from morality, the dual nature of humanity, aesthetics, human thought, meaning and purpose in life, the enduring belief in the afterlife, and the power of religious experience. Then in chapters four, five, and six we examined the "Case for Christ," as based upon fulfilled messianic prophecy, a refutation of the Jesus myth hypothesis, the evidence for both the Jesus of history and the Christ of faith, and the reliability of the biblical record. By the conclusion of chapter six an overwhelming case was made for the Christian faith, beginning with the evidence for a personal Creator-God and then working deeper toward the understanding that God is most fully known to us in the person of Jesus Christ. Along the way the worldviews of atheism, pantheism, and deism were severely challenged.

In chapter seven we examined the relationship between faith and reason. Many skeptics of Christianity are quick to proclaim that the way of Christ is nothing more than a blind faith based upon an archaic collection of writings, which has no room for the use of logic and reason. However, of the four relationships between faith and reason that were discussed in this chapter, only the positive integration of faith and reason provides for a healthy worldview.

Finally, in chapter eight we examined the apologetic model of Paul in Athens, which is still the preeminent case study available to Christian believers when considering how to best share their faith with those from different worldviews. When putting together the "Case for Christianity" as found in this book, I followed Paul's approach by beginning with creation and natural revelation, and then working toward the evidence for the Christ of faith.

In our examination of Christianity among the dominant worldviews, I have made every attempt to be both thorough and methodical, but something important has so far escaped discussion – and it needs to be addressed. When in dialogue with deists, pantheists, and especially atheists, the problem of how a good and loving God could allow for so much suffering in the world will be an issue that always comes up, and for good reason: All people wrestle with this theological dilemma. It may very well be the number one objection to the Christian faith that is posed by skeptics of all stripes.

THE PROBLEM OF SUFFERING

For me personally, the problem of suffering is perhaps the most serious objection against the Christian faith today. That's how I felt about it when I was a skeptic, and I still recognize this conundrum as being a serious challenge to my faith today. I'm just being honest about it. Atheists, agnostics, and skeptics of all stripes are quick to say, "If God exists he would have done something about the problem of suffering. Since nothing has been done about it, God therefore does not exist." Other skeptics have come to the conclusion that if God does exist he does not care about suffering, or maybe he is powerless to do anything about it. None of those options are good, of course.

When examining the problem of suffering, the word "theodicy" will often present itself. Theodicy is derived from two Greek words: *theos*, meaning "God" and *dikei*, meaning "justice." Therefore, "a theodicy is a justification of the ways of God given all the evil and suffering that exists in the world."[196] The concept of theodicy, which is attributed to the philosopher Gottfried von Leibniz (1646-1716) in his book *The Theodicy*,[197] is of utmost importance as all people, regardless of their worldview, wrestle with the problem of suffering.[198] The atheist explains the problem away by insisting that there is no God, the deist accounts for suffering by arguing that God is simply not concerned with the affairs of human beings, and the pantheist argues that suffering is an illusion, or that it somehow fits into the scheme of karma and reincarnation. It is the Christian, however, who seems expected to shoulder the burden of providing a reasonable the-

---

[196] Chad Meister, *Building Belief: Constructing Faith from the Ground Up* (Grand Rapids, MI: Baker Books, 2006), 122.
[197] Erwin Lutzer, *Where Was God?* (Carol Stream, IL: Tyndale House Publishers, Inc., 2006), 7.
[198] Paul Copan, *That's Just Your Interpretation* (Grand Rapids, MI: Baker Books, 2001), 91.

odicy. The Christian knows that God exists (Romans 1:20), that his revealed words in Scripture demonstrate that he is very interested in the affairs of humanity (2 Timothy 3:16-17), that suffering and evil is not an illusion (John 20:27), and that reincarnation is a false belief (Hebrews 9:27-28). Yet, accounting for all of these truths, the Christian must explain how a good and loving God, as clearly revealed in John 3:16, can be reconciled with a world filled with suffering.[199]

THE PROBLEM OF SUFFERING: R.C. SPROUL

In response to the question, "Why is there suffering?" apologist R.C. Sproul listed five possible approaches: Docetism, Stoicism, Epicureanism, Existentialism, and Judeo-Christianity.[200] Docetism is a variation of Gnosticism[201] that denies not only the full reality of Jesus' human nature but also the full reality of the physical creation itself. For the Docetist only the spiritual realm is real while the material universe and everything in it is nothing more than an illusion. Therefore, one should make every attempt to keep in mind that suffering is not real, and hopefully that will be enough to get a person through a difficult time in which he or she is suffering. This is the illusory-pantheistic position, as previously described. In our modern world, this approach

---

[199] I do not wish to imply that this world is only filled with sorrow, but rather I recognize that there is also goodness and beauty in the world as well. Although evil and the depravity of the human race is clearly real, we should not focus solely on this problem. I have encountered many Christians who seem to be concerned only with the wickedness of this world, and as a result of encountering their negative-only view I strive to avoid this one-sided thinking. Human beings are both fallen in nature (Genesis 3; Romans 3:23) and made in the image of God (Genesis 1:27). Both realities should be simultaneously acknowledged by Christian believers.

[200] R.C. Sproul, *Reason to Believe* (Grand Rapids, MI: Zondervan, 1978), 131-143.

[201] I am using the present tense when describing Docetism – as well as Stoicism and Epicureanism to follow – because these philosophies are not extinct, as some might maintain, but are still prevalent today even if the vast majority of modern-day Docetists, Stoics, and Epicureans are unfamiliar with these terms.

is held by followers of the Eastern religions, "New Age" practitioners, and followers of Christian Science.[202]

Stoicism maintains that everything which takes place in the material universe is the result of impersonal forces of nature over which we have no control. Therefore, the Stoic strives to control the only thing that we can control: Our response to the situation at hand. Through controlling the emotions to the point that nothing can disturb oneself, the Stoic seeks to deal with the problem of suffering through "mind over matter," which is quite simple, really: If one doesn't mind, then it won't matter. This is the scientific-pantheistic position, as previously described.

Although Sproul used the term Hedonism to describe the next approach, Epicureanism may be a better term, as he noted that the Epicureans refined the earlier and more blatant forms of hedonism.[203] This approach seeks to establish balance between pleasure and pain. If one is experiencing too much pain in life, the best thing to do is increase the amount of pleasure. As Sproul correctly analyzed, this approach is nothing more than escapism,[204] and is the approach to suffering that alcoholics and others with various addiction tendencies employ.

Existentialism, at least in its atheistic form, is generally marked by the idea that "life is absurd." The atheist philosopher Friedrich Nietzsche advocated the principle of "dialectical courage,"[205] which is the type of courage that manifests itself in the face of ultimate meaninglessness. Sproul declared the battle cry of atheistic existentialism: "Be of good cheer, for life is absurd."[206] This is another way of saying

---

[202] Interestingly, both Hinduism and Buddhism pre-date Docetism by several centuries. Since Buddhism had made its presence known in the Mediterranean region before the time of Christ, some might argue that Docetism developed as a result of Buddhism's influence.

[203] R.C. Sproul, *Reason to Believe* (Grand Rapids, MI: Zondervan, 1978), 133.

[204] Ibid.

[205] Ibid.

[206] Ibid.

that life has no meaning, so you might as well forget about your problems and forge ahead with this thing called life. Not surprisingly, this philosophy can lead to exaggerated forms of hedonism at one extreme, and suicide at the other.

In the end, Sproul noted that only the Judeo-Christian worldview can adequately make sense of the problem of suffering. Unlike adherents of the previously described philosophies, the Christian can state with confidence that (1) suffering is not an illusion, (2) impersonal forces of nature do not account for what happens in our lives, (3) pleasure-seeking does not negate or ease in any meaningful way the difficulties in our lives, and (4) life is not absurd and meaningless, but rather life is a gift from God and has been instilled with meaning in this life as well as hope for the eternal life to come. We obviously live in a created world (Romans 1:20), yet it is also obvious that as a race we are fallen in nature and have chosen to rebel against God (Romans 3:23), and hence the sad state of affairs that we witness daily in our lives. We will do well to always temper the knowledge of being created in God's image with the knowledge that we are fallen in nature and therefore self-centered rather than God-centered.

THE PROBLEM OF SUFFERING: C.S. LEWIS

C.S. Lewis was almost without a doubt the most influential apologist of the twentieth century. Lewis developed a three-pronged approach to addressing the problem of suffering in his classic treatise *The Problem of Pain*. For Lewis, the biblical approach involved the free will theodicy, the soul-making theodicy, and the natural law theodicy, with all three approaches being complimentary to one another.

Free Will Theodicy

Also referred to as the free will defense, this approach to the problem of suffering is perhaps the most commonly appealed to by Christians. God created thinking beings endowed with the ability to make choices for both good and evil. Although it is preferable to make choices which promote goodness, as this is in the best interests of everyone, thinking beings are truly free only if they are capable of decision-making without limitations. If God created beings without the ability to make choices, these beings would not be truly free – they would be nothing more than spirit-infused robots. Love is possible only when choice is possible; one being can love another being only when he or she *chooses* to love. God could create beings capable only of making good choices which please him, but they would not be capable of truly loving God and others because they lack the ability to choose to love. Without choice, there is no such thing as free will.

The free will defense, therefore, rests on the foundation that the decisions which beings sometimes make are immoral and evil in nature – that is, they go against the goodness of God – and as a result of these decisions suffering is perpetuated in the world. The biblical explanation for the malevolent behavior of God's created beings originated within the angelic realm and spread to humanity in part due to the influence of Satan upon the first humans. History is a lesson in the fallen nature of humanity. The history of the human race is a continuous story of suffering, filled with immoral behavior directed against other people, animals, and even God himself.

Needless to say, there are some skeptical challenges to the free will defense. First is the problem of intervention. Although an individual may wish to engage in murder, torture, rape, and other heinous activities, others may oppose those actions. Therefore, life is often a contest of opposing free wills. Although this is deemed a challenge to the free will theodicy by some, I tend to think of this as supporting the next theodicy to be described: Maybe opposing a rapist is actually a soul-making (soul-building) endeavor.

Second, although free will is considered by most people to be a gift, the power to inflict harm upon others is almost always considered to be bad. Opponents of the free will defense may argue that free will would be best if the ability to inflict harm upon others was impossible. However, as already discussed, if that were the case people would not truly possess free will.

Third, much suffering is attributed to natural causes such as tornadoes, hurricanes, earthquakes, diseases, etc. These evils do not readily appear to be caused by immoral actions; they are, in fact, classified as natural evil.[207] The free will defense does not adequately account for natural disasters from the environment and biology, but this is not so much a refutation of the free will defense as it is a point to be noted. Scripture provides the answer to the problem of natural evil: The fall of mankind affected not only the moral condition of human beings, but the entirety of the creation itself, including the patterns of nature (Genesis 3:17-19; Romans 8:22).

Some Christians argue that much of the suffering in the world is caused directly by immoral supernatural beings (fallen angels). Although this is clearly supported by the entirety of Scripture, and perhaps best supported by the book of Job in particular, to say that all suffering is caused by Satan and his minions is assuming too much. No Christian should ever be like the "Church Lady" from Saturday Night Live, who constantly blamed everything bad on Satan. The consequences of the fall of mankind accounts for the lions' share of the moral failings of this world.

Soul-Making Theodicy

The soul-making theodicy was championed by the late John Hick, although its roots may be traced all the way back to the early Church Father Irenaeus in the second century.[208] This theodicy maintains that suffering exists for the purpose of exercising our ability to make proper moral choices and to teach us valuable lessons so as to build our moral character and bring us more in line with how God intended us to be. Only by struggling against the evils of this world can we develop ourselves to be more like Christ. As Christian philosopher Jim Spiegel notes, "Our trials and afflictions do serve a

---

[207] Ron Rhodes, *Why Do Bad Things Happen if God is Good?* (Eugene, OR: Harvest House Publishers, 2004), 22.
[208] Jim Spiegel, "Free Will and Soul-Making Theodicies." http://jimspiegel.com/articles/free-will-and-soul-making-theodicies/

good purpose, the betterment of our souls."[209] He goes on to say:

> What sense could be made of the trait of courage in a world in which there was no danger and nothing to fear? How could one show sympathy if there were no sorrow or affliction with which to sympathize? How might one forgive where there has been no offense? And how can one be said to "persevere" through perfectly pleasant circumstances? These characteristics – courage, sympathy, forgiveness, perseverance – are not just good traits. They are among the greatest of all character traits. And, according to Hick and other proponents of the soul-making theodicy, it is worth God's permitting evil in order to realize these goods.[210]

I like to think of the soul-making theodicy as the "character development program" instituted by God. Most Christians will be inclined to agree with Spiegel's statement, but nonetheless a significant difficulty with the soul-making theodicy must be addressed: How can the suffering that people undergo immediately prior to death contribute in any significant way toward a more righteous character? This is a formidable question. It is almost certain that in some cases this may be a step in the direction of salvation. I have seen more than a few people in my thirty years as a radiation therapist seek after God with all their might in their last days.

Natural Law Theodicy

The natural law theodicy rests upon the foundation "that in order for our choices to have real consequences, there must be a common nature [constant laws of nature] that surrounds us."[211] Art Lindsley, an apologist with the C.S. Lewis Institute, declares, "God could constantly intervene [upon the physical world] so that no evil consequences could follow from evil choices, but that would make the formation of

---

[209] Ibid.
[210] Ibid.
[211] Art Lindsley, "The Problem of Evil."
http://www.cslewisinstitute.org/webfm_send/636

character impossible."[212] He gives examples of how a wooden beam cannot be made as soft as grass when it is used as a weapon, since a person must suffer the consequences for harming another person, and also how the air cannot refuse to carry sound waves carrying the lies or insults of ill-tempered people, for these people must suffer the consequences of their intended slander.[213] The physical creation must remain constant, and cannot be modified to prevent suffering. He further states, "God could turn wooden beams into grass, turn bullets into marshmallows, and thus eliminate evil consequences, but then what would that do to the seriousness of moral choices?"[214]

Most of the things of this material world have the capacity to bring us either pleasure or pain, depending upon how they are used. God has created a world in which the laws of nature are unchanging (barring miracles, of course), and as a result people should know what to expect in any given situation. Wooden beams and bullets hurt and even kill, and these are consequences that people understand and they must be taken into consideration when making moral choices. Natural law theodicy states that our physical environment is such that it provides for the best possible means of both testing and developing our moral behavior, and therefore it compliments both the free will and soul-making theodicies.

There is a perceived difficulty with the natural law theodicy that skeptics are quick to point out, however: The Bible describes many instances of divine intervention upon the laws of nature, so as to produce a favorable outcome for some. C.S. Lewis counters this objection:

> *That God can and does, on occasions, modify the behaviour of matter and produce what we call miracles, is part of Christian faith; but the very conception of a common, and therefore stable, world demands that these occasions should*

---

[212] Ibid.
[213] Ibid.
[214] Ibid.

be extremely rare.[215]

The parting of the Red Sea at the time of the Exodus (Exodus 14:21-22) is one of the most well-known interventions upon the laws of nature, and the life of Christ is filled with many instances where Jesus manipulated the constants of the physical world. The Christian believer is quick to point out that these examples from Scripture happened for a purpose, which was to point people in the direction of the one true God of the universe. God does not modify the constants of nature haphazardly, as if he's experimenting with his creation, but rather every miracle that God performs serves a useful purpose, ultimately directing human beings in the direction of salvation.

STRENGTH IN COMBINATION

The only way that the challenges to each of these theodicies can be effectively countered is if all three approaches function together, an idea supported by the late Ronald Nash: "Since this book [*Faith and Reason* by Ronald Nash] adopts the view that the most adequate theodicy is one that combines elements of the appeal to free will, natural law, and soul-making, I suggest that any reader having reservations about a free will theodicy put them aside temporarily until I have a chance to show how all three approaches can be merged."[216] Nash goes on to quote Michael Peterson, the author of *Evil and the Christian God*: "...there must be some kind of natural order within which free creatures can operate. Free rational action requires a world of natural objects governed by natural laws."[217] These free will choices, made in an environment of physical constants, accumulate and contribute to our character (soul-making). Although Lewis has successfully integrated all three theodicies, it is noteworthy that the free will explanation for the problem of suffering appears throughout the entirety of the book, much more of-

---

[215] C.S. Lewis, *The Problem of Pain* (New York, NY: Harper One, 1940), 25.
[216] Ronald Nash, *Faith and Reason* (Grand Rapids, MI: Zondervan, 1988), 200.
[217] Ibid.

ten than the other two. The free will defense is the anchor in Lewis' approach to theodicy, but is maximally effective only when combined with the other two approaches.

WHAT I DISCOVERED

Now that we have come to the end of this book, we must ask ourselves the question, "What does all of this information mean to me personally?" Most people who read this book will already share my Christian worldview, so for the vast majority of readers the question will not be, "Should I become a Christian?" but rather, "How do I use the information in this book to impact those around me?" For my worldview brethren, that is the real value of a book such as this one. For those of you who began reading this book from a position of skepticism, it is my sincere hope and desire that you seriously consider the case that was made for the Christian worldview – and accept Christ as your Lord and Savior (Romans 10:9).

As previously stated, it is important to realize that no single line of evidence presented in the pages of this book is sufficient to "prove" the existence of God or the truthfulness of the Christian worldview. The "Case for Christianity" is based upon a number of solid lines of evidence that build upon each other. Yet, this book, and those like it, are just the beginning for many people. Even with the evidence for God and Jesus Christ firmly in place, many unsettling questions may remain. Is Jesus the only way to God? What about those who have lived and died without ever hearing about Jesus? Could a loving God, as portrayed throughout the New Testament, really send people to Hell? Doesn't Canaanite genocide and other "atrocities" found in the pages of the Old Testament disprove the notion of a loving God? What about Christian hypocrisy? The list of difficult questions goes on and on, and every one of them can tear away at the fabric of one's faith. Add to that the unrelenting attacks of the skeptical world, who will give no quarter to Christian believers, and that is why a book like this is only the beginning for most of us. A lifetime of study, contemplation, and serious dialogue is in order for the man or woman who has embraced the life of reasonable faith.

Admittedly, I have experienced many times when my faith was tested by some profoundly difficult question or situation that threatened to shake my belief system to the core, yet it is the evidence for God and Christ, as found in the pages of this book, that keeps my faith not only alive, but strong. That is one of the two major strengths of apologetics, the other being the ability to effectively enter into dialogue with unbelievers (1 Peter 3:15). It is my sincere hope that this book serves each and every reader well. May God's blessings be upon all who read these pages and thoughtfully reflect upon its content, whether in agreement or doubt.

BIBLIOGRAPHY

Ankerberg, John & John Weldon. The Passion and the Empty Tomb. Eugene, OR: Harvest House Publishers, 2005.

Bates, Gary. "Designed by Aliens? Discoverers of DNA's Structure Attack Christianity." https://www.creation.com/designed-by-aliens-crick-watson-atheism-panspermia

Beebe, James R. "The Kalam Cosmological Argument for the Existence of God." http://www.apollos.squarespace.com/cosmological-argument/

Boa, Kenneth D. & Robert M. Bowman, Jr. Faith Has Its Reasons. Colorado Springs, CO: Paternoster, 2005.

Byrnes, Sholto. "Britain's Hidden Religion." https://www.newstatesman.com/religion/2009/04/god-flew-deism-world-atheist

Charles, J. Daryl. "Engaging the (Neo) Pagan Mind: Paul's Encounter with Athenian Culture as a Model for Cultural Apologetics (Acts 17:16-34)." https://www.biblicalstudies.org.uk/pdf/athenian+charles.pdf

Copan, Paul. That's Just Your Interpretation. Grand Rapids, MI: Baker Books, 2001.

Dembski, William. "Intelligent Design." http://www.designinference.com/documents/2003.08.Encyc_of_Relig.htm

Eastman, Mark & Chuck Smith. The Search for Messiah. Fountain Valley, CA: Joy Publishing, 1996.

Eidsmoe, John. Christianity and the Constitution: The Faith of Our Founding Fathers. Grand Rapids, MI: Baker Academic, 1987.

George, Jim. The Bare Bones Bible Handbook. Eugene, OR: Harvest House Publishers, 2006.

Grigg, Russell. "A Brief History of Design." https://www.creation.com/a-brief-history-of-design

Groothuis, Douglas. Christian Apologetics: A Comprehensive Case for Biblical Faith. Downers Grove, IL: IVP Academic, 2011.

Ham, Ken. "Evangelism for the New Millennium." https://www.answersingenesis.org/gospel/evangelism-for-the-new-millennium/

_____ & Stacia McKeever. "Seven C's of History." https://www.answersingenesis.org/bible-history/seven-cs-of-history/

Hannam, James. "Refuting the Myth that Jesus Never Existed." http://www.bede.org.uk/jesusmyth.htm

Harrison, Paul. "Naturalistic (Scientific) Pantheism: Reverence of Nature and Cosmos." https://www.pantheism.net/paul/index.htm

_____. "Varieties of Pantheism." https://www.pantheism.net/paul/variety1.htm

_____. "The WPM Statement of Principles." https://www.pantheism.net/manifest.htm

Heeren, Fred. Show Me God: What the Message from Space is Telling Us about God. Wheeling, IL: Day Star Publications, 2000.

Herbert, David. Charles Darwin's Religious Views. Guelph, Ontario, Canada: Joshua Press, 2009.

Holding, James Patrick. "Secular References to Jesus: Mara Bar-Serapion." http://www.tektonics.org/jesusexist/serapion.html

_____. "Shattering the Christ Myth." http://www.tektonics.org/shattering.html

_____. "The Testimony of Tacitus." http://www.tektonics.org/jesusexist/tacitus.html

_____. "Was the Story of Jesus Stolen from that of the Persian Deity Mithra?" http://www.tektonics.org/copycat/mithra.html

_____. "Was the Story of Jesus Stolen from that of Zoroaster?" http://www.tektonics.org/copycat/zoroaster.html

House, H. Wayne. The Jesus Who Never Lived. Eugene, OR: Harvest House Publishers, 2008.

Humm, Alan. "Josephus on Jesus." http://www.jewishchristianlit.com/Topics/JewishJesus/josephus.html

Jeffrey, Grant. Jesus: The Great Debate. Toronto, Ontario, Canada: Frontier Research Publications, Inc., 1999.

_____. Journey into Eternity. Toronto, Ontario, Canada: Frontier Research Publications, Inc., 2000.

Jones, Timothy Paul. Conspiracies and the Cross. Lake Mary, FL: Front Line, 2008.

Konig, George. "A Tribute to Luke, and his Accuracy as a Historian." http://www.konig.org/wc112.htm

Lewis, C.S. The Problem of Pain. New York, NY: Harper One, 1940.

Lindell, John. "History of Christian Deism." http://www.christiandeistfellowship.com/histdeism.htm

Lindsley, Art. "The Problem of Evil." http://www.cslewisinstitute.org/webfm_send/636

Lutzer, Erwin. Where Was God? Carol Stream, IL: Tyndale House Publishers, Inc., 2006.

Mapp, Alf J., Jr. The Faiths of Our Founding Fathers. New York, NY: Fall River Press, 2006.

May, Peter. "Karl Barth and Natural Theology?" https://www.bethinking.org/is-christianity-true/karl-barth-and-natural-theology

McGowan, Andrew. "How December 25th Became Christmas." https://www.biblicalarchaeology.org/daily/biblical-topics/new-testament/how-december-25-became-christmas/

McGrath, Alister E. Mere Apologetics. Grand Rapids, MI: Baker Books, 2012.

McGregor Wright, R.K. "Paul's Purpose at Athens and the Problem of 'Common Ground.'" http://www.vantil.info/articles/rkmw_ppaa.pdf

McRay, John. Archaeology and the New Testament. Grand Rapids, MI: Baker Academic, 1991.

Meister, Chad V. Building Belief: Constructing Faith from the Ground Up. Grand Rapids, MI: Baker Books, 2006.

Muncaster, Ralph. Evidence for Jesus. Eugene, OR: Harvest House Publishers, 2004.

_____. Examine the Evidence. Eugene, OR: Harvest House Publishers, 2004.

Nash, Ronald. Faith and Reason. Grand Rapids, MI: Zondervan, 1988.

Oakes, John. Reasons for Belief. Spring, TX: Illumination Publishers International, 2005.

Patton, Michael. "What Happened to the Twelve Apostles?" http://www.credohouse.org/blog/what-happened-to-the-twelve-apostles-how-do-their-deaths-prove-easter

Price, Christopher. "A Thorough Review of the Testimonium Flavianum." http://www.bede.org.uk/Josephus.htm

Rhodes, Ron. Why Do Bad Things Happen if God is Good? Eugene, OR: Harvest House Publishers, 2004.

Ross, Hugh. The Fingerprint of God. New Kensington, PA: Whitaker House, 1989.

Sarfati, Jonathan. "DNA: Marvellous Messages or Mostly Mess?" https://www.creation.com/dna-marvellous-messages-or-mostly-mess

Schroeder, Gerald. "The Age of the Universe." http://www.geraldschroeder.com/AgeUniverse.aspx

Sewell, Alida Leni. "Paul at Athens: An Examination of His Areopagus Address in the Light of its Historical and Philosophical Background." http://www.freewebs.com/reformationalphilosophy/Sewell/Acts17.pdf

Sire, James. Apologetics Beyond Reason. Downers Grove, IL: IVP Academic, 2014.

_____. The Universe Next Door. Downers Grove, IL: InterVarsity Press, 1997.

_____. Why Good Arguments Often Fail. Downers Grove, IL: InterVarsity Press, 2006.

Spiegel, Jim. "Free Will and Soul-Making Theodicies." http://www.jimspiegel.com/articles/free-will-and-soul-making-theodicies/

Sproul, R.C. The Consequences of Ideas. Wheaton, IL: Crossway Books, 2000.

_____. Defending Your Faith. Wheaton, IL: Crossway Books, 2003.

_____. Reason to Believe. Grand Rapids, MI: Zondervan, 1978.

Stanback, C. Foster. The Resurrection: A Historical Analysis. Spring, TX: Illumination Publishers International, 2008.

Strobel, Lee. The Case for the Real Jesus. Grand Rapids, MI: Zondervan, 2007.

Sullivan, Andrew. "The Forgotten Jesus." Newsweek (April 9, 2012).

Sunshine, Glenn S. Why You Think the Way You Do. Grand Rapids, MI: Zondervan, 2009.

Tunnicliff, Jeffrey S. "Can We Trust Religious Experience to Help Us Know God?" http://www.renewaloffaith.org/basics/talking/relexp.pdf

Vince, Ron. "At the Areopagus (Acts 17:22-31): Pauline Apologetics and Lucan Rhetoric." http://www.mcmaster.ca/mjtm/4-5.htm

Wade, Rick. "The World of the Apostle Paul." http://www.leaderu.com/orgs/probe/docs/apospaul.html

Waldman, Steven. "Deism: It's Back!" http://www.blogbeliefnet.com/stevenwaldman/2009/09/deism-its-back.html

Wilkens, Steve. Good Ideas from Questionable Christians and Outright Pagans: An Introduction to Key Thinkers and Philosophies. Downers Grove, IL: InterVarsity Press, 2004.

Williams, Peter. "Aesthetic Arguments for the Existence of God." http://www.quodlibet.net/articles/williams-aesthetic.shtml

Woods, Len. Handbook of World Religions. Uhrichsville, OH: Barbour Publishing, 2008

ABOUT THE AUTHOR

Randy Hroziencik, a Radiation Therapist since 1988, has a passion for teaching on the books of the Bible, often emphasizing apologetics in his classes at Bethel Baptist Church in Galesburg, Illinois. A former skeptic, Randy now speaks locally on topics related to science, faith, and reason, and has spoken at both the 2015 and 2016 International Christian Evidences Conference at York College in York, Nebraska.

In 2012 Randy completed the process of ordination through Bethel Baptist Church, and in the following year he graduated with a joint Master of Arts-Doctor of Philosophy (Theology) through Trinity College of the Bible & Theological Seminary, an institution specializing in distance education. In 2014 Randy became the first-ever graduate of the Apologetics Research Society's Certificate in Christian Apologetics, a ten-course program examining the scientific, historical, archaeological, and theological aspects of the evidence for the Christian faith.

Randy currently serves as an elder at Bethel Baptist Church, and has been heavily involved in leading classes geared toward adult learners. Randy and his wife Deb, a Fertility Care Practitioner by profession, have two married children and three grandchildren.

Contact Randy at randyhroziencik@comcast.net.

CPSIA information can be obtained
at www.ICGtesting.com
Printed in the USA
LVHW052057190921
698212LV00014B/582